About the Authors

DONNA BRAZILE, a veteran Democratic political strategist, is an adjunct professor at Georgetown University, author, television political commentator, and former interim chair of the Democratic Party.

YOLANDA CARAWAY, founder of the Caraway Group public relations firm, has played a major role in shaping the goals and objectives of the national Democratic Party.

THE REVEREND LEAH D. DAUGHTRY is a nationally recognized teacher, preacher, speaker, organizer, leader, planner, political strategist, and CEO of the 2008 and 2016 Democratic National Conventions.

MINYON MOORE is a partner at the Dewey Square Group, was formerly CEO of the Democratic National Committee, and served as assistant to the president of the United States and director of the White House Office of Public Liaison, and director of White House political affairs under President Bill Clinton.

Additional Praise for
For Colored Girls Who Have Considered Politics

"When I launched the 'Vote or Die' campaign, I knew I needed to have the Colored Girls' advice and knowledge. With their expertise and commitment to change, we were able to register and motivate hundreds of thousands of young voters and make issues that they care about part of the national conversation. We knew then what continues to be the truth now: what's missing in politics, in our democracy, is the organized voices of young people of color. This powerhouse group of black women who have worked hard behind the scenes for decades to make our country better, are inspiring the next generation of leaders. *For Colored Girls* is the blueprint."   —Sean "Diddy" Combs

"*For Colored Girls* is basically part history book and part biography but wholly significant. I'm so glad this book exists because the stories of these four women, who were instrumental in so many moments of history, needs to be told. I'm honored that we can take a sip of their life tea in this way, because what they've done and been a part of are the watershed moments of this nation's contemporary politics. It also doesn't hurt that it's super juicy. The transparency of the Colored Girls as they tell their stories is admirable. When I finished this book, what I understood is how we have walking icons in our midst, and this was the opportunity to sit at their feet and soak in their lessons, wisdom, and #NoirPixieDust. I'm basically gonna start calling them all my aunties. The Colored Girls are Peak Aunty Goals. I salute you, Leah, Donna, Yolanda, Minyon. Thank you for showing black girls and women that we, too, belong in the rooms we're in."   —Luvvie Ajayi, *New York Times* bestselling author of *I'm Judging You: The Do-Better Manual*

"I first got to know the Colored Girls when they were just young women determined to give a voice to the voiceless in American politics. *For Colored Girls Who Have Considered Politics* is an interesting, informative, inspiring, motivating, and just plain delightful read. These are four colored girls who weren't born on third base in privilege, but came from relatively humble beginnings. They started with menial jobs and through discipline, strategic

thinking, and hard work achieved meaningful careers for themselves and better lives for other people through politics. They considered careers in business, health care, law, and civil rights, but found their calling and fulfillment in politics. When and where they enter, history is made. Their choices benefited all of us."   —Reverend Jesse L. Jackson, Sr., founder and
president of the Rainbow PUSH Coalition

"How blessed we are in these times that fortune deigned that the hearts of these four exceptionally driven, intellectually brilliant, socially conscious sisters would intersect. Their lives, dedicated from the beginning for service to community, family, and nation, is the refreshing cross breeze of authenticity needed in Washington politics. A compelling memoir of cultivated dreams, *For Colored Girls* provides insight into and illumination of the undeniable call to service and the ways in which these four navigated a sometimes perilous and truly circuitous journey."   —Angela Bassett

"This is a remarkable book about four extraordinary black women who through strength of character, humility, and just plain smarts, became indispensable in every Democratic presidential campaign since 1984. They played a major role in building the modern Democratic Party and, perhaps most importantly, mentored a generation of young people who became activists and candidates in their own right. Finally, this book is a great window into modern African American history as it is still being written. It would be a mistake for anyone who aspires to build a better America not to read this."

—Governor Howard Dean, former chair of the Democratic Party

"We who are faithful have never doubted the power of women with hearts set on justice, equality, and opportunity to shape and sharpen the conscience of a nation. These African American women, known collectively as the Colored Girls, have written the handbook on movement building and changing the world through progressive politics. This is a book I will be sharing with my daughters and every activist woman I know. As the mothers of the church used to sing, 'I'm glad she didn't keep it to herself.'"

—Reverend William Barber, president and lecturer of
Repairers of the Breach

For
Colored Girls
Who Have
Considered
Politics

For Colored Girls Who Have Considered Politics

Donna Brazile, Yolanda Caraway,
Leah Daughtry, and Minyon Moore,

with Veronica Chambers

Picador
St. Martin's Press
New York

picadorusa.com • instagram.com/picador
twitter.com/picadorusa • facebook.com/picadorusa

Picador® is a U.S. registered trademark and is used by Macmillan Publishing Group, LLC, under license from Pan Books Limited.

For book club information, please visit facebook.com/picadorbookclub
or email marketing@picadorusa.com.

The Library of Congress has cataloged the St. Martin's Press edition as follows:

Names: Brazile, Donna, 1959– author. | Caraway, Yolanda, author. | Daughtry, Leah, author. | Moore, Minyon, author. | Chambers, Veronica, author.
Title: For colored girls who have considered politics / Donna Brazile, Yolanda Caraway, Leah Daughtry, and Minyon Moore with Veronica Chambers.
Description: First edition. | New York : St. Martin's Press, 2018. | Includes index.
Identifiers: LCCN 2018017175 | ISBN 9781250137715 (hardcover) | ISBN 9781250137722 (ebook)
Subjects: LCSH: African American women politicians—Biography. | African American women—Political activity—History. | United States—Politics and government—20th century. | United States—Politics and government—21st century.
Classification: LCC E185.96.B829 2018 | DDC 328.73/092 [B]—dc23
LC record available at https://lccn.loc.gov/2018017175

Picador Paperback ISBN 978-1-250-13773-9

Our books may be purchased in bulk for promotional, educational, or business use. Please contact your local bookseller or the Macmillan Corporate and Premium Sales Department at 1-800-221-7945, extension 5442, or by email at MacmillanSpecialMarkets@macmillan.com.

First published by St. Martin's Press, an imprint of St. Martin's Publishing Group

First Picador Edition: October 2019

10 9 8 7 6 5 4 3 2 1

somebody/ anybody
sing a black girl's song
bring her out
to know herself
to know you
but sing her rhythms . . .
sing her sighs
sing the song of her possibilities
sing a righteous gospel
the makin of a melody
let her be born
let her be born
& handled warmly.

—NTOZAKE SHANGE

For the women

    who ride the early bus
    who work the late shift
    who teach the children, clean the offices, nurse the sick
    who stand guard and keep watch

    who build, create, and sustain
    who cut new paths and swim in unchartered waters
    who light the path and lead the way

    who stand up, step up, sit down, and always keep moving
    who do the everyday extraordinary work of family, community, and
    liberation.

We sing this song for you.

Contents

Acknowledgments

Writing this book was an experience that challenged and inspired us more than we could have imagined. We had so many remarkable stories to tell . . . not only of the events we experienced in politics but also of all the living we've done . . . the historic moments we have witnessed, the amazing men and women of valor we have worked with, and reflections on the present moment. We offer our heartfelt thanks to those who supported us as we attempted to capture these stories, most especially:

. . . Our sister, Tina Flournoy, the fifth Colored Girl, who walked these long roads with us. Though her name does not appear on the book jacket, she is present in every one of these stories and has her own stories to tell.

. . . Our families, our friends, our coworkers, and the many, many colleagues over the years who have stood with us in promoting justice and equality for all.

. . . Members and contributors to the "Bank of Justice," our work is not over. Let's continue to lift up those struggling to overcome poverty, racism, and all forms of bigotry and oppression.

. . . All of those who played a role in the journey that is our lives and our careers. We name many of them in the book, but there are many,

many dozens more. There are not enough pages to name you all nor words to express our gratitude for what you did to make us better, to make us stronger, to make us braver, tougher, clearer, and more compassionate.

. . . Felicia D. Henderson, filmmaker and showrunner extraordinaire, who first told us that the story of our friendship was worth telling.

. . . Isiah Thomas, thank you for recognizing our history even before we began this book-writing process. Your clarity and your words encouraged us to think long and hard about our individual and collective achievements.

. . . The incomparable Veronica Chambers, who started as our writing partner and became our friend who became our sister—we thank you for your grace, your patience, your wit, your skill, your creativity, and your passion for this project and for us . . . working with one author is challenging enough, but combining four voices into a cogent, coherent, and interesting read is a major feat! We are grateful.

. . . Activists Zerlina Maxwell and Reverend Mark Thompson, both of whom host shows on Sirius XM (among other things), and inspired the title for this book. And on that note, we thank the brilliant Ntozake Shange, author of *For Colored Girls Who Have Considered Suicide / When the Rainbow Is Enuf.* Her seminal work has inspired women for decades, encouraging and emboldening sisters everywhere to tell their stories and live their truths.

. . . Those who spent time reading our drafts, commenting on passages, saying brava, or simply telling us to "delete."

. . . The awesome team at St. Martin's Press and especially Michael Flamini, our incredibly kind, incredibly fun (and funny) editor and guide through this mysterious process called book publishing.

. . . Gail Ross, our fabulous agent, who took us on when this book was just an idea, and kept four busy women on track and on task over many months.

. . . Darrell Miller, Esq., our eagle-eyed attorney, for his expert advice and advocacy, dotting every "i" and crossing every "t."

. . . **To our mentors**, those who have gone on and to those who are still with us, Rev. Willie T. Barrow, Coretta Scott King, Dr. Maya Angelou, Dr. Betty Shabazz, Dr. Myrlie Evers, Mrs. Jacqueline Jackson, Dr. Dorothy Height, Congresswoman Shirley Chisholm, Congresswoman Eleanor Holmes Norton, and the incomparable Cicely Tyson. We are blessed and humbled that our lives crossed paths with yours. We owe you a lifetime of gratitude. May your living never be in vain.

. . . Finally, we worship and praise an awesome God whose grace gives us focus and whose mercy allows us to continue to give back and pay it forward.

And now, some personal acknowledgments:

DONNA

I would like to thank my ever-expanding large and diverse family, especially my sisters and brothers: Cheryl, Chet, Lisa, Demetria, Kevin, Zeola, and my phenomenal nieces Janika, J. Mallore, Brianna, Aailyah, Kaliyah, Kiristin, and Whitney. And to my amazing nephews: Kevin Jr., Elmore Jr., Roderick Jr., Colin, Chet Jr., Malik, Kevin III, Karim, J'oel, and Jace. To all my cousins and that includes my first, second, third, fourth, and well, you know. I am grateful to God for the many blessings of my beautiful family. They have stuck by my side and provided me with unconditional love and a lot of laughs.

There are so many friends who have lifted me up, came over to share a cup of coffee or a glass of wine; you know who you are because I cannot thank you enough. Ellen, Sophie, Julie, Nicco, Nancy, and my Boston circle of friends at the Shorenstein Center on Media, Politics and Public Policy who helped me get back on the dance floor of life. Special thanks to Mia, Betsy, and my little godson Kai for their love and personal support on so many levels.

To my former colleagues at the Democratic National Committee (and Ro'Chelle Williams) who answered the call to serve and never surrender, you all are honorary members of the Bank of Justice. Don't forget to repay your dues through acts of goodness and kindness. The movement is fueled by love and hope. Let's not grow weary in doing good.

Special thanks to Georgetown University and ABC News who helped me get up from the cyber storm that virally rippled through the 2016 U.S. presidential election.

Finally, to my sisters Minyon, Leah, Yolanda (and Tina who remains smarter than us all), God is not finished with us. You all are my favorite roadrunners in the battle for justice and mercy. Your rare gifts, combined with intellect and compassion, are truly a sight to behold. I see our ancestors in you. At a time when some of those who never really believed in any of us came after me, you didn't join the choir. At least you allowed me to speak. Thank you.

Thank you.

P.S. When I started this book, my little doggie Chip heard all my stories. At times, he barked along with me, but he also groaned. Like, *Mommy, please don't go there.* Chip, I miss you. You were magical to me.

YOLANDA

First and always foremost, I would like to acknowledge and thank the Father—I've always known he didn't bring me this far to leave me. I am so grateful to you for the many blessings that have been bestowed upon me throughout my life.

I would like to thank Minyon Moore, Leah Daughtry, Donna Brazile, and Tina Flournoy for being my ride-or-die girls for all of these years. I couldn't imagine a better group of sister-friends to have on this journey. #ColoredGirlsForever!

To Earl Harris, Wendell Phillips, and Theron Tucker, Jr.—I miss you every day.

To my mother, Cecile Harris, for teaching me the joy of entertaining—thus the "Black Martha Stewart" nickname; and for instilling in me, at an early age, that I was as good as anyone else.

To my big sister, Dorothy, who raised me. And always provided me with a place to land when I needed one. I will be forever grateful.

To my nephew, Wendell, my "guy" BFF, for allowing me to help raise his daughters Clarke and Logan. They give me joy and hope.

To those who mentored me: Rev. Jesse L. Jackson, Sr., Honorable Ron Brown, Alma Brown, Alexis Herman, Congressman William H. Gray III, Honorable C. Delores Tucker, Rev. Willie Barrow, Addie Wyatt, Congresswoman Maxine Waters, Honorable Percy Sutton, Mayor David Dinkins, Honorable Basil Paterson, Congressman Charlie Rangel, Mayor Richard Hatcher, Caroline Jones, Frank Mingo, Ernie Green, Ann Lewis, Bertram Lee, and Bob Johnson. I thank you all for sharing your knowledge and wisdom with me.

And to all of the young men and women I have mentored over the years, both in business and politics, I've learned as much from you as you did from me. I feel blessed to have had each of you in my world. We made history together.

LEAH

All praise and thanksgiving to Creator God, the Source of all supply, the lifter of my head, and the giver of every good and perfect gift. I am grateful for every blessing and every obstacle. I will always be your worshipper.

To **my family:** My grandparents, Alonzo, Emmie, Vermell, and Earl, who laid a firm foundation. My parents, Herbert and Karen; my siblings, Sharon, Dawn, Herb Jr., and my sister-in-love, Danielle; my beautiful nephews, Lorenzo, Herb III, and Myles; my niece-in-love, Sarah, and my first grandniece, Lauren Joy. Your love, prayers, presence, and support have been like air for me and have made all my work possible. Some may be as blessed as me, but none more.

The members of the best church in the world, **The House of the Lord**, for loving me from the beginning, for being my shelter, my laboratory, and my well, and for always giving me room to grow.

To the **politicos, activists, and organizers** who helped to shape the way that I think about politics and community. Michael Amon-Ra, Adeyemi Bandele, Khadijah Bandele, Atchudta Bakr, Mayor David

Dinkins, Congressman Floyd Flake, George Gresham, Ron Herndon, Honorable Bill Lynch, Nomzamo Winnie Madikizela-Mandela, Honorable Velmanette Montgomery, Joshua Nkomo, Sam Pinn, Viola Plummer, Congressman Charles B. Rangel, Honorable Annette Robinson, Congressman Ed Towns, Kwame Toure (Stokely Carmichael), Oba T'Shaka, Honorable Al Vann, and Baba Jitu Weusi.

My mentor turned friend turned sister, the **Honorable Alexis M. Herman**, advisor, protector, cheerleader, cajoler, and fairy godmother; you shaped me in too many ways to count. What would I do without you?

To **my extended family,** including Pat Lattimore, Jacqueline Williams, Alissa Williams, Mara Rudman, Marsha Trant, Viva Hardigg, and Lucia Jackson. Thanks for surrounding me with love, backing me up, and being ever present.

To **black activist Brooklyn**, the people of Uhuru Sasa and the East, Brooklyn CORE, Sista's Place, and many more, for giving me an example of what it is to be black and proud, committed to culture and community.

To **the Congressional Black Caucus,** the conscience of the Congress. In my early days in Washington, you were a beacon of hope and a source of strength and light. To walk the halls with giants was a privilege and an honor. I remain proud of you and all you do, every day, against tremendous odds to be the voice that this nation needs.

To **Governor Howard Dean and Congresswoman Debbie Wasserman Schultz**: you trusted me with one of the biggest enterprises of your DNC Chairmanships, leadership of the 2008 and 2016 Democratic Conventions. Thank you for your friendship and your faith in me.

My **DNC and Convention** teams: you are simply the best in the business and the world knows it; thanks for taking the ride with me. You were there for me and I will always be there for you.

To **Randi Weingarten,** president of the American Federation of Teachers, who, unbeknownst to her, saved my life and then, as a bonus, put me on a path to some of the most fulfilling work of my life: Reconnecting McDowell.

To the **young women and men I've mentored** along the way, most especially Latoia Jones, Lisa Hargrove, Patrice Taylor, Julie Greene, Heather Barmore, Jess Torres, Ashanti Gholar, Jotaka Eaddy, LaDavia Drane, Maya Goines, Amaya Smith, Jamie Richards, Shavon Arline-Bradley, Christopher Huntley, Chris Cobbs, and Charles Olivier, and my baby girls who started it all: Djanaba Nicole Bird Lester, Shakeema Bryant, Latoya and Tamara Mack, and Iesha McConnell; you have enriched my life, made me smarter, and given me more than I could have ever given you.

And lastly, my most heartfelt thanks to my girls, Minyon, Yolanda, Donna, Tina—and now coauthors!!!—with whom I've journeyed these last many years; all we ever wanted was to make a difference and make our people proud.

Now thanks be unto God Who always causeth us to triumph. To God be the Glory!

MINYON

To my family, your love and support has been immeasurable. You've never allowed me to stray too far from home base. To my mother who is a solid rock. You were my first example of what it means to be loving, hardworking, and to persevere, sometimes against amazing odds. To my uncle Dennis, thank you for your love and for holding the family down. Your sacrifices have not gone unnoticed. I am grateful to you every day. To my sister, Diane, and brother, Carl, it's impossible for you to understand my love for you both. Every achievement I've made, it was because you were the "wind beneath my wings." Corionna (London) Sierra and Christopher each day you make me proud to be your aunt. You will always have my full support and unwavering love. To my extended family, Marvin, Regena, Penny, Bobbi, Lisa, Connie, Cookie, Lavette, Mattie, Carlton, and Lawanda, you knew before the titles. I am grateful for your presence in my life.

To my Third Baptist Church family, thank you for giving me the greatest teachings of my life. My faith and my walk with God has sustained me. **To My Rainbow PUSH Family,** my journey in public service began with you. Thank you for nurturing and supporting me throughout my career. The foundation and confidence you instilled in me allowed me to walk into rooms with my head held high, knowing I was more than qualified to be there. My gratitude can't be measured in words. **To my colleagues at Dewey Square,** it is an honor and a privilege to work with each of you. Sixteen years later, I remain in awe of the integrity, comradeship, and commitment you bring to your work and our clients. **To Michael and Charlie,** I can't think of anyone I would rather be in the foxhole with. You are indeed my brothers. Although our foxhole is missing **Chuck,** we know he is with us in spirit. **Ginny,** thank you for your friendship, our late-night laughs at work and your constant encouragement, while trying to ease me into areas where I tend to shy away.

To Hillary Clinton, a person whom I admire and respect. You personify dignity and grace and continue to raise the bar on the meaning of public service. Expressing gratitude for your service and your commitment to others seems woefully inadequate, so I will simply say thank you for never giving up on America.

West Coast Colored Girls, Angela Bassett, Felicia Henderson, Gina Prince Bythewood, Erika Alexander, Mara Brock Akil, and Ava DuVernay, you unlocked a passion in me that allowed me to understand the power of images and words. I owe you for inspiring me to learn how I could use my perch to promote these messages and images, especially to our young women and girls.

Cora Masters Barry, thank you for picking me up at the White House on many occasions. Those drives to Southeast, DC, kept me focused on what was real—our young people. Watching your vision of the tennis and learning center unfold has been a joy and is a testament that dreams can come true.

To Sean Combs, thank you for being my North Star and a guiding light. Through **Vote or Die,** you used your voice and resources to raise awareness around issues that impact young people and communities of color. You made sure these communities were never forgotten. We are all better off because you have chosen to step up and not sit on the sidelines. I am better off after having had the privilege of working with you.

A number of young people started with me at the DNC and they grew in number with each new position and campaign. My life was made easier because of your dedication and hard work. Thank you to Janna Pasqual, Jessica Briddle Zielke, Julie Kim, Alix DeJean, Samantha Slosberg, Andre Anderson, Jua Johnson, Lisa Mushaw, Alison McLaurin Perry, Greg Moore, Angelique Pirozzi, Jocelyn Bucaro, Jamie Collins, Vincent Fry, Emma Christman, Kim Selden, David Huynh, Jorge Neri, Denise Horn, De'Ara Balenger, Ebony Meeks, Nadia Garnett, Vida Benavides, Patrice Taylor, LaDavia Drane, Ashley Etienne, Jotaka Eddy, Symone Sanders, and Zerlina Maxwell. You made me a better person and a better professional. The leadership gap is shorter because of you.

To the CGs, you are my oars and anchors. When my days are off and on, I can always count on one of you to be by my side. My life is richer because of your friendship. I love you my sisters.

And finally, from all of us . . .

To our beloved sister Tanya Lombard, a woman of integrity, purpose, and honor, who exemplifies what it means to be a Colored Girl.

Thank you for believing in us and in this book from the very beginning. In word and action, you have helped to amplify and spread our story across America. We are deeply thankful for you and your friendship. We know that Ms. Barbara is proud of your success.

FOREWORD

In 2011, having recently been elected as the Democratic leader for the Georgia House of Representatives, I faced my first election cycle. But this was no ordinary time. Georgia, like dozens of states, had fallen into firm conservative control—the result being a gerrymandered map that allocated more than 65 percent of Georgia House seats to the GOP. I had the dubious responsibility of beating back a Republican supermajority with limited resources and little faith in the potential outcome. To fund our campaigns, we secured Governor Howard Dean, the former chair of the Democratic National Committee, to headline our first major fund-raiser. Afterward, the governor offered to introduce me to a group of women who might be able to help me even further: the Colored Girls.

I had heard of the famed quartet of Democratic powerhouses: Donna Brazile, Yolanda Caraway, Leah Daughtry, and Minyon Moore. The first black woman to helm a presidential campaign, Brazile hailed from Louisiana, next door to where I grew up in Mississippi. Caraway, a comms expert, had navigated both the Fortune 500 and political environs. Like my mother, Daughtry ably served a religious congregation, and she'd also excelled as chief of staff for Dean at the DNC. Moore held court at one of the nation's leading political consulting firms, advising unions and candidates alike.

With his introduction in tow, I secured a late-winter audience with the Colored Girls. In a dimly lit restaurant in Washington, DC, I sat enrapt for more than an hour as they peppered me with thoughtful questions and lifted me up with sage advice. By the time our dinner concluded, I had received a decade's worth of tutelage in how to lead our flagging state party forward and block a Republican sweep. While I have not been successful at getting all four women together at the same time, this masterwork, *For Colored Girls Who Have Considered Politics*, ably re-creates that extraordinary dinner and the years since.

With clarity, accessibility, and wit, they expose the layers of complexity that are modern politics, and the tensions invariably present in a big tent party. Sharing their paths to leadership, each woman opens her story up for those who cannot yet figure out how their stories begin. Yet, the most affecting aspect is the constancy of a friendship that has survived presidents, ersatz scandals, tragedy, and outrageous victories. Like any successful quartet, they manage to harmonize their skills on the written page and in the work they have done to grow the party and the nation they love.

As Americans grapple with questions of identity, electability, and a murky future, the Colored Girls are a welcome antidote to potential despair. Instead of dwelling solely on the racist and misogynistic hurdles they have traversed, each woman places these obstacles into critical context and then proves how ineffective her worst enemies have been at trying to slow progress.

During my tenure, the GOP never achieved their supermajority. And each year thereafter, I duly made the trek to DC to confab with the Colored Girls. Minyon opened doors to political stars who didn't yet have Georgia on their minds. Donna helmed fund-raisers that pushed our caucus and our party into swing-state territory. Leah rained down righteous fire on those who questioned my bid for the governorship. Yolanda quietly shored up the work by calming those worried about what my candidacy might mean. Separate or together, they are the banner women for justice and lived experience. For nearly a decade, I have been an admirer of the Colored Girls. And by the end of this award-winning book, you will be, too.

—Stacey Abrams

July 26, 2016

On the second evening of the 2016 Democratic National Convention in Philadelphia, former president Bill Clinton took the stage. He began his speech with a love story, "In the spring of 1971, I met a girl," and then he went on to describe how this young woman, wearing no makeup and large, oversize glasses, blew him away with a "strength and self-possession I found magnetic." Through good times and hard times, he explained, this woman had been the love of his life. Of course, he was talking about his wife, the soon-to-be-confirmed nominee of the Democratic Party for president of the United States, the first woman ever to achieve that distinction: Secretary of State Hillary Rodham Clinton.

We sat facing him, on the convention stage. Who are we? We're the Colored Girls, four African American women who had been a part of his political life since he first entered politics on a national level. It was an unprecedented moment because we have, throughout our lives, been somewhat hidden figures in American politics. That moment on the stage was a rare public show of who we are and what we were determined to do. The roles we played in the 2016 election were ones that our early mentors, ranging from Coretta Scott King to Shirley Chisholm to Reverend Willie Barrow, might have hoped for but could never have fully imagined. Let us tell you who we are and what we were doing at the 2016 Democratic National Convention: I'm Donna Brazile, and I was the 2016 interim chair of the Democratic Party. I'm Leah Daughtry, and I was the CEO of the convention, the only person in America of any race or either gender to hold that position twice. I'm Minyon Moore, and I was there in my role as senior advisor, and one of the Super Six, the inner circle of Hillary Clinton's campaign leadership. And I'm Yolanda Caraway. I ran podium ops, meaning I was the one behind the scenes directing everything that was happening onstage. None of us knew what would happen on November 8, 2016. That was all ahead of us, but behind us was a story we've never told. Until now.

For
Colored Girls
Who Have
Considered
Politics

1

A Call to Serve

In the summer of 1964, Rochester, New York, was still a gleaming destination of the Great Migration. Eastman Kodak was there, and by the middle of the decade, Kodak had been joined by big companies such as Xerox and Bausch and Lomb. It was the kind of city that epitomized the hope of the Great Migration: where any hardworking black person who aspired to could get a good job. Yolanda Caraway was a long-legged, beautiful teenager with hair that swung like a Supreme's and a brain that held facts and figures like a human computer. Hers was a community of have-somes, and her ambitions matched the achievements of the men and women around her. She was inspired by the Freedom Riders and remembers that by the time she attended high school, she had only one ambition: to help people. She toyed with the idea of being a social worker, but medicine called her, too. Her best friend's aunt was a doctor. That same friend, Anne Micheaux, had a grandfather who was a doctor, too, "the black doctor" in their town.

The year she turned fourteen, Yolanda got a summer job as a candy striper at St. Mary's Hospital, the very same hospital where she had drawn her first breath. Years later, she would admit, "I think I was really attracted to the cute little candy-striped dresses. The boys seemed to really like them—and I liked that." But things did not work out the way she planned. She flunked algebra and needed to retake the course to get a passing grade. Yolanda went to summer school in the morning. Then, at noon, she went to St. Mary's with her girlfriend Delores Leach—who did become a nurse. Life in the hospital was not as glamorous as Yolanda had imagined. She spent her afternoons emptying bedpans, running errands for doctors, checking people into the emergency room, and cleaning up all manner of vomit and excrement. "It took me about two weeks to realize that I was definitely not cut out for that," she says. "The first time some very bloody person was wheeled in—I was out. Never could take the sight of blood, even on myself." There was more blood than usual in Rochester that summer. A case of police brutality had ignited the city's first race riots, and angry protestors had taken to the streets. Yolanda didn't know it at the time, but the influence of that event—so close to home, and prompting feelings of injustice and frustration— would tilt her attention toward politics.

It was Freedom Summer, 1964. Lyndon B. Johnson had become president after the assassination of President John F. Kennedy. The hope and potential of the modern civil rights movement hung in the balance. In June 1964, a coalition of four branches of the movement gathered with the united purpose of registering as many African American voters as humanly possible. They were SNCC, Student Nonviolent Coordinating Committee, the young people's wing of the movement; CORE, Congress of Racial Equality; SCLC, Southern Christian Leadership Conference; and the NAACP, National Association for the Advancement of Colored People, the more than fifty-year-old organization started by W. E. B. Du Bois, Mary White Ovington, and Moorfield Storey.

Over the course of the ten-week nonviolent initiative, the Ku Klux Klan and organizations such as the white supremacist Citizens' Council brought down a reign of terror on the volunteers. They used every tool at their disposal as members of the white Southern elite: volunteers were beaten and murdered; evicted from their homes and fired from their jobs; intimidated, arrested, and harassed. Dozens of black churches and homes were bombed and burned. Fannie Lou Hamer, a former share-cropper, was so powerful in her testimony before the credentials com-mittee of the DNC that summer that President Johnson called a press conference to divert the television cameras from her story. She wanted the right to vote, she told the committee members. Voting was what stood between her current status and the right to become a first-class citizen. With all the death and destruction being rained down upon nonviolent volunteers who were simply trying to get people to the ballots, Hamer let the country know, "I question America."

That fall, when Yolanda started the ninth grade, a friend asked if she wanted to volunteer to work on Bobby Kennedy's Senate campaign. Pres-ident Kennedy had been assassinated just the year before, and his younger brother Robert had left the administration and moved to New York to be able to run for Senate. Yolanda can still remember her excite-ment at the invitation: "Well, all black people *loved* JFK and were dev-astated by his murder; so of course we loved his brother Bobby. I was always looking for something to do after school so I didn't have to go home; I was happy to have somewhere to go."

Yolanda was the youngest and only child of her mother's second mar-riage. As the only kid at home, she remembers bearing the brunt of her mother's unhappiness, "which made me a very confused and unhappy kid." But her father balanced the scales: "I simply adored my father, who was just the opposite. He was loving and affectionate, kind and funny, and very handsome." Each parent had other daughters from a previous marriage.

Every day after school, she'd take the bus from East High School all the way to the west side of town to volunteer on Bobby Kennedy's cam-paign. It was the first time she had ever done anything like that. She'd type letters, make calls, answer phones, stuff envelopes. The work was just as lowly as being a candy striper, but it had a far different effect on Yolanda. She remembers feeling as if she had "come alive." In the campaign offices, she had an up-close and daily history lesson about the slain president's brother and his family. When campaign staffers discussed Bobby's platform, Yolanda understood that they were trying to communicate the goals and governing style that would guide the candidate's tenure should he be elected. "For the first time in my very young life, I really began to understand how important those people were who were *leaders*. I began to see this was another important way to help people.

"By the end of the campaign, I was knocking on doors after school, explaining to people why they should vote for Bobby Kennedy. To my own teenage surprise, I sounded like I knew what the hell I was talking about." Bobby won that election, and Yolanda was confident she felt every bit as triumphant as he did. For her service, she received a thank-you letter signed by Senator Kennedy. Knowing, even decades later, that the letter might well have been signed by a secretary using a signature stamp didn't diminish the impact of the gift. The letter hangs on her office wall to this day.

Yolanda had been bitten by a bug she wasn't aware existed and didn't yet fully understand, but politics would come to be a part of her, what she would describe as "one of the great passions of her life." As she grew older and gained more experience, she discovered that it was a mutual love affair: she had a gift for management, for parsing complex political issues and communicating their importance to voters. She had great political instincts. Bobby Kennedy was the first inspiring candidate she backed, but he was far from her last.

"That August, during that candy striper summer and right before my fifteenth birthday, I went to Baltimore to visit with my sister Dorothy and my brother-in-law, a minister named Wendell Phillips, and their one-year-old son, Wendell, aka Poo. I was what was then called a 'change of life baby.' There was a sixteen-year difference between Dorothy and me. When Dorothy got married, I was only ten years old." While Yolanda was often estranged from her mother, she was inextricably close to her big sister. Wendell, in turn, became the big brother she'd always longed for but had never had.

The visit to Baltimore made it one of the best summers ever. Yolanda remembers, "Wendell had a very active youth fellowship at his church, Heritage United Church of Christ, and I made so many new friends. I absolutely loved Baltimore. Well, I probably would have loved anyplace other than Rochester, but I remember telling my parents, 'I've never seen so many colored people in my life.' I didn't want to go home. So, I stayed."

Politics became a natural, intrinsic part of Yolanda's life in Baltimore, too. Wendell was a well-known activist in the city, and a key player in every election. Yolanda, now in her early twenties, volunteered for every candidate Wendell backed. In the late seventies, Wendell ran for state delegate and won. Still in her twenties, Yolanda ran his Annapolis office. The visibility of that position led to her supporting and campaigning for Ted Kennedy in the Democratic primary against the incumbent president, Jimmy Carter. As part of the senator's on-the-ground Baltimore team, Yolanda organized a church event for Kennedy. And it was in that church basement where she first met Ron Brown, one of Senator Kennedy's deputies. Brown would later become the first African American chairman of the Democratic National Committee and U.S. secretary of commerce. But more than that, he became Yolanda's good friend and other "big brother."

That church basement event proved to be the site of many firsts for Yolanda. Maria Shriver attended the event with her "Uncle Teddy." One of Maria's close friends, a local TV journalist named Oprah Winfrey, came by to see her—Yolanda remembers the two women "screaming and hugging like two teenagers; you could see how close they were." Once Yolanda got her own place in Baltimore, she began to throw parties at her apartment. Winfrey, the new anchor at WBAL, came to one of them with Sue Simmons, also a news anchor. Yolanda remembers Winfrey as a little shy, "but it was right after she'd moved to town, and she probably didn't know many people."

Everyone used to throw house parties in the seventies. Literally every weekend, someone was having a party. These were parties where, Yolanda says, "anyone and everyone showed up. You could put out the word on Friday and have a full house on Saturday." For her parties, Yolanda would make a big pot or two of chili, some of her special brownies—and that was it. "It was such a different time. We never worried about anyone showing up with a gun and going postal," she says. "People got together, had some drinks, danced, and had a good time. It was as simple as that."

Despite the magic of the Kennedy name, or maybe because of it, that campaign ended in a bitterly fought primary and President Carter's being re-nominated. Still, it was Yolanda's first time attending the Democratic National Convention, an opportunity that allowed her to make a connection that would change her life's path. She was getting off the elevator in the Kennedy headquarters hotel when she ran into Terry Taylor, her brother-in-law Wendell Phillips's former campaign manager in Baltimore. (Yolanda's connection to Taylor went back even further: they had attended the same high school in Rochester, and even went to the junior prom together as friends; they had always been very close.) Taylor introduced her to Ann Lewis, who was administrative assistant to then-Congresswoman Barbara Mikulski, a Democrat from Maryland. Lewis was also the sister of Congressman Barney Frank, a Democrat from Massachusetts. Lewis mentioned that Mikulski's team was looking for a legislative correspondent, and Taylor helped Yolanda set up an interview for the following week.

Yolanda still remembers how exciting it was to drive from Baltimore to DC on that late-summer day. She parked her car on the Senate side of the Capitol and had to walk many blocks to get to the Cannon House office building. She'd dressed for the interview in an outfit worthy of *Vogue*: a stylish skirt suit and three-and-a-half-inch-high heels, which made her look even more like a slim Amazon than she did in bare feet. She loved fashion, and even though she had already turned thirty, people still stopped her on the street and asked if she was a model. On that walk, she had time to think about her life and what she'd made of it so far. She was divorced, with a ten-year-old son, and was living with her boyfriend of several years. A job in Washington sounded glamorous and intriguing, but she worried about child care and the commute. Her boyfriend was encouraging and supportive, though. "Go and get that job," he'd told her. "We'll make it work."

When she arrived inside the building, she approached the "Members Only" elevator, not fully understanding what the sign meant. She knew a couple of the black members of Congress already, but she knew nothing about congressional protocol, and as she *was* going to see a member of Congress, she figured it would be okay. When the door opened, a group of men and only one woman got off. One of the men was Congressman Ron Dellums, who represented Northern California. For someone as enamored of politics as Yolanda was, it was like running into one of the Beatles. She remembered that her mouth literally dropped open. "This was my Hollywood," she would later explain. "One of my greatest desires in life was to attend a Congressional Black Caucus dinner. I was more starstruck by this small group of dedicated black people to our cause than I was to any movie star. This was my Oscars, and I knew that my moment to work side by side with them would come."

Dellums asked where she was going and then very kindly explained the elevator system. By the time he pointed her in the right direction, she had totally lost whatever cool she had assembled before the interview. She can still remember "shaking and feeling faint" while riding the correct elevator up to the third floor, where she was to meet with Ann Lewis in Congresswoman Mikulski's office.

She aced the meeting with Lewis and was asked to stay and meet with Mikulski. Yolanda was breathless. The only congressperson she knew personally was Parren Mitchell. The term *goon squad* has a slightly menacing definition in mainstream society, but in Baltimore, Parren Mitchell's Goon Squad—they took the name from a *Baltimore Sun* reporter who often referred to them as such—was something altogether different:

a group of highly educated, Christian men who helped Mitchell navigate the political waters so that he could ensure that black citizens enjoyed the rights promised to them in the Constitution. The group consisted of Wendell Phillips and Parren Mitchell; Gus Adair, head of the political science department at Morgan State College (as it was before its university accreditation); Pat Scott, who ran the art department at Morgan and was (and still is) a gifted artist; the Dobson brothers, Vernon and Harold, both ministers; Maryland Supreme Court judge Joe Howard; the Rev. Marion Bascom; the Rev. Frank Williams; and Lalit Gadhia, a civil rights attorney.

There was just one woman in the Squad: Madeline Wheeler Murphy. Her husband, William Murphy Sr., was a judge, and the Murphy family owned the *Afro-American* newspapers in Baltimore and Washington. Madeline's daughter Laura Murphy remembers those men and their egos being no match for her ladylike, picture-perfect, poised mother. As Laura said, "No, honey. She said she went to those meetings. She said she cussed them out. She'd march with them, she'd do whatever she had to do to move the mission of civil rights forward."

At the time, there were four black women in Congress: Shirley Chisholm, who ran for president in the 1972 Democratic primary; Cardiss Collins, who was elected to fill her husband's seat (George Collins in 1973); Yvonne Braithwaite Burke; and Barbara Jordan. These were the women Yolanda idolized. She would end up meeting them all, but first she had to win over Mikulski.

She had to wait for the congresswoman to come back from voting. Lewis indicated a spot on the couch, and Yolanda sat—and immediately felt out of sorts, like Alice in Wonderland: as if her knees were touching her chin and the furniture around her was becoming smaller. She wondered if her nerves were getting to her. This was before the age of social media or even Google, so she didn't know anything about Mikulski that she hadn't read in the paper or seen on TV. Then Mikulski walked in, and Yolanda understood: the congresswoman was both larger than life and just under five feet tall. Yolanda remembered being impressed by Mikulski's booming voice and commanding presence.

The interview lasted all of five minutes, and then Mikulski welcomed her to the team. Yolanda had the job.

"I was going to my Hollywood on the Potomac!

"A few months later, I was sitting at my desk when an assistant came in and asked if I would meet with an unexpected visitor. She explained that the young lady didn't have an appointment, but she thought I might want to take the meeting anyway. I looked at the stack of paperwork on my desk and wondered why anyone would ask me to meet with an unscheduled visitor. Then, when the young woman walked in, I got it: we were both black."

Because Yolanda's office was so tiny—more a nook than a proper office—the two women met in the hallway. The woman's name was Donna Brazile, and she was lobbying congressional offices to get support for the Martin Luther King Jr. national holiday.

"The more Donna talked," Yolanda says, "the more excited I became, because I was doing what I had always wanted to do. I was representing the congresswoman about an issue that might actually get traction."

Later that week, Yolanda tried to channel Mikulski's voice and presence when she reported on the important meeting she'd had with an emissary from civil rights heroine Coretta Scott King. "I didn't know yet that meeting Donna was the beginning of a new and exciting chapter in my life."

Minyon Moore was a girl from the South Side of Chicago. In the 1960s, when it seemed that the world was in turmoil, her home and her church (Third Baptist) were her safe havens. She knew her parents to be "hard workers and great providers." Her stepfather worked for the postal service; her mother worked for GTE, the General Telephone and Electronics Corporation. As with Yolanda Caraway, Minyon's was a community of "have-somes," but also families who were barely making it and living paycheck to paycheck. With so much hope and hopelessness in close proximity, Minyon's mother was known to be the strictest mom on the block. Minyon and her siblings were called "the streetlight kids," meaning that when the streetlights came on, they had better be back in the house. The punishment for letting the streetlight catch you out and about was clear and severe: "either your Saturday skating privileges would be revoked or, worse, you wouldn't be allowed to sing in the Sunday choir."

The winter Minyon turned nine, Chicago was hit with the worst snowstorm in the city's history. It was January 23, 1967, and the city was pummeled with twenty-three inches of snow. Winds whipped through the streets at an astonishing fifty miles per hour, and some of the snowdrifts were more than fifteen feet tall. Minyon's mother, like so many of the city's residents, was stranded in her office building overnight. The city streets and highways were littered with more than a thousand abandoned buses and, by some counts, fifty thousand abandoned cars. It was the most catastrophic natural event to hit the city since the Great Chicago Fire of 1871.

The next morning, Minyon waited by the window for her mother to come home. Sandra Marie Moore was a petite woman, just five foot two. "After hours of waiting, I saw my mother's slight figure, making her way down the street. She was holding two white bags. She had managed not only to make it through the storm, but also to bring home our favorite takeout from White Castle, one of the few restaurants in the city that remained open for business. As I was growing up, I wanted to be like my mother and have her mix of stamina and selflessness."

Minyon's uncle Dennis was the great storyteller of the family. She says, "He seems to have archived our family tree in his brain. He is known for making the stories come alive with facts and flourishes. He continues to connect so many of the dots of our family tree. He is a strong example of a man who cares for family. The sort of man that made Chicago seem less like a cold big city and more like an outpost of the South."

Minyon (whom everyone called "Minnie" back then) was a born defender. In elementary school, when a teacher kept picking on a fellow classmate for no apparent reason, Minyon jumped to the girl's defense. Then, one afternoon, the teacher came up to Minyon and slapped her hand with a ruler. "You're not the savior of the world," she told Minyon, "and I don't know why you think you can save her every time she gets in trouble." Minyon shakes her head at the memory of it. The sting of the ruler is still vivid all these years later—as was her response: "It didn't stop me," Minyon remembers. "It hurt, but it did not stop me."

Minyon's mother would save up all year, and each summer, her grandmother, whom she called Momma, would take her and her siblings to the family home in Terry, Mississippi. Every summer until she was sixteen, she spent her school vacation on the farm with her great-grandparents Papa Bud and Momma Lovie. Those trips down South shaped her vision of what her adult life would be like, because, as she said, "They were always people that I saw helping, and I was trying to figure out how I could do the same. How could I help people? How could I do things to help change people's lives?"

Minyon attended Chicago Vocational Career Academy (also known as CVS, Chicago Vocational School). The South Side high school had opened in 1941 and, because of the intense need for wartime labor, was put under the control of the U.S. Navy. Later, the school would be instrumental in helping returning GIs complete their education and set themselves up for the next phase of their career. In the early 1970s, when Minyon was there, the school saw a shift from a predominantly white student body to a predominantly African American one. The leaders of the school community took seriously the job of creating a generation of black professionals. The school principal, Reginald Brown, an impeccably dressed, no-nonsense leader, inspired respect and affection from both the students and the teaching staff. Under Brown, CVS boasted the best band and football team in the city. Also, Minyon was able to take black history classes at CVS, a new field back then, and one that wasn't always taught in public high schools. The teacher of the course, Ms. Almeda McPherson, was young and hip, and related each lesson to the times the students were living in. While Reginald Brown modeled a strong, positive image of what a black man could be, McPherson and the assistant principal, Ms. Willie Mae Crittenden, were especially powerful role models for young women such as Minyon. "Just the way they carried themselves," Minyon remembered, "made you want to carry yourself in a way that showed you respected yourself, your people, and the opportunities you'd been given."

For a while, Minyon thought she might want to be a doctor, so she volunteered at Northwestern Memorial Hospital. She thought she might want to be a Supreme Court justice, so she flew to Washington to visit her cousin, who was able to get her a ticket to sit in on an afternoon session of the Court. "See, there's a pattern with me," Minyon explains. "If I'm interested in something, I learn it first. I dig into it a little. I take myself to where it's happening. That's why I tell young people all the time, 'Spend some time volunteering, spend some time just putting your foot in the water. You will eventually find your comfort zone.'" After high school, Minyon enrolled as a part-time student at the University of Illinois while she worked part-time at the post office to pay her way through college.

That post–civil rights era was full of icons who inspired not only Minyon's career choices but also how she would move through the world. For example, Minyon grew up in a generation of women who dressed well for every situation. Barbara Jordan, the first African American congresswoman to come from the Deep South, was no exception to that rule. Minyon never forgot the speech Barbara Jordan delivered to the 1976 Democratic National Convention. "It was the most riveting speech I had ever watched on TV. The fact that she was the first African American woman to deliver a keynote address to a national convention wasn't lost on me, even at eighteen years old. While I was barely aware of the political importance or influence this speech would have on the nation, what wasn't lost on me was the fact that she looked familiar, she sounded familiar, and she spoke with that deep preacher-like voice that caused you to hang on to her every word. She was someone that you wanted to emulate. Her moral clarity raised our consciousness. To this day, her speech is considered, along with President Obama's, one of the best speeches of any political party. And it rings true today. 'We are a people in a quandary about the present,'" Minyon begins, quoting Jordan's speech. "'We are a people in search of our future. We are a people in search of a national community. We are a people trying not only to solve the problems of the present, but we are attempting on a larger scale to fulfill the promise of America.'"

No one was more central, at the time, to the conversation about the promise of America and its African American citizens than Jesse Jackson. Jackson had been a protégé of Dr. Martin Luther King Jr., and in 1966, King appointed him head of Operation Breadbasket, a job placement agency based in Chicago. As King explained in 1967, "The fundamental premise of Breadbasket is a simple one. Negroes need not patronize a business which denies them jobs, or advancement [or] plain courtesy. Many retail businesses and consumer-goods industries deplete the ghetto by selling to Negroes without returning to the community any of the profits through fair hiring practices." Jackson was a theological student in Chicago when he took the helm of Operation Breadbasket's Chicago branch. Under Jackson's leadership, the Chicago Breadbasket targeted and boycotted the big dairy companies, the Pepsi-Cola Company, Coca-Cola, and supermarkets. In its first two years, Operation Breadbasket helped create more than two thousand jobs and bring an additional fifteen million dollars in income to the neighborhoods where those companies operated. King called the boycott "spectacularly successful." Under Jackson's leadership, Operation Breadbasket helped Chicago evolve into the financial powerhouse of black America. In *Jesse: The Life and Pilgrimage of Jesse Jackson*, author Marshall Frady cites Chicago as "the most sizable and powerful financial base of any [black community] in the United States—a complex that included six banks, three savings-and-loans, and two insurance companies. Of the nation's one hundred black-owned enterprises with annual sales of over a million dollars, eighteen were in Chicago, a count second only to New York, and all eighteen had been demonstrable beneficiaries of Jackson's efforts."

In 1971, Jackson founded Operation PUSH (for "People United to Serve Humanity"). Increasingly, he had begun to broaden his scope from race-based operations to those that focused on economic and class issues. As he told the *New York Times*, "When we change the race problem into a class fight between the haves and the have-nots, then we are going to have a new ball game."

Operation PUSH's offices were in a stately stone building, complete with columns, in the Kenwood section of Chicago. Minyon was impressed before she even walked through the front door. "I was going and coming, back and forth to the PUSH offices. I got to know Reverend Jackson's aide, Craig Kirby. My whole attitude was 'I'm *getting* this interview.' And we would show up at PUSH every week—either it was my cousin or it was me. I ended up meeting Rev. Willie Barrow."

As she describes it, "I was an eighteen-year-old college student in Chicago, enrolled in a literature course. My study group decided to do our final paper on the topic 'When Blacks Become Mainstream, Do They Lose Their Identity?' We actually wanted to interview Reverend Jackson because the professor gave us the impression that if we got the interview with Reverend Jackson—who was, at the time, the most prominent leader in town—we would automatically get an A before we even wrote a word. So, because I was always determined and unafraid, I sought that interview! I ended up interviewing the legendary Rev. Willie Barrow, who was a key figure in the leadership of Operation PUSH and had fought to open doors in corporate America for young, educated blacks."

Like Minyon's mother, the Rev. Willie Barrow was a petite woman, standing just four foot eleven. In fact, she was known in the civil rights movement and throughout Chicago as the "Little Warrior." Reverend Barrow had marched in Selma with Dr. King after having found her gift for community organizing at a young age. When she was just twelve years old, she led the charge to integrate her Texas school bus. For years, the black children walked miles to school while a half-empty bus of white children rumbled past them. One day, Barrow walked right up to the driver and said, "We all alike—we've all got butts, and all we got to do is just sit down on the seat. And you got plenty of room—so why you want me to get off just 'cause I'm black? Nooo, we got to change that." And from that day forward, the black children were permitted to ride the bus.

When Minyon met Willie Barrow, it turned out to be an auspicious moment for both of them. Minyon had been well raised by her mother and grandmother. She had been groomed for leadership by the principal and teaching staff at Chicago Vocational School. She had landed a job as an advertising associate at Encyclopedia Britannica. Minyon was not only one of the few blacks there but also one of the youngest in the corporation. She showed up for work each day wearing a crisp silk blouse and a perfectly pressed suit. It's a uniform she wears to this day. Even if she's attending a march, Minyon Moore would be neatly dressed.

Then in her fifties, Reverend Barrow was ready to pass on what she had learned in the trenches of the civil rights movement. She had been close friends with Addie Wyatt, the first African American woman elected vice president of a major labor union (the Amalgamated Meat Cutters and Butcher Workmen of North America). Along with hundreds of others, the two women showed up in Selma a week after its Bloody Sunday (when state troopers attacked those attempting to cross the Edmund Pettus Bridge at the beginning of the Selma-to-Montgomery March) to continue the work of forwarding the cause of civil rights. Their host family was a schoolteacher who, along with her children (with the exception of the four-year-old), had been beaten and jailed during the Selma march. The two young women volunteered for kitchen duty at a local black church, but even that seemingly harmless task required training on how to navigate the constant threat of violence and what to do in the event of an attack. Every night there were meetings at which freedom songs were sung and plans were hatched to move the cause along. Addie Wyatt would later write, "This is a tense battle of nerves, but the power of love and endurance is evident in their battle-scarred and worn faces."

Those years, while terrifying and dangerous, had an energy and a momentum that gave leaders such as Willie Barrow a great deal of clarity. The enemy, so to speak, in the Jim Crow South was always in plain sight. The path to change was difficult but not mysterious. Reverend Barrow could see the arc of the 1980s on the horizon: things were changing and fast, for the better and for the worse at the same time. She believed that "if these youths don't know whose shoulders they stand on, they'll take us back to slavery." Barrow had learned how to lead, she said, by opening her home to "Coretta Scott King, Dorothy Height, Addie Wyatt. We have to teach this generation, train more Corettas, more Addies, more Dorothys."

Enter Minyon Moore. When Reverend Barrow looked at Minyon, she saw in her a kindred spirit, a young woman who would give as much, if not more than, she would get. "By the end of our first meeting," Minyon says, "I knew that I didn't need an interview with Jesse Jackson to land an A on my paper. An afternoon with Reverend Barrow had made history come alive for me."

Reverend Barrow was also a part of a generation of women leaders who would not take sides against themselves. Whereas previous generations of black women might have been content to let black men lead, Reverend Barrow and her peers decided simply and without much proclamation that they must fight on all the fronts that mattered to them. Indeed, Barrow was noted not only as a civil rights activist, but also as someone who stood on the front lines for women's rights and the labor movement. When her only son came out in the early 1980s and later died of AIDS, in 1983, Reverend Barrow became a champion for gay rights and an early HIV/AIDS activist.

"Reverend Barrow and I went on to become very close. She was a mentor, second mother, and friend," Minyon says. "After graduation, I went and got a fancy job at Encyclopedia Britannica, and that's when she said to me, 'You need to come back to PUSH. You need to serve your community. You need to start volunteering. You need to be active in our efforts . . .' So, I started volunteering every free moment I had. It was a moment when the civil rights leaders wanted black Americans to shift their focus from what Reverend Barrow called 'paper money' and dig deep into wealth building. 'Buy your first home, but also own radio stations, own TV stations, make sure you own your black businesses.' It was a very radical idea back then."

PUSH believed that every committed person could use his or her station to uplift the race. Minyon never forgot the lessons she learned from Reverend Barrow and the PUSH leadership team. "When you're in corporate America, what is your role in corporate America? They're spending our dollars, so how do you make sure that they give back to the community? You're in politics; how do you make sure that your elected officials are investing in your neighborhoods? Are our kids safe, and are they getting a quality education?" Indeed, as Minyon recounts, "it was Reverend Jackson who would visit high schools and speak truth to power to our young people. He talked about reducing teenage pregnancy and about black-on-black crime before they became hot-button issues."

As for Reverend Barrow, Minyon says, "she taught me one of my earliest and biggest civic lessons: the difference between wealth and *wealth*. She explained to me that wealth was no more than a transfer of paper. I can still hear her voice now, so rich with wisdom, but so down-home at the same time: 'Ain't nobody got no money! This is all about paper wealth! Paper wealth! You're just trying to get some paper wealth!' I thought, 'Well, that makes sense.'"

Minyon believed deeply that the "line for leadership is short." The key, she learned early on with PUSH, was that no task was too big or too small to take on. The skills she learned in corporate America blended well with the life lessons she learned in the civil rights movement. Even as a young businesswoman, she continued to be active in PUSH, sharing what she learned in the corporate boardroom with the leaders there. It was, she believed, an even exchange. The lessons she learned in both worlds gave her a foundation grounded in values and principles that, she says, guide her to this day.

"My first exposure to high-level politics came in 1982," Minyon says, when Rev. Willie Barrow took her to the first organizing meeting of Harold Washington for Mayor. In the corporate world, Minyon had earned a seat at the table; but at this particular meeting, she humbly took another place: in the corner, holding Reverend Barrow's purse, while the key players sat around a polished mahogany board table. Even before the first person sat down, the massive size of the table conveyed to Minyon that this was a room of real power and real decision making. Every black leader in Chicago was there, trying to convince Washington to run for mayor. Harold Washington looked around the room and said, "Our patch isn't big enough." The leaders looked at one another, puzzled. Minyon was relieved that she wasn't the only one who didn't get Washington's lingo. The reluctant candidate went on: "You will have to help me raise money. You have to help me register voters. And you have to help me broaden my coalition. Until you all tell me how we can accomplish *all* of these things, I am not ready to jump into this."

The men and women at the table were stunned at how hard Washington was pushing back. "The leaders and the community wanted him to run for mayor more than he did—or so it seemed from my little corner," says Minyon. So the group reconvened in a few weeks with a bona fide plan. That plan launched Washington's candidacy.

Minyon's first major political experience was as a youth organizer for the Harold Washington campaign. She remembers, "Nobody was reaching out to the young people, and so I gathered up some of my friends—Ken Bennett, Mark Allen—and we all went down to the campaign office and decided that we were going to organize the college students and young people. It was just that simple. It wasn't like somebody told us to do it. We saw a need and we became the youth organizers for the campaign.

"Ken, Mark, and I were all Operation PUSH buddies, the young people who would hang around the office. We took it upon ourselves to start doing voter registration and outreach in the youth community. The slogan was 'Come Alive October 5.' It was the early days of hip-hop; the rhyming helped.

"Mark is one of the most skilled organizers I know. There was nothing he couldn't organize. He went on to become a radio announcer, but he was just a really gifted organizer.

"Ken is the exact same as he was when he was growing up—just a good, decent, really thoughtful human being. Yeah. I mean as respectful as they come. Ken is the type of person every mother and father would want as their child. He was just that steady, and he went on to work for President Obama as his state director in his Senate office for Illinois, and then he went on to work in his White House.

"They'd give us our walk sheets and we'd go out walking. Walk sheets lay out the areas where you go and you knock on doors. You knock on doors and you pass out literature and say, 'You come vote.' We were primarily focused on making sure that students on college campuses were registered and they were voting.

"This was an exciting time for us. It was the 1980s, and people in Chicago hadn't lost faith in the promise of the 1960s. In fact, I think we were gaining faith, because to see this Congress member named Harold Washington come back home and become the first black mayor of Chicago, that was exciting for us. It was certainly an exciting time at Operation PUSH, because every Saturday our forum was about making sure you got registered to vote, making sure we built the right coalitions. To be exact, we weren't just organizing African American students; we were organizing any student and any young person. We were introducing young people to the concept that they could make a difference, that if they voted, then this candidate could actually be a candidate that they could say they were partly responsible for putting in office. We were doing more by teaching them about the power of the vote as opposed to changing their minds.

"Harold Washington's race was just a natural progression of progressive politics in the city of Chicago. One thing that people don't understand about my hometown—it is a very activist city. I mean, people are active. They are active organizing, they are active building, but they are really great community organizers. It's no doubt that President Obama said he was a community organizer because we are just noted for that whether we're organizing around issues or campaigns. Chicago is always very active."

Later, when Washington won his historic bid and became the first African American mayor of Chicago, Minyon worked her connections to get Washington to visit her church. She had organized her fellow churchgoers, worked tirelessly on outreach, and delivered the votes. Now that he was elected, all over town, people wanted to spend a moment with the man who had made history. Minyon says, "Once he was elected, I worried the crap out of his then scheduling director, Ed Hamb. Believe me when I tell you, I worried the stew out of him. I would not take no for an answer. I said, 'Well, we worked for him, so he can come work for us in the community now, right?'

"The first couple of times, I would just go down to city hall and I'd ask to speak to Ed, but he was always busy. Of course, I didn't know anything about making appointments. I made an appointment, and then he finally saw me and I told them what I wanted. A month or two later, he finally put it on the schedule. I think that surprised everybody at my church, too. They were walking around saying, 'She really got the mayor to come to the church.'"

When Washington won, becoming the first African American mayor of Chicago, he paved the way for all the leaders who would follow him as mayors of major American cities: Harvey Gantt and Carrie Saxon Perry, David Dinkins and Willie Brown. Yolanda notes, "But after Washington was elected and after Jesse ran in '84, for the next decade, we had black mayors in every major American city: New York City, Los Angeles, Houston, Dallas, Detroit, Atlanta, Birmingham, Baltimore, Berkeley, Charlotte, Cleveland, Columbus, Compton, Dayton, Denver, Durham, East Orange, East St. Louis, Flint, Hartford, Kansas City, Little Rock, Memphis, Minneapolis, New Haven, New Orleans,

Newark, Oakland, Philadelphia, Raleigh, Richmond, Seattle, St. Louis, Trenton, Washington, DC. You could add Wellington Webb [Denver, 1991] as an example. Point being: black mayors ran pretty much every urban city in America."

One day, Reverend Barrow looked over at Minyon and said, "You need to quit your good-paying job and come work for me." "And I did," Minyon remembers. "I was twenty-five years old and I gave up my benefits, quit my good-paying job, and went to work for my people. I simply decided that was a worthy journey. I started there as a personal aide: typing up speeches and accompanying Reverend Barrow to the many events she attended. Then I became her executive assistant, and it was through the family leadership retreats that Drs. Tom and Barbara [Williams-] Skinner organized that I got to know figures such as Dr. Betty Shabazz and Dr. Maya Angelou, Coretta Scott King, Myrlie Evers-Williams, and Dr. Dorothy Height. I became so close to Reverend Barrow that people started calling me 'Little Willie.'"

Minyon came to feel, very quickly, that at PUSH, she had found her place. "I was inspired by the work they did on behalf of our community," she says. "I was inspired by their grace and grit. Their tenacity to fight for the betterment of black people without recognition was always humbling; to always be willing to stand up and take on the tough issues. I was just inspired every time I sat in a PUSH forum and listened to the community leaders speak."

Every generation has its calling. "I am so grateful to God that I was born when I was born," Minyon says with pride. "That I was able to experience all that I have and continue to experience. I didn't march with Martin Luther King, but I knew his wife and children. I didn't know Malcolm X, but I knew his wife and children. That connected me to [those leaders] in a very special way. It also taught me how to be humble in the midst of greatness. It taught me to be selfless, probably too much so, but that's okay. It also taught me that hard work pays off. Sometimes I think about the many nights I have stayed at one of these offices (from a field office to a corporate office to the White House, just trying to make a difference) and everybody else has gone home. That all started for me at PUSH headquarters, 930 East Fiftieth Street. That time, that place, that era taught me how to serve."

Donna Brazile is a Southerner through and through. Her home was the bayou, so close to the levees around the Mississippi River that she liked to say, "Every time it rained, we had waterfront property." Donna grew up with eight siblings in a two-bedroom, one-bath house. She remembers the April night in 1968 when her world changed forever. Rev. Dr. Martin Luther King Jr. was shot shortly after 6 p.m. It was dinnertime in the Brazile household. Donna's grandma Frances was home with the kids, as Donna's parents got home late each night from work. When the news broke about Dr. King, Grandma Frances called all the children into her bedroom and made them get on their knees to pray for King, who had been rushed to the hospital. The family were devout Catholics, and as Scripture mandated, they prayed without ceasing, both during Mass and at home.

That night, Donna and her siblings prayed for Dr. King's recovery. And when they were not praying, they sat glued to the TV. The top of the giant wood-encased set served as a kind of altar, where pictures of the family heroes were displayed: Jesus, John F. Kennedy, and Dr. King alongside family photos and objects from Mardi Gras season.

Later that evening, when Donna's parents returned home from work, they gave the children the bad news: Dr. King was dead. While her brothers and sisters cried, Donna remembers being *furious*. "Why would anyone kill Dr. King? I *loved* Dr. King," she says, her voice full of the kind of passion that blurs the present and the past. "I supported civil rights because it meant freedom, equality." Big words for a child, but words that found a place in Donna's vocabulary early on.

Donna couldn't stop questioning the morals of a world in which a man like Martin Luther King Jr. would be murdered. Her mother,

Jean, distraught and used to Donna's soliloquies, urged her daughter to be quiet—or, as Donna remembers it, my mother said, "Shut up, Donna." But Donna also remembers that "I couldn't shut up. I was angry."

The murder of Dr. King ignited a defiant streak in Donna Brazile, one that left her ready to defy whoever got in her way, including her parents. Her father, Lionel, and her mother were both proud supporters of the civil rights movement. At the same time, they were not public people. They did not want to shake things up. Donna, who wasn't yet ten years old, was in mourning. The night after King's death, she sought some vestment that could mark her grief. She took her mother's black headscarf and draped it across the door like a flag. "It was a small act," she says, "but for me, it was powerful. I had made it official. Just like those Baptist preachers who called down Jericho on the sinners every Sunday morning, I was ready to raise a little hell."

Brazile continues: "As a child growing up in Louisiana, one of my early heroes was Shirley Chisholm, the first black woman to be elected to Congress and the first woman to run for a presidential nomination in the Democratic Party. I knew all about her '72 race," Donna says. "I knew everything about her history, about [her] being the first black woman elected to the statehouse in New York. I knew about her feistiness, her fire." Donna was eleven at the time, and decorated her room with pictures of Chisholm that she had cut out of magazines such as *Jet* and *Ebony*. When she wrote an admiring letter to Chisholm's office, they sent her a button, which Donna hung on her bedroom wall. "On my bedroom wall, Shirley Chisholm shared wall space with posters of Michael Jackson and the Jackson Five."

Recently, Donna went to visit her alma mater, Louisiana State University. She was asked about being "controversial," and she reminded the faculty and the administration that she was "controversial on *this* campus." Among other things, in 1977, she became the first black female elected dorm president. In 1978, she began writing weekly columns for the student newspaper, the *Daily Reveille*, calling for the naming of Dr. King's birthday as a national holiday. She asks out loud, "Do you understand how controversial that was, back in 1978, when some people wanted to believe that he was a Communist and a traitor because he stood up for civil rights? I got in trouble in 1979 when I said I was a feminist and I was pro-choice. And again in 1980, when I called for the release of Nelson Mandela from prison. I've always been out there. I have never been afraid to put my pen to paper and to tell my story. If you're going to be involved in the public sector—if you're going to be involved in any sector, really, including academia—you have to be willing to know your truth and to tell it without being fearful of the consequences."

In college, Brazile interned for Congressman Gillis Long of Louisiana, chair of the House Democratic Caucus. One afternoon, as she walked down the hall of the Rayburn Building, Shirley Chisholm walked by. Donna, ready as ever for her moment, stopped her and said, "Hi, I'm Donna Brazile. I'm from New Orleans. I'm up here with Gillis Long. I'm also interning for Lindy Boggs, and I just want to let you know, I've admired you since I was a little girl. I remember when you ran for president."

Shirley Chisholm looked at her and said, "You're a little young to know me."

Donna then told Chisholm about cutting out pictures of her from *Ebony* and *Jet*. The two women developed an instant rapport. Every time Chisholm saw Donna in the hallway, she'd ask, "How's the little woman from Louisiana?" To which Donna would answer, "Great. I'm doing just great."

Brazile had political ambitions, and she'd met many of her icons (Bella Abzug, Rep. Parren Mitchell, Senator Ted Kennedy, and Mayor Andrew Young), but there was no easy road map for someone who wanted to be a civil rights activist in the late 1970s, what was already being called the *post*–civil rights era. Donna decided to volunteer for every person she felt could help her fulfill her dream of being a "worker in the vineyard of justice." She remembered that she "met Jesse through Coretta. And I met

Coretta through Ralph Abernathy. And when they all come into your life, you're never the same person you were before. Once these civil rights leaders got to know you and trust you, you worked for them—most of the time without pay. Service comes cheap, but it's highly rewarded. You're instantly in the family. Not like your biological parents—the civil rights movement connects you to another form of DNA. When it metabolizes, you're hooked for life. In service until the end."

When Coretta Scott King hired Donna Brazile straight out of a Southern college, it was over the objections of many. The movement people idolized the Ivy League just the way the rest of Washington did. Eleanor Holmes Norton, the civil rights icon, women's rights leader, and future congresswoman from DC, famously asked Coretta, "Why would you hire some young kid with no deep experience and unknown to work on the twentieth anniversary of Dr. King's historic 1963 March on Washington?" (It took "a long late-night call, some cussing, and a reminder that she was also young and unknown when she served as legal counsel to Fannie Lou Hamer" for Donna to, in her own words, "set Eleanor straight." Brazile went on to run Norton's first congressional campaign, in 1990.)

But it was back in 1982, during her work on the King holiday campaign, that she met Jesse Jackson for the first time. She said, "He was so charismatic. I kept thinking how lucky to meet someone who actually knew Dr. King."

It was, Brazile believes, her youth and vigor that got her in the front door of the King national holiday campaign, where she landed what she considered the job of a lifetime: director of mobilization. Her end goal feels inevitable to us now, but back then, it seemed impossible: to mobilize Americans in support of granting a national holiday in honor of Martin Luther King Jr. She says, "I promised the leaders, including Coretta Scott King, that I would never fail them. I was twenty-two, but I had the experience of those who had come before to organize, mobilize, and build a movement. And I was out to prove that they'd taught me well."

Sometimes this made for unlikely bedfellows. Brazile says, "I've got a picture of me, Coretta Scott King, [Dr. King's son] Dexter King, and DC Delegate Walter Fauntroy, and Michigan Congressman John Conyers from the same King holiday effort back in 1982. Me with my big Afro."

Those years of the campaign made Brazile feel vital but lonely. "I never went home," she recalls. "I didn't have a lot of money, but I'd send what little I had—fifty dollars, a hundred dollars—home to my mom. When she asked, 'When are you coming home?' I would say, 'Oh, soon. Soon.' She'd press me further: 'Well, what are you doing now?' and I'd tell her, 'Oh, I'm working on a very important project.' I had a day job because I had to eat, but my real job was to make sure that we got the holiday and to help organize the twentieth anniversary of the historic 1963 March on Washington. All those buses and buses of people. And getting millions of signatures on the petitions. I did not go home for Christmas. I was broke, and what little money I had I sent home to help my parents. I spent every Christmas working until we got a King holiday. I spent every Christmas licking envelopes, getting things in the mail, soliciting for money, getting help. I think back now when people say, 'Well, how come you don't do this, you don't have that?' Because I was so committed to the movement, so committed to making all of this happen. And the leaders of the movement put a lot of responsibility on my shoulders to get it done. And I felt like I couldn't fail them."

At that first celebration of his birth, at least a quarter of a million people came to honor Dr. King, as well as his dream and a legacy for jobs, peace, and freedom for all. "But when you're twenty-one, twenty-two, having this responsibility," Donna says. "It was huge. Huge. Huge! Because I had on my shoulders the responsibility of continuing a great march for justice, freedom, and equality."

The legislation declaring the King holiday passed, and Donna remembers how honored she was to be invited to the White House for the signing of the bill into law. She says, "I never thought I would get inside the White House. . . . I'll never forget that President Ronald Reagan wore a brown suit. Brown suit, brown socks, brown shoes, brown hair, and brown eyes. I mean, I studied him. But I was there to witness the signing of [the bill]. And that was my first visit. I was struck by the scale of it. It looks so big from the outside, but once you get in it, it's a big house. It reminded me of some of the mansions I would see—we called them plantations back where I was from."

She continues: "The signing took place in the East Wing of the White House, in the East Room. First there was a small meet-and-greet with leaders of the Congressional Black Caucus and Stevie Wonder, who had been instrumental in the final push for the holiday. Then we all went out later for the signing. It really felt like I was part of history, but I was still so young. I was twenty-three when the bill passed. I'm not sure I fully understood what it all meant. Here was a campaign where we were actually making history by getting the third Monday of January designated in honor of Dr. Martin Luther King, who inspired so many of us to get involved and become engaged in the movement for change." From that moment, Donna says, she felt as if she had acquired "wings" and could claim a seat at the table. Yet her next step was a controversial one in terms of the civil rights movement: she wanted to work for the Rev. Jesse Jackson.

Leah Daughtry's first recollection about her meeting Reverend Jackson was that he was "just really tall, so tall." She admits that her perception of him had been skewed ever so slightly by her age: she was six years old when she met the six-foot-three reverend. She already knew that he gave powerful speeches. Year after year, throughout her childhood, she watched him bring the house down with them. "I'm a church girl," she explains decades later. "So my definition of great speaking is pretty high. The Reverend was an amazing speaker, a really extraordinary preacher."

Jackson's Afro also made an impression on Leah. "It's hard to remember, but growing an impressive Afro wasn't something you just did. A great Afro takes maintenance: the right balance of washing and moisturizing; African American hair tends to be dry. Detangling is an art form—you want to use a wide-tooth comb—and regular trims are a must. And even with all of that, the 1970s and early 1980s are full of famous examples of lopsided, ungroomed, just not cool Afros. So Reverend Jackson's Afro was not just a statement of cultural pride to the world. It also signaled to the community, like a well-made suit, that he was a man who could handle his business."

Leah's father, the noted civil rights activist the Reverend Herbert Daughtry, was working with Reverend Jackson on Operation Breadbasket to improve the economic conditions of black Americans in communities across the country. "Some of my earliest memories are of doing boycotts with those two men," Leah says. "Reverend Jackson would come to town, and he and my father would lead these boycotts of the A&P supermarkets because they wouldn't hire black people." Reverend Daughtry was the chair of Youth in Action, a key partner of Operation Breadbasket. "The headquarters of our activism was our church, The House of the Lord," Leah adds. Regular visitors included globally well-known activists such as Stokely Carmichael (Kwame Ture), Maulana Ron Karenga (the creator of Kwanzaa), poet and author Amiri Baraka, artist-activists Ossie Davis and Ruby Dee, and South African freedom fighter Joshua Nkomo. In New York, Leah's father's church was an essential stop for anyone seeking to heighten their political influence or connect with the community. These men—and they were mostly men—came to her father seeking guidance and support, and Leah therefore got to know them and interact with them at a different level, and form a different vision of who they were outside their fiery speeches and public personas.

Donna Brazile remembers that a trip to see Reverend Daughtry and his church was a key stop for any young African American activist at the time. "I met Leah's dad while still in college at LSU. We drove an entire day from Baton Rouge to Brooklyn to meet this fiery black nationalist Pentecostal preacher. At the time, I didn't know Leah—she was a younger version of what we all thought of ourselves at the time: warriors for the cause. But Leah was coming up."

Many of the guests at Reverend Daughtry's church became lifelong friends to a young Leah. "I first got to know Dr. Betty Shabazz, widow of Malcolm X, through Dr. Betty's regular visits to my father's church. After worship, Dr. Betty would come to the pastor's office for chitchat and she'd ask me to get her a plate from the kitchen of whatever the church ladies had cooked up for the Sunday meal, asking, 'Baby, can you fix me a plate?' Later, when I learned to bake, I'd slip Dr. Betty a slice of cake or pie. 'Baby, did you make that? That's good!' Or she would say, 'Baby, can you bake me a cake?' Dr. Shabazz loved chocolate cake, yellow cake with chocolate icing, and especially pies. She would light up at the sight of one. 'Oh, baby, you made me a pie!'"

Leah continues: "Dr. Shabazz was beautiful—and brilliant. She could get up and make a speech on any subject with little or no notice. She was proud she'd earned her doctorate, that it wasn't honorary. She taught at Medgar Evers College, and she was always well dressed." She adds: "Dr. Shabazz was a St. John girl. She liked to show off her legs."

Although Leah's father's base was the church, his circles were wide and concentric. And Leah got to know them all: the black nationalists and the Pan-Africanists, the post–civil rights era capitalists and the dyed-in-the-wool socialists. Her father's friends and colleagues included Muslims and black Hebrew Israelites. Every representation of black political thought was present. Despite their philosophical and theological differences, they all knew the power of coalition. Reverend Daughtry's church was the meeting place, and he was the leader. It was a valuable lesson for a young Leah, who learned that you can get along with just about anybody if you unite around a common goal.

Leah was her father's firstborn, and every bit a daddy's girl. She was born the day before the March on Washington, an event the civil rights leadership expected her father to attend. Dr. Martin Luther King Jr., the Rev. Jesse Jackson, and Ralph Abernathy all knew, with confidence, that on that historic day, the Rev. Herbert Daughtry would be there. In the days leading up to the march and Leah's birth, her father went back and forth on his decision. Then, at the very last moment, he decided to stay home and wait with his wife for the birth of his first child. Leah's mother likes to joke that his decision is one of the reasons their marriage is fifty years strong and counting.

Reverend Daughtry believed in the importance of having one foot in both worlds—and by that, he meant the world of the white power elite and that of the strong African American community in which Leah was raised. Leah and her siblings were all educated in predominantly white schools. When the time came to go to college, Leah didn't feel pressured to consider a historically black college. When the time came to go to college, Leah's father said, "You should go to the school you deem the best. Don't worry about learning our culture; that should not be your primary consideration. Besides, you've got that already. And if I'm waiting until now to get you culture, it's too late. So, if you want to go to a black school, fine. But if you decide to go to a white school, that's fine too; go up there where the white folks are and learn what they're giving out up there."

Leah says, "My father always stressed the importance of having people who were your *inside* men and women, who worked within the traditional structures and the white-majority seats of power, and the *outside* people, who worked with and on behalf of the people first and foremost." From her earliest days at Dartmouth, with her success and her ability to traverse worlds, Leah was marked as a classic inside woman. Still, she says she couldn't have done it without the love and support of the people at home. "My community was always supportive of me being on the inside," she says. "They loved me and they nurtured me; they got it." She was becoming a political interpreter: translating to the inside folks what was happening on the streets, and elucidating to the outside folks what was happening on the inside. She carried both worlds with ease because her intent was clear and her compass true: "I work on the inside, but I have never lost sight of where or who I've come from or where or who I represent."

These are the stories of how we began. While we're united in friendship and in our efforts to make a better world, we come from very different backgrounds and have very different styles of how to get the job done. The idea that black women are a monolith has always made Washington a tough place to navigate for black women some view as not fitting what their white colleagues consider to be "the norm."

In 1977, during her confirmation hearing for the post of secretary of housing and urban development, Patricia Roberts Harris was asked by Senator William Proxmire, the Democrat from Wisconsin, whether she had sympathy for the poor. "Senator, I am one of them," she replied. "You do not seem to understand who I am. I am a black woman, the daughter of a dining car worker. I am a black woman who could not buy a house eight years ago in parts of the District of Columbia. . . . If you think I have forgotten that, you are dead wrong."

Each of us is old enough to remember when black folks couldn't vote or live where they wanted; to remember the assassinations of our heroes and the images of ordinary black people being beaten in the streets. The years went by, and we rose up the ladder. Today, you'll find us to be well-dressed and well-coiffed, powerful black women who earned our place at the highest levels of government in these United States. But if you look at us and think for a second we have forgotten where we came from or who nurtured us, you are more than mistaken. You're dead wrong.

2

Brooklyn, 1980: Before Black Lives Mattered

In the 1970s in New York, unchecked police brutality resulted in a string of high-profile murders of young black men. Leah remembers them vividly. Among the deaths was that of ten-year-old Clifford Glover, who was shot by an undercover white police officer. Glover, who was with his father, was shot twice while running away from the officer. The bullets ripped through his back and emerged through his heart. The officer, Thomas Shea, was acquitted by a jury of eleven whites and one black citizen. After the trial, there were riots resulting in more than two dozen injuries, including among fourteen police officers.

Decades before the death of Trayvon Martin, Clifford Glover captured the imagination of a city that could not see the logic in shooting a weaponless child in cold blood. The Rolling Stones even sang about Glover in their song "Doo Doo Doo (Heartbreaker)."

Clifford Glover haunted the dreams of the great poet Audre Lorde, who wrote about the young boy in one of her most famous poems, "Power." The poem throws down the gauntlet with a line about the centuries of African Americans, from slavery to the present day, who could not protect their children from injustice and harm. Lorde wrote:

The difference between poetry and rhetoric
is being ready to kill
yourself
instead of your children.

Lorde goes on to use Glover's killing and the one black woman in the jury as a parable about the abuse of power and about how power is stolen away:

A policeman who shot down a ten-year-old in Queens
stood over the boy with his cop shoes in childish blood
and a voice said "Die you little motherfucker" and
there are tapes to prove it. At his trial
this policeman said in his own defense
"I didn't notice the size nor nothing else
only the color." And
there are tapes to prove that, too.

Today that 37-year-old white man
with 13 years of police forcing
was set free
by eleven white men who said they were satisfied
justice had been done
and one Black Woman who said
"They convinced me" meaning
they had dragged her 4' 10" black Woman's frame
over the hot coals
of four centuries of white male approval
until she let go
the first real power she ever had
and lined her own womb with cement
to make a graveyard for our children.

That same year, a fourteen-year-old boy named Claude Reese was in the basement of his apartment building, decorating the room for a party with a group of six other teenagers. Suspecting that a burglary was in progress, someone called police to the scene. A twenty-four-year-old police officer named Frank P. Bosco shot at Reese because he believed the teen was holding a weapon. When Reese's body was found, he was holding an eighteen-inch saw with a pistol grip. Bosco was acquitted of the murder.

On Thanksgiving Day 1976, fifteen-year-old Randolph Evans was hanging out with friends in the Cypress Hills housing project in the East New York neighborhood of Brooklyn. Responding to a report that there was a man with a gun in the projects, Officer Robert Torsney shot Evans point-blank in the head. According to reports, Torsney did not check on Evans's condition, and his own partner, Matthew Williams, said that after the shooting, Torsney got in the squad car and calmly replaced the bullet that had been discharged from his gun. When Williams asked Torsney what he had done, he allegedly replied, "I don't know, Matty. What did I do?" Torsney claimed he'd had a psychotic break due to epilepsy, a condition he'd never evidenced before the shooting, and never evidenced again after the shooting. The jury acquitted him by reason of insanity.

In the summer of 1978, thirty-five-year-old businessman Arthur Miller, from Crown Heights, Brooklyn, was strangled to death in a struggle with police. Leah was a junior in high school at the time. "By the time Randolph Evans was murdered," she says, "we were beginning to ask, 'Okay, really? How many of these are there going to be?' Evans and Miller became a catalyst for the black community to come together. My father and a group of men in New York City"—together known as the Big Four—"formed an organization called [the Coalition of] Concerned Leaders and Citizens to Save Our Youth. The 'leaders' were my dad, Assemblyman Al Vann from Brooklyn, Sam Pinn of Brooklyn CORE, and Brother Jitu Weusi, whose previous name had been Les Campbell." The Coalition started boycotts in downtown Brooklyn. "That was my first hands-on, up-close witnessing of activism in motion," says Leah.

While dozens of people were involved, these four men made for a unique leadership combination. Albert Vann had been born and raised in Brooklyn's Bedford-Stuyvesant neighborhood. He joined the military at the age of eighteen, rising to sergeant in the U.S. Marines. He went on to earn degrees from Toledo University, Yeshiva University, and Long Island University; spent decades as a public schoolteacher; and founded New York's African American Teachers Association. As a community board member, he was instrumental in the founding of Medgar Evers College and Boys and Girls Memorial High School, in Brooklyn. As an assemblyman, he worked diligently for better representation of community colors in New York City. His work in that area led to the creation of two additional congressional districts, three additional state senatorial districts, and six additional assembly districts in New York State. Al was the original cool: slim, well dressed whatever the style of the era, and known for wearing a single earring stud. He was a family man, with a beautiful wife, Mildred, and two adoring daughters.

Sam Pinn was also from Bedford-Stuyvesant. In 1971 he became the head of the newly formed Brooklyn branch of CORE, the Congress of Racial Equality. It was a time of great turmoil in New York City, and the *New York Times* reported that one of the things Pinn and CORE did was to gather witnesses to the increasing number of "line-of-duty" shootings of young black men by white police officers. Pinn told the *New York Times* in 1971, "We don't want them coming in here shooting first and asking questions later. This is a tense community and it is always on the verge of exploding." An aide told the *Times* reporter that one of the things CORE hoped to do was to "cool the young brothers out so that they don't give the cops an excuse to come in and shoot up a lot of people." Sam Pinn was sure and steady. He had the look of an established businessman. Always in suits and ties, he gave you the feeling he was going to or coming from a meeting, and that the briefcase he carried contained the secrets to our liberation.

Jitu K. Weusi, born Leslie Campbell, was raised in Bedford-Stuyvesant and was, along with Al Vann, a founding member of the

African American Teachers Association. A black nationalist, he founded a cultural organization called The EAST and the Freedom Now School, or Uhuru Sasa Shule, the first black independent private school in New York City. EAST Jazz became a prominent venue that featured performances by legends such as Sonny Rollins, Betty Carter, and Pharoah Sanders. Weusi's leadership in the community had been cemented during the Ocean Hill–Brownsville struggle for community control of schools. He was quiet, studious. Seven feet tall and always attired in traditional African fabrics, he had an easy smile and laugh, but make no mistake— he was a stone-cold master organizer. All the plans the Big Four came up with he was in charge of executing.

Black leadership has never been a monolith. From the days of W. E. B. Du Bois and Booker T. Washington, through the seemingly opposing camps of Martin Luther King Jr. and Malcolm X, there has always been dissent over strategy, method, governing principles, and endgames. "My father, Vann, Pinn, and Weusi were the most unlikely of compatriots," Leah says, "but they decided, 'We can put aside whatever our political differences are and whatever our economic or religious philosophies. We can sit in these rooms every Friday morning and plan around this thing even though we may not agree on who should be mayor and what the governor is doing. Doesn't matter. This is about a particular issue and how we move our community forward.'

"The four men would meet every Friday morning at our home or at Al Vann's home. . . . They would sit for two hours and just plan, and organize, and think. Each one had a role. Each one had a different community that they touched," Leah says. "I watched them go from a seedling of an idea to the rollout of this massive protest. You'd show up at these rallies and there'd be ten thousand people. It was an amazing thing that I could see was seeded in my mother's dining room. It was powerful to watch. That movement, in which we boycotted the downtown stores, happened because of the coalition they were able to build."

The Big Four decided that if the people could not get justice in the courtroom, then they would agitate for economic justice. On November

7, 1978, Reverend Daughtry led more than a thousand protestors across the bridge from downtown Brooklyn to Wall Street. It was Black Solidarity Day, and the *New York Times* sent a young reporter named Anna Quindlen to cover the march.

Quindlen reported that "the demonstration was led by the Rev. Herbert Daughtry, pastor of the House of the Lord Pentecostal Church, who has led several other such marches since a Crown Heights civic leader, Arthur Miller, was killed in a scuffle with police in June. . . . Their presence was as much a sign of a continuing protest against the quality of police protection in their community as against the Koch administration's policies on minority rights."

Standing on top of a car on Wall Street near Broadway, Reverend Daughtry told the crowd, "We have not been satisfied that police are going to stop killing our children. We are not satisfied that police are going to stop killing our model citizens like Arthur Miller."

Reverend Daughtry marched that day with Arthur Miller's widow, Florence. As Quindlen reported:

"Somebody's making an awful lot of money from the way we live, and some of those who are making the most money are located where we are going now." Later he said: "We want to touch all the bases, you understand. We'll be able to go back in the file and document every step we've taken along the way so that when the day of reckoning comes, somebody's going to say, 'Did you go?'"

"Yes," the crowd yelled back.

"Did you meet? Did you see? Did you talk?" he continued, and "Yes," the crowd responded to each question.

"We're tired of talking," he said.

The policemen who worked the march seemed not to take issue with Daughtry or his followers. Quindlen reported that one officer told her, "We've been on duty with them before. They have a point to make and they make it. They don't cause trouble."

The Big Four were, however, just getting started. Most of the black residents in Brooklyn shopped at the big downtown department stores: A&S, Mays, Korvettes, and Martin's. Leah explained that the plan the Big Four set out stated, "If we can't get the justice from the criminal justice system, then here's what we want from the merchants. This is where we spend our money. There's no place else in Brooklyn to shop. Brooklyn people don't go to other boroughs. If it's not in Brooklyn, they're not going to get it." The Big Four then discussed the ten-point plan they had presented to the city's merchants. "So we want the merchants to fund the scholarship fund. We want summer jobs for young people. We want a crisis fund for people who are having challenges in their lives. And [the] merchants said no. We're not funding it. It's not our problem. It's not our business. Take your problems elsewhere."

So the Big Four launched a boycott. They got all the organizations that were part of the Coalition of Concerned Leaders and Citizens to Save Our Youth and, every single day for an entire year, their members boycotted the downtown stores. In the beginning, they boycotted all the stores, but the effort was too diffuse; they couldn't make a big enough impact. So they began a targeted boycott. They decided they would go from store to store, starting with Martin's, because it had only two doors: one on Fulton Street and one on a side street. Every organization took its turn standing out in front of the store and announcing the boycott. They talked to passersby about the murder of Randolph Evans and Arthur Miller. And they said, again and again, until the stores were closed for the evening, "Boycott. Don't shop!"

It was the holiday season, and with the steady pressure from the protestors standing guard in front of both its doors, people chose not to enter Martin's. Within six months, it closed. The store actually went bankrupt. When the other merchants saw Martin's declare bankruptcy, they said, "Okay, let's negotiate." During the negotiations, the boycott continued, now focused on Abraham & Straus department store. In the end, the Coalition got everything it had listed on its ten-point plan.

Leah says with a smile, "We still give scholarships in Randolph Evans's name, though we fund them ourselves now. All these years later, every year, there are kids who go to college on behalf of Randolph Evans."

That catalytic event would spawn the Black United Front in New York (and later, the National Black United Front nationwide). In the meantime, the Big Four continued to organize demonstrations, now under the umbrella of the Black United Front, tackling a variety of issues, such as police brutality, greater job opportunities for black citizens at Brooklyn's Downstate Medical Center and at construction sites throughout the borough, fighting the closure of Harlem's Sydenham Hospital. They would go on to be instrumental in the election of David Dinkins, New York City's first black mayor.

"My father and my mother would go to these other cities who expressed interest and meet with the organizers and activists," Leah recalls. "They would drive around the country and meet with people. The Black United Front was born on the strength of their car and gas." The first national convention was held in June 1980, with more than a thousand people attending from forty-eight states and five foreign countries—including a young Donna Brazile, who made the twenty-hour journey with some friends in an old station wagon. "My father was elected chair," Leah says. "We had all these organizations that had long, complicated histories with each other. They didn't necessarily trust each other, but they all could agree on my dad. They trusted him, so they elected him chair. He was the chair of the Front for five or six years."

This was around the time that Dr. Betty Shabazz began to frequent Leah's father's church. "She was always in Brooklyn," Leah recalls. "She lived in Mount Vernon, but she was always in the orbit someplace. So she was always around. She and my mom became very good friends. So, when my mom, Dr. Karen S. Daughtry, was launching her organization, Sisters Against South African Apartheid, Dr. Betty was part of that. Ours was the activist church in New York before activism became popular. So everybody came here."

Reverend Daughtry was a moderating force for some of the more nationalist, more radical people who didn't want to deal with the "establishment types," and a radicalizing force for the establishment folks. When he was there, everybody was welcome. They would meet at the church. Steering and committee meetings were held in the fellowship halls around a big square table. "Not round," Leah specifies. "A square table. No theater seating, so everybody had a seat at the table."

She continues: "The Front made its name on a door-to-door brand of activism. Remember, this was before the internet. This was before cell phones. . . . This was before black radio; we didn't have any black radio. Now we have WBLS and WWRL, where you can go on and make an announcement. Back then, you didn't have any of that. It was true word-of-mouth. It was true talking to your neighbors, handing out a flyer. I used to do the flyers on a mimeograph machine. That's when you had to crank it up and then put the stencil on with the blue ink and run. When you had ten thousand people show up at a rally then, it was because we *touched* ten thousand people. Or we probably touched twenty thousand to get ten thousand there. But that was hand-to-hand, knocking on doors: 'Hey, sister, let me tell you about this event.' Or 'Hey, brother, do you know what's going on downtown?' We'd gather a bunch of kids, a stack of flyers, and we'd just hand them out, talking to people. Sometimes we pasted them on the telephone poles, back when there were telephone poles. That was how you organized back then."

Leah was, by this point, a high school student, and she paid careful attention to how her parents were turning a moment into a movement. Her younger brother has fewer fond memories of that time. At the rallies, the Front would give children signs to carry. There's a photo of Leah's younger brother carrying one that reads, "Am I Next?" He was ten at the time, just five years younger than Randolph Evans at the time of his murder. Years later, Leah learned how troubled her brother felt by that sign and his connection to Evans. "For many years he used to sleep with a baseball bat or a knife under his pillow," she says. "He felt unsafe.

"He wasn't the only one. My father began to get serious death threats during this time. The church was getting bomb threats. My parents were traveling more as the Front grew in stature both nationally and internationally, and they began to fear what might happen with the kids home alone." Reverend Daughtry moved the family to New Jersey, around the corner from Leah's grandparents. "We went to their house two nights a week for dinner," Leah explains. "If anything happened, they were right there. It gave my parents more peace of mind. But what it meant for us was that we couldn't go to the meetings. We were missing the boycott. We were missing the rallies because we were in Jersey."

As the oldest, Leah in particular missed the energy of activism that surrounded her father's church. She remembers thinking, "Oh, my God, we don't know what's going on." As in the Marvin Gaye song, "What's going on?" became a constant refrain around her family dinner table. Eventually, on Fridays, her father would drive to New Jersey from his office, pick Leah and her siblings up from school, and bring them back to Brooklyn so they could boycott, so they could be a part of what was going on.

For Leah, the training was invaluable. She learned that there's a lot of work that has to happen in any movement. "You don't just wake up and there's a movement," she says. "You don't just decide, 'Oh, let's go have a march.' There's a lot that goes behind that. Not just the planning but the conceptualization, the mission of it, the *why* of it. That's one thing I took away from it."

She learned also that "just because you are in coalition with people doesn't mean that you lay all of your values down or that you separate yourself from the community." Each leader of the Front had his own community. When they got ready to roll things out, Jitu brought the EAST. Sam brought Brooklyn CORE. Al brought his governmental political establishment people. And the Reverend Daughtry brought the church people in his network. As Leah says, "They didn't leave their people behind because they were in conversation with others. That's what I think made the movement strong and made it grow. These four modeled for us what it was like to be in coalition and collaboration with one another. So, I took that into my work. I can talk to anybody. There's something we have in common if it's only our humanity. If we can be respectful enough to have conversation, then we can move forward. Also recognize where you come from and who people are bringing to the table with them. That's what makes you strong."

Leah adds, "I learned from that, that you got to talk to people. That you can find common ground with anybody around a cause. If you can agree on the cause, then you can find a way forward. That only comes through conversation and through deciding that you're going to be open enough to have conversations." The people drawn to the Front's rallies could have said, "I don't know these people. I'm not coming." But, Leah says, "They decided that the stakes were too high for them to be separate. That the stakes were high enough that they needed to come together despite their differences." In some ways, the Big Four was a brain trust parallel to what we would become when we became the Colored Girls.

3

Jackson '84

On November 4, 1983, at the Walter E. Washington Convention Center, Jesse Jackson made the announcement that he was running for president. He was just forty-two years old. "I stood at the door," says Donna, who was twenty-three, "collecting names and giving out bumper stickers. I was excited. The press showed up in great numbers. We had six TV cameras, and I knew Reverend Jackson would be pleased with the huge turnout and coverage." Filling that large room had been an effort. Donna (along with Anita Bonds, field director for Jackson '84) took to the streets with pamphlets and went straight to the pulpit with scripts of Reverend Jackson's plea that our time had come.

The press would be a pivotal part of the campaign because Jackson was evolving his image from an outside agitator to an inside power broker. A *New York* magazine reporter named Michael Kramer reminded Jackson that when he'd first met him in 1972, the venue was the first National Black Political Assembly, in Gary, Indiana. Jackson had told the reporter then that "I do not trust white Republicans or white Democrats. I want a black party." Twelve years later, dressed in a conservative suit, he told Kramer, "I've learned a lot since then. I enjoy my role. I was born to lead."

At that point, each of us had met the Reverend, at some early, pivotal moment in our lives. Minyon Moore was a twenty-year-old college student when she met him. "I met Reverend Jackson at Operation PUSH one Saturday in the back-office area," she says. "He was introduced by one of his aides at the time, Craig Kirby. I remember thinking to myself what a towering figure in real life. He was always surrounded by lots of people—especially in the back offices of PUSH. I am sure it was uneventful to him, but to me it was like I had met a president or something."

Leah remembers that the Reverend was in and out of her father's church whenever he was in town. When he was considering his first presidential campaign in '84, "Run, Jesse, Run" was the slogan of the day, used by people trying to convince him to run. But the Reverend had concerns. Leah recalls that "the first exploration meeting was actually at our church. All of these elected politicians and activists came to talk with him about a potential presidential run. I remember he said to them, 'Look, I don't want *Run, Jesse, Run* to become *See Jesse Run.*'"

It was at that meeting in 1983, while Leah was home from college, that Jackson made the decision to run. She admits, "I was skeptical, because I didn't know enough about the presidential process to know whether it was actually possible. In those days, my definition of winning is that in the end, you are the president. I could not see, in that time of Ronald Reagan Republicanism, how the country would be ready for a black president. I was skeptical."

Yolanda Caraway was dressed in a ball gown and rushing toward the 1982 Congressional Black Caucus Gala when she first met Rev. Jesse Jackson. "I was attending the gala and running late. I was rushing through the revolving doors and literally bumped into him," she remembers. "He was with his daughter Santita and was very nice about it. The interaction lasted all of about fifteen seconds. But you would've thought I bumped into God."

Amelia Parker, the staff person for the vice chair of the Democratic Party (Richard Hatcher, the mayor of Gary, Indiana) and the DNC Black

Caucus (which comprised all the black DNC members), needed to fill the table purchased by the DNC, so Parker had invited several of the black staff members, including Yolanda. "I was so excited—this was my first CBC Gala. It was a balmy Saturday night in September, and I drove into DC from Columbia, Maryland, which is where I lived at the time. (I can't believe I used to make that commute every day.)

"I was running late, which is why I was flying through the revolving door and ran into the Reverend. I don't remember what I was wearing, but it was probably something by St. John. I didn't have a date. I don't remember anything about the actual gala. Running into Jesse L. Jackson was the most exciting thing that happened to me that night—that and to be up front and personal with so many of our leaders at that time, not just politicians, but business leaders (John H. Johnson, Bertram Lee) and civil rights leaders (Jesse Jackson, Dorothy Height), actors and entertainers (Ossie Davis and Ruby Dee, Stevie Wonder).

Back in Chicago, Reverend Barrow took the reins at Operation PUSH. On Saturdays, when Reverend Jackson wasn't on the road, he would come back to PUSH and would be our speaker. Minyon remembers, "Man, oh, man. That place was electrifying when he would come home. One of the things that I remember was that Reverend Jackson's pilots were African American. One of his lead Secret Service agents was African American. (I later learned he happened to be the father-in-law of one of my good friends, Isiah Thomas.) Emma Chappell, she was his chief financial officer. African American woman. I think what happened when all these people started showing up, it took your mind to a whole new level. We were all saying, 'Oh my God, look at all these professional people. Look at all of them doing all these exciting things.' I'm looking at black Secret Service agents, black pilots, black CFOs, and all I could think was 'Whoa.'

"On those visits to Chicago, what Jackson did was make it clear that he wasn't leaving us behind. He said, 'Okay, come on. Go with me on this journey. You've held me up and I'm going to make sure people see you.' But I think what he didn't understand was little people like me who were watching from afar were saying, 'I can do this, too.'"

While Donna was the only one to work on that first campaign in a formal capacity (Leah volunteered for the campaign in New Hampshire), we all saw Jackson's 1984 run as the birth of political possibility and a path to power. Donna joined Jackson's campaign as a regional field organizer and was later political director and convention floor manager. "That campaign was organic," she remembers. "One day we would be in a church talking about the boats stuck on the bottom, and the next day, we would venture into the community to do voter registration. We didn't have a traditional campaign, but it was a combo of a political movement and a revival."

Jackson's campaign did more than become the first credible race for an African American, since he won more than 18 percent of the vote in the primaries. His Rainbow Coalition brought unprecedented numbers of black, Latino, Native American, gay, lesbian, and other progressive members of the party to the table. Many credit both his campaign and the constituents he was able to rally as two of the elements that allowed the Democrats to take control of Congress in 1986, leading to their regaining the Senate and setting the stage for Clinton's run in 1992.

On a deeper, even more subtle level, what happened in the wake of Jackson's campaign was that a whole swath of Americans who had never seen themselves in the political process began to broaden their imaginations and ambitions about what was possible. From a young Barack Obama, who has spoken about Jackson's influence on him, to the successful local and national campaigns that followed, Jackson's campaign rippled out inspiration and strategy. In 1989, David Dinkins became the first black mayor of New York City, and black candidates became mayors in Seattle, Memphis, and Denver. When Douglas Wilder became governor of Virginia in 1990, he became the first African American elected governor of any state since the Reconstruction era.

"When Reverend Jackson went to meet the Pope, he took my father," says Leah. "I remember my father saying, 'I never thought I'd meet the Pope, but here I am.'"

During the '84 campaign, Leah got to see Jackson up close. "I came to admire how engaging and charismatic he was. And funny. He was funny. He could wrap up his comments into phrases like 'I don't want *Run, Jesse, Run* to become *See Jesse Run*,' and everybody laughed, because we all knew what he meant. He used his humor in his talks in a way that engaged people."

New York City was going through a challenging time in the early 1980s. The city's residents were hardened to the idea of politicians and saw little hope or promise in the courting rituals of campaign cycles. Leah watched with interest as Jackson nimbly "broke through that concrete veneer of disbelievers. As I worked with the campaign, in New Hampshire, and we hosted him at Dartmouth, I was always amazed how white people responded to him, once they got in the room with him. Even the ones who said, 'There's no way he can win' were fighting to get seats, to get into the auditorium to hear him speak. Then, once they heard him, the response was often 'Wow, he's making some really good points.'"

She continues: "I don't think that they expected him to be as clear and as knowledgeable about the issues as he was. Everybody thought he was going to focus only on social justice issues. The fact that he could also talk about economic policy, hard economic policy, like what the Federal Reserve was doing, surprised people. But he was knowledgeable about it all: all of the key domestic and international issues of the time. It surprised a lot of people." But more than being conversant, on the '84 campaign, as the American citizens discovered, not only did Jackson understand the issues, but he spoke about them in a way that people could understand. He had a gift for taking complicated facts, figures, and timelines and distilling them in a way so that, as Leah explains, "regular people who didn't think about Russia every day, or who didn't think about the Fed every day, could understand why the Fed or why Russian policy was important in their lives. The only other person I've seen do that is Bill Clinton. Bill Clinton can explain anything. You feel smarter just by being on the receiving end of that conversation. 'Oh, so *that's* what that means! Okay.' He and Reverend Jackson have the same quality of being able to help people understand issues without making them feel stupid. They can explain it in a way that you would find relevant and understand the relevancy without feeling like you didn't have the proper education or that somehow you missed something in school."

Leah was just a college student then, but she took on organizing Jackson's Hanover campaign. New Hampshire held the first primary that year, and a crowd of fifteen hundred, mostly young people turned out to hear Jackson speak at the University of New Hampshire. On a chilly October day, he would lead them on a mile-long march to the Durham city hall to register to vote. But first, he spoke for twenty minutes, brilliantly and without notes. Then he led the crowd in some good old-fashioned call-and-response. "I am!" Jackson began.

"I am!" the crowd responded.

"Somebody!"

"Somebody!"

"Respect me!"

"Respect me!"

"Protect me!"

"Protect me!"

"I can be!"

"I can be!"

"Whatever I want to be!"

"Whatever I want to be!"

"I am!"

"I am!"

"Somebody!"

"Somebody!"

Reverend Jackson routinely did this chant at the end of every PUSH service on Saturday. He would conclude the morning forum with "I Am Somebody." He would also do this when he visited colleges, high schools, and jails. It was his way of letting people, especially young people, especially in the inner cities, know that "you may be born in the slums, but the slums weren't born in you." With each chant, people got louder and more emboldened. It was our generation's form of empowerment.

"I didn't know what I was doing," Leah notes with a smile. "I don't think *any* of us knew what we were doing on the campaign that first time. None of us had worked on national politics at that level before. We were learning as we were going. Which is good and bad, you know?"

For Donna Brazile, the opportunity to do what had never been done before was always good. She also had a high level of tolerance for working without a blueprint or a safety net, a quality that held her in good stead during the Jackson '84 campaign. "Reverend Jesse Jackson will always have a special place in my growth and development because he took a chance on a young woman from Louisiana to manage many of his state-wide campaigns during his 1984 historic bid for the White House," she says.

Shirley Chisholm once said, "If they don't give you a seat at the table, bring a folding chair." Donna remembers that Jackson '84 represented a transformative moment, when a whole generation of young people came to see themselves as "no longer a bystander in history, but living in the moment. The crew who survived the politics of the 1970s all found a way to the table. And many of us could bring in the folding chairs."

Having grown up with a brother-in-law who was heavily involved in the civil rights movement as pastor of Baltimore's Heritage United Church of Christ, Yolanda knew who the key African American players were in national politics. In those years, no one was more electrifying than Jackson. In 1983, while working at the DNC, Yolanda attended a DNC Black Caucus meeting chaired by the late congressman Mickey Leland. Reverend Jackson had requested this meeting to discuss his potential run. "This was the first time he actually spoke with this group about the possibility of him running for president in '84," she said. "I think most of the DNC members in the room thought he had lost his mind, but he actually did make a good case for it. And his reasoning holds true today: we need to stop being used and disrespected by the Democratic Party." Yolanda noted, "I've always speculated that the Rainbow was originally intended to become a new political party."

In 1984, Yolanda was thirty-two and director of education and training for the DNC. She planned and led three-day regional campaign training seminars across the country. Between 75 and 125 aspiring candidates, campaign managers, and workers attended each session. It was an exciting glimpse into the very earliest stages of a political career. In each seminar, a handful of the most talented and ambitious men and women would eventually run for, and win, seats in Congress, the Senate, and other state and local bodies. The most notable candidate whom Yolanda trained? Rahm Emanuel, who would go on to be a prominent congressman, chief of staff to President Obama, and mayor of Chicago. Yolanda remembers that "Rahm was a student at Northwestern and worried the hell out of me for student discounts on the training workshops. He told me he could get a bunch of students to participate if I got them a discounted rate. I did, and he made good on his promise. He showed up with a ton of his classmates, which helped me with attendance and bringing in young people. And at the end of the day, this is what we were trying to do: widen the tent."

For Yolanda, the job signaled both independence and agency. "It was the first job where I was pretty much on my own to plan and execute every aspect of the program, including selection of speakers, materials, travel—*everything*! I worked with two great interns, Bill Cramer"— Cramer still volunteers on her team at the Democratic Convention every four years—"and Brad Kiley. They were two college-age white boys who worked their asses off and loved it. In fact, we all worked our asses off and loved it. Looking back over the years at what I've done, it was probably my favorite job."

"In 1984, I went to the Democratic Convention in San Francisco to serve as floor leader," says Donna. "My job was to help Jackson get enough signatures to have his name placed in nomination. So I went to every state delegation asking for help. It was a big job, and I had less than a day to get it done. Once I had gained the seven hundred fifty signatures necessary, time was running out, and I ran back to the Hilton hotel where Reverend Jackson was staying. Mrs. Jackson told me he was in the bathroom shaving. I knocked on the door and said, 'Reverend, I need your signature. We have enough names to place you in nomination and you *will* address the convention.'"

Jackson's remarks that evening were words for the ages. He told the crowd:

Tonight we come together bound by our faith in a mighty God, with genuine respect and love for our country, and inheriting the legacy of a great party, the Democratic Party, which is the best hope for redirecting our nation on a more humane, just, and peaceful course.

This is not a perfect party. We are not a perfect people. Yet, we are called to a perfect mission. Our mission: to feed the hungry; to clothe the naked; to house the homeless; to teach the illiterate; to provide jobs for the jobless; and to choose the human race over the nuclear race.

We are gathered here this week to nominate a candidate and adopt a platform which will expand, unify, direct, and inspire our party and the nation to fulfill this mission. My constituency is the desperate, the damned, the disinherited, the disrespected, and the despised. They are restless and seek relief. They have voted in record numbers. They have invested the faith, hope, and trust that they have in us. The Democratic Party must send them a signal that we care. I pledge my best not to let them down.

There is the call of conscience, redemption, expansion, healing, and unity. Leadership must heed the call of conscience, redemption, expansion, healing, and unity, for they are the key to achieving our mission. Time is neutral and does not change things. With courage and initiative, leaders change things.

No generation can choose the age or circumstance in which it is born, but through leadership it can choose to make the age in which it is born an age of enlightenment, an age of jobs and peace and justice. Only leadership—that intangible combination of gifts, the discipline, information, circumstance, courage, timing, will, and divine inspiration—can lead us out of the crisis in which we find ourselves. Leadership can mitigate the misery of our nation. Leadership can part the waters and lead our nation in the direction of the Promised Land. Leadership can lift the boats stuck at the bottom. . . .

If, in my low moments, in word, deed, or attitude, through some error of temper, taste, or tone, I have caused anyone discomfort, created pain, or revived someone's fears, that was not my truest self. If there were occasions when my grape turned into a raisin and my joy bell lost its resonance, please forgive me. Charge it to my head and not to my heart. My head—so limited in its finitude; my heart, which is boundless in its love for the human family. I am not a perfect servant. I am a public servant doing my best against the odds. As I develop and serve, be patient: God is not finished with me yet. . . .

America is not like a blanket—one piece of unbroken cloth, the same color, the same texture, the same size. America is more like a quilt—many patches, many pieces, many colors, many sizes, all woven and held together by a common thread. The white, the Hispanic, the black, the Arab, the Jew, the woman, the native American, the small farmer, the businessperson, the environmentalist, the peace activist, the young, the old, the lesbian, the gay, and the disabled make up the American quilt.

Even in our fractured state, all of us count and fit somewhere. We have proven that we can survive without each other. But we have not proven that we can win and make progress without each other. We must come together.

"At the 1984 convention," Yolanda says, "I was the lead whip for the Northeastern delegation, which included the late congressman William H. Gray. I will never forget Reverend Jackson's amazing speech, after which the house orchestra played the O'Jays' 'Love Train.' Everyone in that hall was singing and dancing and hugging and kissing—it was quite a moment. Bill Gray came over to me and said, 'I'm running for House budget chair. If Jesse can run for president, I'm going to run for budget chair—and I'm going to win.' And he did. First and only African American ever. It's a fact that has often been lost in the skirmish of history, how Jackson's run made the impossible seem possible, and in the process, he changed the game."

We'll never forget that Jesse always used "We," not "I." He was a collective; he made a whole generation of leaders proud of their history. We remember the ripple effect of Jesse's presidential races. A lot of people we knew said, "If he can do *that*, we can do *this*." Bill Gray did become chair of the House Budget Committee. Ron Dellums became chair of the Armed Services Committee. Bill Clay chaired the House Committee on the Post Office and Civil Service. Cardiss Collins joined the powerful Government Ops Committee. As Yolanda remembers, "People were walking around singing 'Love Train': 'If Jesse can do that, we can do this.'"

For us, it was a movement, not a moment. We saw and experienced how Jesse Jackson was ahead of his time, how hundreds of people gained powerful roles in the political process because of him.

Walter Mondale was eager to build bridges to the movement that Jackson had brought to the Democratic Party. He sought advisors and staff to help expand his campaign and the party's reach. Donna was brought on to work with Gayle Perkins, Mondale's deputy press secretary; Paul Tully, the campaign's political director; Gina Glantz, the campaign field director; and Nikki Heidepriem, who was responsible for women's outreach. Her first assignment was to organize a rally for vice presidential nominee Geraldine Ferraro in Harlem on 125th Street. To do this, she reached out to legendary political strategist and organizer Bill Lynch for help.

After the convention, Yolanda was asked to design and implement a training weekend for the Mondale-Ferraro staff. "That's when I met Ernie Green, one of the Little Rock Nine—the first to graduate—who had worked on the Reverend's campaign and he'd now gone over to the general election campaign, by his admission, 'as deputy campaign manager, in charge of all things Negro.' Preston Love, who was also with the Reverend's campaign, suggested to Ernie that he hire me as *his* deputy. I interviewed with him the week after the convention and knew what an important opportunity it was. I had never worked on a presidential campaign before. I thought it would be an interesting challenge. So the DNC let me take the leave, and I moved over to the campaign."

Ernie had already hired a young woman named Licia Green as his assistant. Licia was a student at Howard University and had taken off a semester to work on the Mondale campaign. Later, Yolanda says, "It was Licia who encouraged Ernie to hire me over the others he had interviewed." The two women became fast friends, and as Yolanda says fondly, "she became my little sister of sorts. She is still one of my best friends today."

The team's first assignment was to plan a black leadership meeting in Mondale's hometown of St. Paul, Minnesota. Congressional Black Caucus members, mayors, state and local representatives, civil rights leaders—all waited in a big conference room for the candidate to show up. "Little did we know," says Yolanda, "that Mondale was at his home, meeting with Jackson."

Later that evening, Yolanda met Jackson officially. Ernie Green, Yolanda, the Reverend, and Licia all met at the hotel bar. Yolanda's job, she would learn during the Mondale campaign, would be to serve as

Jackson's scheduler. "Not fun," she notes. "Because he was always chang-ing his schedule. He drove Licia and me crazy."

Ernie Green was on the plane with Mondale while Yolanda and Licia stayed behind in DC to hold down the fort. Yolanda recalls that "as we got closer and closer to Election Day, we realized that the campaign had no real get-out-the-vote strategy. That was the campaign where Andy Young had coined the phrase 'smartass white boys.' He was surely right about that."

Flo McAfee, a friend of Yolanda's from the Kennedy days, worked at the campaign in the communications department. Flo was beside her-self: she told Yolanda she had nothing to do. "Imagine that!" Yolanda says, still incredulous decades later. "Nothing to do on a presidential cam-paign that was winding up. Unbelievable."

Together, Flo, Yolanda, and Licia came up with their own get-out-the-vote plan. They called it "48 Hours," after the then-popular Eddie Murphy movie. Their plan was so powerful that the campaign adopted it. "We launched the Sunday before the election with events across the country, calling out, 'Forty-eight hours to save your future,'" Yolanda says. "It was a great idea, and it might have helped if they'd adopted it and launched it earlier. But we didn't win. We actually lost in forty-nine states."

Mondale lost that election by a huge number, but we began to see, as did many of our friends and colleagues, that Jackson didn't need to clinch the nomination to win on a much bigger scale. Leah says that because of Jackson's '84 campaign, "my definition of winning has changed. In those days, in '83, my attitude was 'What? He's gonna do *what*? Mm. Okay, all right. We'll see. I don't know how this is going to work.' But then I saw this room of black leadership coming together and saying, 'Okay, we support you. If you choose to do this, we will support you.' From my work on the Black United Front, I knew that these moments were rare. Getting this array of black leadership to agree on anything, particularly in a political enterprise, is a major undertaking. So that was a win."

As the campaign took off, we were all impressed by the crowds Jackson drew, by how well he held his own in political debates. "The positions he took were unlike anything we'd seen in a presidential campaign," Leah recalls. "More radical than I'd ever seen from a main-stage politician in my short life."

For us, the '84 Jackson campaign ended up being so much more than "See Jesse run." It was a master class in presidential politics for an entire generation of African Americans, the Colored Girls chief among them—and we were right in the middle of it. Before Jackson '84, Leah remembers thinking, "Conventions were something that happened on TV. You saw them on television, and you thought, 'They're having a convention. Change the channel to whatever's next.' Jackson '84 made us part of the 'they' of American politics. That was the presidential election where we got our first real taste of being in the room where it happened, the back rooms where deals were really made."

We all speak a common language when the conversation turns to Jesse Jackson. There was the way Jackson taught all of us who were working with him to learn the democratic process. He told us, "Once you learn the rules, you can break them with dignity." As we like to say, "He had coattails." Another Jackson-ism we all use a lot is the term *swinging people through*, meaning the responsibility you have to keep the doors of opportunity open and helping those coming behind you to walk through those doors as well.

Leah remembers her time working for Jackson '84 as an education in the little things that were big things. "Where do you get credentials? You have to negotiate for credentials. Okay. Oh, you have to negotiate for hotel space. Okay. These were things we didn't even know anything about. You just turned on the television and you watched the convention. We weren't aware that there was a whole set of enterprises and operations behind the scenes. We didn't know anything about election night boiler rooms, where people were getting numbers and people were making phone calls and calculations and projections."

Of that first Jackson presidential bid, Leah says, "We were building the airplane as we were flying it. We were just regular black people living our lives, and now, because of this man and his campaign and his influence, our vision has been raised. The idea of what's possible was different. He took us into rooms and into spaces we never imagined we would be in, some of which we hadn't even known existed. He made the space for us to experience American politics at the highest level. And we said, 'Okay, this is how it works. Got it.'"

4

Ron Brown

Born in 1941 in Washington, DC, where he'd rise to national recognition, Ron Brown was raised in New York in a unique setting that bred his affability and ambition. He was a son of New York City and, more specifically, a son of Harlem. His parents were graduates of Howard University who moved to New York City to manage Harlem's famed Hotel Theresa. Ron grew up doted on by loving parents and lived on the twelfth floor of the hotel. He was raised in part by the hotel's guests: athletes, artists, musicians, and politicians who opened his mind.

We understood that to have grown up at the Theresa made Ron a kind of black royalty: he'd grown up and been exposed to the crème de la crème of Harlem. And of course, Harlem had a very rich, strong black political community. Percy Sutton, David Dinkins, Charlie Rangel, Carl McCall, and Basil Paterson—all of them were part of that circle, and the circle that Ron was raised in.

Ron Brown attended the prestigious Hunter College Elementary School, where he was the only black in his class and later became the first African American member of the Sigma Phi Epsilon fraternity while attending Vermont's Middlebury College. After university, Brown joined the army—but not before marrying Alma Arrington, a Brooklyn native and Fisk University graduate, in 1962. On their first date, Brown famously accompanied Arrington from Greenwich Village to her home in Brooklyn. Exhausted, he fell asleep during the cab ride. Many suitors might have felt embarrassed by dozing off on a first date. But Brown, by Alma's account, woke up refreshed from his catnap and began to plan date number two.

Alma championed Brown's career and was a fervent civic activist in her own right. "There was always something different about him," she told the *New York Times* in 1994. "He was more mature than the other boys, and sure of himself."

A full two decades before the invention of Facebook, Brown was lauded for being the ultimate connector. James Hackney, a Brown colleague and confidant, estimated in 1994 that Brown had between "15,000 and 16,000 friends." This before most people had cell phones and when email was just beginning to be a thing.

As he scaled the political ladder from executive director of the National Urban League's Washington office to deputy campaign manager for Senator Ted Kennedy during his 1980 presidential run, Brown developed an ethos that the *New York Times* described this way: "The sum of Ron Brown's style could be printed on an index card: Maximize your time. Focus on your goals. Know who runs what. See them. Make your point. Don't linger. Never look back."

"I first met Ron at my church, in 1980," says Yolanda. "Heritage United Church of Christ in Baltimore, Maryland. My brother-in-law, Wendell Phillips, was president of the Interdenominational Ministerial Alliance of Metropolitan Baltimore. At the Alliance's annual conference that year, the guest speaker was Ted Kennedy. In my neighborhood, as in so many African American neighborhoods across the country, we were big Kennedy supporters. Atif Harden and Michael Frazier did advance work for Kennedy," Yolanda says. "And it was at an advance meeting that I met this tall, strikingly handsome and smooth man, who was deputy campaign manager Ron Brown. All three of those guys had worked for Kennedy in his Senate office and were now on the campaign trail with him. Atif, Michael, and I became great friends and are still close to this day."

Vernon Jordan ran the National Urban League, and Ron ran the Washington office and was their chief lobbyist before he worked for Kennedy. Ron, at one time, wanted to be DC mayor, but he moved on from that once he got into national politics. "Little did I know when I met this guy at my church," Yolanda recalls, "that we would make history together. God always has a plan."

The next year, in 1981, Yolanda went to work at the DNC. The office was located on Massachusetts Avenue, in the Air Line Pilots Association Building. Yolanda was working for then-Congresswoman Barbara Mikulski. Mikulski's chief of staff, Ann Lewis, left to work at the DNC after Carter's loss, and asked Yolanda if she would like to go with her.

Ron and Yolanda started work at the DNC on the same day in 1981. He was a deputy chair and general counsel, and she was administrative assistant to the political director, Ann Lewis. Senator Kennedy was chair of the Senate Judiciary Committee, and Ron was the committee's general counsel until the Dems lost the White House and the Senate in 1980. Then, Senator Kennedy worked out a deal for Ron to become general counsel of the DNC. In 1981, he joined the Commission on Presidential Nominations. As Harvard University's Elaine Kamarck wrote, "His 1980 race had concluded in an especially bitter and contentious convention fight between President Jimmy Carter and Senator Edward Kennedy. The convention fight had centered upon Rule 11 (H) that bound delegates to support the candidate in whose name they were elected." This committee was chaired by North Carolina governor Jim Hunt and was therefore named the Hunt Commission. The changes that commission put into place would become critical for Jackson '84 and Clinton '92.

Working for Kennedy gave Ron broad experience and broad connections. We all agreed: "Frankly, he wasn't just Ron the black guy. Having worked with Kennedy, he had that exposure with this old royalty of the

Hill. So, he learned the Hill and knew all the ins and outs of Washington, DC."

In 1988, at the Democratic National Convention, Brown was chief negotiator for the Jackson campaign within the party, and part of what he negotiated for was a study about voting in America: about the history of voting, the constituents, and protecting voting rights. Ron was charged with putting the study together. He was great to work for. He'd worked at Patton Boggs and Blow, a prestigious DC law firm, so he was used to a certain level of privilege. He'd say to his team, "Let's do our staff meeting at the Four Seasons and have breakfast." Yolanda says, "Not that he was taking advantage of his privilege, but when you worked for Ron, you learned that working hard didn't have to be all misery."

We all came to know and revere Ron's intelligence, the way he worked with people, the way he interacted, and how he was such a people person. Jackson represented one kind of ambition. Brown, with his deep history in the corridors of privilege and power, represented a different kind of ambition. "His eyes were on the prize," Yolanda notes. "I'm sure he was thinking down the road. The voting study was a great foundation for a race that would eventually come: the campaign to be DNC chair."

During the 1980s the DNC Black Caucus was made up of a majority of state and local elected officials and very high-level activists such as Hazel Dukes, who was president of the New York NAACP; Mayors Richard Hatcher (Gary), Ernest "Dutch" Morial (New Orleans), Wellington Webb (Denver), Lottie Shackelford (Little Rock), and Harvey Gantt (Charlotte, North Carolina); former New York State senator and secretary of state Basil Paterson; former secretaries of state for Pennsylvania and Oklahoma, respectively, C. Delores Tucker and Hannah Atkins; labor leaders Addie Wyatt and Bill Lucy; congresspersons Cardiss Collins (Illinois) and Mickey Leland (Texas); and state comptroller Roland Burris (Illinois). During that period, the DNC Black Caucus was as powerful in its own right as the Congressional Black Caucus, in terms of fighting for issues of importance to the black community.

"Back when I started working at the DNC," Yolanda remembers, "there were twenty-five at-large members who were appointed by the chair, for the strict purpose of diversity—to balance the states that lacked diverse or female members. They generally included African Americans, Hispanics, women, labor organizers, state and local elected officials, and high-profile activists. In 1988, the day after the convention, one of the concessions to the Jackson campaign was that DNC chairman Paul Kirk would add twenty-five at-large members, and Jackson would choose twenty of them. That's when I became an at-large member of the DNC, along with Ron Brown, Harold Ickes, Jim Zogby, and sixteen other supporters of Jesse Jackson '88. Opening the tent—that's what we did in that campaign. Between '84 and '88, we registered millions of new voters for the Democratic Party. We changed the rules. We had our say in the platform. We were winning. And we were about to win the biggest prize yet: chairman of the Democratic National Committee."

Minyon met Ron Brown right before the 1988 convention. At the time, he was the Jackson campaign's convention manager and lead negotiator for Jackson. "I remember saying to myself, 'He is so polished,'" she remembers. "When he enters a room, you knew he was important. Ron possessed a very unique skill—he could sit at the table with white and black leaders and command the same level of respect. Some of it was just confidence. I also think it helped that Ron had worked for the National Urban League, which gave him a unique perspective into the civil rights community. It didn't hurt that he was also a lawyer and had worked with many of the Democratic leaders—he had gained the trust and respect of both sides. I would often reflect on the way Ron conducted himself in meetings and how he was always prepared, and no topic caught him off guard. His leadership style was worth emulating."

Minyon became even closer to Brown when he became commerce secretary. "Everyone knew President Clinton had so much respect for him and valued his opinion. [Ron] was always drawn into issues that had absolutely nothing to do with his job as commerce secretary. Because he had such a broad perspective, the president always felt confident in his recommendations."

Donna first met Ron Brown through the legendary political operative and strategist Paul Tully. "When the campaign ends at the convention," she says, "when the primary season is over with and the general election starts, the winning candidate always seeks to bring on board individuals from the losing campaigns because . . . for whatever reason: they're impressed with your work, or they want you to continue your service. The Mondale campaign picked me up to work on their campaign in '84, and I got to go and work for Paul Tully over in the Mondale campaign. Paul Tully was very close to Ron Brown because Ron Brown came out of the Kennedy campaign. Ron Brown was someone I got to know as a result of knowing Tully, not the other way around. It's a weird world." Tully and Brown were like soul brothers. Tully had the rhythm of campaigns down to a science. Brown understood the lyrics, the optics, and the policy.

Confidence was a key Ron Brown asset, Leah remembers. "All of those rooms we talked about, that we didn't know about—Ron gave you the sense that he had been *born* in those rooms. Which I knew wasn't true, because he grew up in Harlem and all of that. You knew he didn't grow up privileged. You knew it intellectually, because you knew the facts of his life, but when you met him, you just felt like he belonged in those rooms. That he had grown up there and that that was his culture. That he understood all of this. I think some of it was his schooling. It was one of the things that we shared. He went to Middlebury, in Vermont. I went to Dartmouth, in New Hampshire. We understood this rich, white New England culture because of our experience in school. That's what we would talk about often."

Leah remembers that Brown was always well dressed. "Oh, my goodness," she says. "Immaculately dressed. With the white shirt collars that had the high point. They were always pointed collars. My nana would say you look like you just stepped out of the bandbox, which means you are dressed to the nines. That was Ron. His English was perfect. [He] just easily, seamlessly moved from meetings of the Congressional Black Caucus, of activists and organizers, into high-cotton meetings with senators. Some of that I think was because he worked for Senator Kennedy for years."

There was a big difference between the Senate culture and the culture of the House of Representatives. As Leah explains, "On the House side, we say about the Senate, 'That's rarefied air over there. They think they're special.' We call anybody who worked over there—we called them the Senate-side Negroes. They just didn't socialize with all those people on the House side. I think because he had spent so much time with Senator Kennedy, who was the lion of the Democratic Party, [Ron] understood, and he had been in those rooms. He became party chair; he had these relationships already. He just transferred them. He could seamlessly move through these different spaces."

For her part, Donna was learning some of Ron Brown's diplomacy and art of the deal. After Jackson '84, she served as executive director of the National Political Congress of Black Women. Her higher-ups there included "Dorothy Height, Shirley Chisholm, all of the black women: Willie Barrow, Addie Wyatt, C. Delores Tucker, Mary Frances Berry, Eleanor Holmes Norton, Attorney Dovey Roundtree, Maxine Waters. I was the executive director of this whole organization that sought to identify, recruit, and promote black women to run for political office. I was just twenty-five years old."

5

Icons

When Martin Luther King Jr. was assassinated on April 4, 1968, many looked to his young wife, Coretta, to step into the void of leadership created by his death. She would, in time, use her strong voice and her position, but first she had four children to raise and guide through the ravages of grief.

Betty Shabazz was just thirty years old when she witnessed the assassination of her husband, Malcolm X. She was sitting in the audience of the Audubon Ballroom in New York City, waiting for her husband to take the stage, when she heard the shots. Instinctively, she grabbed her daughters and pushed them underneath the bench upon which they were sitting, shielding their bodies with her own. When the shooting stopped and she could see through the crowd, she saw her husband bleeding onstage. She had been a licensed nurse, and she ran to him, quickly administering CPR. An ad hoc stretcher was concocted, and he was carried to Columbia Presbyterian Medical Center, just two blocks away, where he was pronounced dead on arrival. Her children would carry forever the scar of having watched their father's murder. Shabazz would have to balance the task of being a single mother to six daughters with the side effects of crippling insomnia. Every time she closed her eyes to sleep, she relived the events of that day in the Audubon Ballroom so vividly that she felt they were real.

Myrlie Beasley of Vicksburg, Mississippi, was just eighteen years old when, on Christmas Eve 1951, she married Medgar Evers, her high school sweetheart. The young couple had three children and quickly threw themselves into the work of creating a better America for them. Following the historic *Brown v. Board of Education* decision that ruled that segregation was illegal in all state-funded schools, Medgar Evers applied to the University of Mississippi's law school. He was denied admission on the basis of race. Later that year, the NAACP appointed Evers to be its first field secretary in Mississippi. His young wife joined him in his work, and over the next decade, the couple organized and strategized tirelessly, with an intense focus on voting rights, the desegregation of the University of Mississippi, and equal rights for African Americans.

As the Everses' profile grew, so did the threats against them. They became official targets of the Ku Klux Klan, and death threats were a constant. A Molotov cocktail was thrown into their carport; their home was firebombed. Because of this, they trained their three young children how to respond in the case of bombs and fires. One evening in 1963, Medgar Evers narrowly escaped with his life when a car attempted to run him over as he left the NAACP offices. The threats grew so great that the FBI assigned two cars to protect him, and the local police department assigned yet a third car to follow him on his commute to and from work.

Just hours before, on June 11, 1963, President John F. Kennedy gave his first and only nationally televised remarks on the subject of civil rights. He stated, "We preach freedom around the world, and we mean it . . . but are we to say to the world, and much more importantly, to each other, that this is the land of the free except for Negroes?" The White House was flooded with telegrams that night, more than two-thirds of them from white citizens who were pleased with the stand the president was taking.

That night, Medgar Evers worked late. He called his wife to say he'd be home soon, then left the office. His FBI escorts and the police car assigned to him were suspiciously absent. It was not the first time, or unexpected. The NAACP understood that some members of the Southern government offices and police departments were also card-carrying members of the Klan. Evers arrived at his home and drove into the carport. As he exited his car, holding newly made T-shirts printed with a new message, "Jim Crow Must Go," an unseen assailant opened fire with a sawed-off shotgun. The bullets ripped through Evers's back and exploded his heart. He staggered forward thirty feet—an astonishing distance, given the extent of his injuries. His wife opened their front door to find her husband dying on the steps. She was thirty years old.

Coretta Scott King, Betty Shabazz, and Myrlie Evers were the founding members of an organization that no one would ever choose to join: the Civil Rights Widows' Club. Despite their husbands' differences in life (most notably the rift between Martin Luther King Jr. and Malcolm X), the women made a vow always to be there for one another. It was a "death till they parted" vow they all kept. As Myrlie Evers later wrote, "Coretta, Betty Shabazz, and I were a threesome. The public perception, fanned by the media, was that we were jealous and competitive. In reality, we three had lost our husbands, the loves of our lives. What about that was something to be in competition over? How foolish."

The women, all strong-willed, were not just keepers of their husbands' legacies. Each emerged to be a leader in her own right, with a point of view distinctly her own. They came to understand the value of the years in the civil rights movement, what it meant to have had, truly, a front-row seat to the years in which America changed course on the issue of race, justice, and equality—though they were well aware there were many rivers still to be crossed until true equality could be achieved. These three women were also well acquainted with the gender battles within the African American community—how hard it was for a black woman to step forward, step up, and take charge. As Coretta Scott King wrote in her memoir, "Liberated, independent women intimidate some men and my daughters inherited those traits from me. My girls knew Coretta [not

"Coretta Scott King"], and Coretta was an independent woman. I had to learn to make it as a single parent at an early age."

Dorothy Height understood well that these women had more to offer than lives as professional widows. Of Mrs. King, she said, "Much of our male leadership that honored Dr. King, worshipped Dr. King, find it hard to recognize the strength in a woman like Coretta King. It is easier for them to think of her as the widow of the martyr than giving leadership in her own right."

These three women wanted to pass their life lessons down to the next generation. Yes, they wanted to pass the lessons down to their own daughters, but they also wanted to pass them down to the daughters of the movement, and that's where we came in.

In the early 1980s, a Harlem-born minister named Tom Skinner and his wife, Barbara, conceived of something that didn't exist in previous incarnations of the movement: a retreat where the elite of the African American leadership could gather both to refill their depleted energies and to collectively strategize for the future. It was at the Skinner family retreats, with the aid of this young couple, that we finally met these women we admired.

"The first retreat that I attended," says Minyon, "was in the early nineties, in Nassau, Bahamas. You needed to be sponsored by a mentor or invited by Tom and Barbara." Minyon attended with the Rev. Willie Barrow. The retreats lasted from Thursdays through Sundays, and represented a who's who of the black community, from politicians such as Governor Doug Wilder to executives such as Toni Fay (then a high-ranking VP at Time Warner) to writers and entertainers such as Dr. Maya Angelou. "Tom and Barbara were nothing short of visionaries," Minyon says. "As the black community began to thrive on a political and economic level, they believed that they also needed a place to recalibrate. They embarked on this bold and ambitious undertaking of bringing very notable leaders together to build relationships of trust. They believed our leaders needed time together to relax and get to know each other off the public stage."

Tom Skinner himself told one reporter that the idea behind the retreats was to make sure that black leaders, across fields and genres, had a familiarity that would build both trust and power. "If we are going to talk about the healing of the city," he said, "we've got to talk about the healing of relationships. . . . In fact, the great problem that divides people is that we no longer hang out."

It was at one of those retreats that Minyon first got the opportunity to "hang out" with Coretta Scott King. "Mrs. King was considered First Lady of the civil rights movement. [She] was a bit more reserved than the other women. A bit more guarded, and fiercely protective of her children. But once you gained her trust, you became like family. I loved to hear her pronounce my name. It had some extra syllables or something." Minyon recalls that when Mrs. King said her name, "It would make you sit up straight if you were slouching in your chair or if the phone rang and she was on the other line. I always felt it must have been hard to have the expectation laid at your feet that you would have to be the standard-bearer for dreams and hopes of a people because of the unfortunate and untimely death of your husband. 'Grace under pressure' is probably not an adequate description, but she picked up the torch and became our modern-day Esther in the Bible."

It was during a time when the African American community did not always embrace the treasures they had in women such as Mrs. King. As Juan Williams reported in the *Washington Post* at the time, "Twenty-one years after her husband's killing, many of the old messages of the civil rights movement seem hollow to young blacks today. King herself has yet to develop a relationship with younger Americans who see her as an aging symbol of her husband's increasingly distant life."

We knew better. We embraced our time with women such as Coretta Scott King and understood that she, Shabazz, and Evers were warriors with lessons to impart. As King herself said, "I don't want to be a queen. I've never wanted to be a queen, because my concept of a queen is someone who is a figurehead and someone who is told what to do, who is treated with a certain kind of deference but not really taken seriously.

And I have always wanted to be taken seriously as a human person with intelligence and a serious purpose in mind."

Tom and Barbara Skinner were especially instrumental in helping us keep our compass when times were tough, which was often. "Tom was a gentle giant," Minyon recalls. "He was respected and loved; he was especially beloved by the young people. He took time with us. He counseled and loved us. Both he and Barbara opened their home to us. They became a safe haven when leaders needed a spiritual rejuvenation. What I loved about them both was: their love and leadership was unconditional. You could come broken, tired, and scared or you could arrive full of life, hope, and love—they treated you the same."

Maya Angelou would also praise Tom Skinner for his unconditional love. "What he had was a great inclusiveness," she said at the memorial held after Skinner's death from leukemia at the age of fifty-two. "Tom would say, 'So you shot your mother and kicked three children. Well, God loves you. Now let's see what we can do about it.'"

Those retreats at the Skinners' helped us not just personally but professionally, too. Dr. Angelou did a few DNC public service announcements for us, as did Ossie Davis and Ruby Dee. Dr. Betty Shabazz became a member of the newly created Women's Leadership Forum (WLF), which was a fund-raising arm of the Democratic National Committee. It was created so that women could show their financial and political strength and power within the party. Minyon says, "It might surprise many people to know that Dr. Shabazz was a member of the WLF. We were so honored to have her involvement. She was loved and admired by many of the leaders of the WLF. Dr. Shabazz was also very strategic. She understood what it meant to empower the black staff of the DNC. She was very generous with her contributions. While her money gave her power, she empowered us by always giving the donations through us. David Mercer, one of the first African American fundraisers for the DNC, was one of the recipients of her generosity. It was so liberating to have a donor at her level and a person of her prominence become a voice for women in the party. When she attended the WLF conferences it was like royalty walked in the room. People were simply in awe. Dressed in one of her famous St. John suits, she was always smiling, down-to-earth and very approachable. I am sure, had it been another type of conference, people would have been lined up to ask her for her autograph; instead they lined up just to say hello. I'm thankful that so many people got to know Dr. Shabazz through this forum. Her openness became a mirror to her family, and it allowed them a glimpse into a man that they had only read about in the newspapers or in books."

Coretta Scott King, like Dr. Shabazz, was smart. She had been a concert pianist, and she taught Donna "so much about order and discipline. In the aftermath of Dr. King's death, Coretta saw herself as a leader. Mrs. King understood that if Dr. King's legacy was to be told correctly, she would need to be at the forefront of shaping his story. She did not let Andy Young or Joe Lowery or any of the other men from the Southern Christian Leadership Conference push her aside."

"King taught me to cross every *t* and dot every *i*," Donna says. "She taught me how to fund-raise. She'd say, 'Call them and tell them what you need.' She taught me how to write reports—and I wrote reports nonstop, I can tell you that. I remember handing in reports to King as late as nine and ten o'clock in the evening. That's when Mrs. King would get energized. All of the older generation loved conference calls," Donna remembers. "They loved that technology. They wanted to be in touch with everybody. That taught me the value of maintaining relationships, writing down phone numbers when you meet someone, and sending notes to follow up."

Maya Angelou had come into the King orbit as a grassroots organizer. The young Angelou had earned her place with a bit of bravado, telling the Southern Christian Leadership Conference that "if you want someone who has titles before or after his or her name, that's one thing. But if you want someone to get the job done, I will be your best choice."

On the surface, Mrs. King and Dr. Angelou seemed to be very

different, but as Angelou would later recall, "We just liked each other from the start. I was a southern woman and she was a southern woman. We had the same attitude toward things, like being very respectful of elderly people, even when they were boring. That is really southern black. We were proud of doing certain things that we thought were feminine. We loved to cook, to dress nicely, to sing a little bit. She felt good about being a wife, a mother, and a spokesperson."

"When I wasn't working on the King holiday," Donna recalls, "I had the opportunity to be a fly on the wall as Mrs. King socialized with the women. A frequent combination was Dr. Shabazz, Dr. Maya Angelou, and Mrs. King. They were more than friends; they were family." Dr. Angelou once wrote about Mrs. King, "I knew how to make her laugh. I'd sneak up on her and whisper something in her ear or tell her a joke. I couldn't enjoy myself better than to catch her off guard. She would do her best to control herself, but she'd laugh."

"On special occasions," Donna remembers, "I'd go out and get them drinks. Dr. Shabazz liked Chateau Ste. Michelle. Dr. Angelou had her favorite 'libation,' as she called it. And Mrs. King liked champagne. *They* were the original Colored Girls."

6

Jackson '88: Democratizing
the Democracy

It was not so long ago, but many of us have forgotten how vicious the Reagan era was to the poor, to people of color, and to the disenfranchised. It was an era when the social safety net was being ripped out of the country. The villainized "welfare queen" became the symbol of black women in the popular (white) imagination. Reagan rolled back civil rights. We were engaged in a constant march, a constant fight to make sure the economic conditions for the poor and middle class were seen and heard. In fact, it was the draconian policies of the Reagan administration that led to the rise of the Rainbow Coalition.

"We didn't misunderstand Reagan; we lost sight of the moment," Donna notes. "America was at the crossroads, and many of the traditional civil rights leaders had become uncomfortable challenging the status quo. So, they punted. Reverend Jesse, no doubt, frightened the traditional old black political model, where you had to ask permission from white folks in order to run. He unleashed black power in the political veins of our democracy. He was a game changer. We saw it firsthand, and there was no turning back."

In between deriding the "welfare queen" and attacking the drug-addicted, the Reagan administration made time to turn more than three hundred thousand mentally ill patients out onto the streets in a shameful repeal of Jimmy Carter's 1978 Commission on Mental Health. One report from Los Angeles in 1985 estimated that "30 to 50% of the homeless were mentally ill." This spike in the deinstitutionalization of the mentally ill directly correlated to violence committed by citizens who might have thrived with the proper treatment. Many of the most publicized multiple homicides of that era were directly tied to the lack of care and treatment of the mentally ill.

Yet it wasn't just the homeless and mentally ill who were suffering. Reagan's refusal to address the plight of gay men caused the deaths of thousands, including many of the nation's most talented individuals, during the HIV/AIDS crisis. By the time Jackson ran for the presidency a second time, in 1988, AIDS had devastated the nation and affected millions.

At the same time, the heartland was suffering as a generation of white farmers faced foreclosure on their family farms. In Mississippi, when whites showed up at Jackson rallies with "sacks over their heads," Jackson's team worried. It turns out the farmers were merely hiding their identities from the American Farm Bureau. Jackson visited farms. Jackson visited AIDS hospices. He visited poor whites in West Virginia and poor blacks in Tunica, Mississippi.

We've come so far, it's easy to underestimate the power of the imagery that Reverend Jackson projected into our communities and into the nation at large. "It was unprecedented at that level of American politics for a candidate to hire so many people that looked like us," Minyon says. "There were women, Hispanics, Asian Americans, gay and lesbian staffers, Arab Americans. When he stood up at the mic and said, 'You are somebody,' it really resonated because he put it into actuality."

Jackson threw the doors of the party open. And by his side, and in increasingly influential positions of power, the Colored Girls were doing the work of "democratizing Democracy." As Jackson put it: "We said, 'If we could leave the racial battleground for economic common ground, we can find the moral higher ground.' That's how we got the rhythm."

Leah remembers that as a college student during the Reagan era, "Dartmouth became even more of a bastion of conservatism, and during several of my Dartmouth years, I shared the campus with students who would become icons of the conservative movement: Dinesh D'Souza and Laura Ingraham, most notably. They were as fervent then as they are now—maybe more so. The newspaper they founded, the *Dartmouth Review*, was—for students and faculty of color and for the LGBT community, and really, for anyone not a white male—the bane of our existence."

In the fall of 1985, Yolanda left the DNC to become the first political director of the National Rainbow Coalition, the incubator for Jesse Jackson '88. (The organization later became Rainbow PUSH.) One of the biggest problems for the '84 Jackson campaign had been that those involved didn't understand presidential party politics. Back then, it was really an insider's game. The Jackson camp didn't understand the primary rules until it was too late, so they were never really able to put together a strategy. So, '84 was definitely a movement, but not a campaign. That all changed in '88.

Reverend Jackson started trying to hire Yolanda after her stint with the Mondale campaign. She says, "I remember every time the Reverend came to DC, he would call me and Michael Frazier (a friend from the Kennedy campaign) and spend time picking our brains about the party and our experiences on presidential campaigns.

It was a standard practice, if you worked for Reverend Jackson, that you would eventually make the sojourn to Greenville, South Carolina, Jackson's hometown. His mother, Helen Jackson, affectionately known as Momma Helen, had the biggest heart. And she opened her home to all of us. When you walked in the house it would be filled with pictures of Reverend Jackson and his brother Chuck, who was a big music producer. Photos of famous people lined the walls. Family photos of the Jackson family were throughout the house. When we arrived, Momma

Helen would greet us with a big smile, a hug, and great food. During these short visits, her entire house would be occupied by Jackson staff. She never seemed to mind having a houseful of people. She was always so happy to see her son, so if this was the way she got to see him, she was perfectly content. It was funny how everyone knew when the Reverend was in Greenville. The late Lottie Gibson, a former city councilwoman and head of the South Carolina Rainbow Coalition, was always the first to arrive. Lottie had a big presence and a big personality, and you knew when she was in the house. She was a mover and a shaker in South Carolina. She knew everything that was happening in the state and was the first to brief the Reverend on everything, even the gossip. She would organize any events for the Reverend during his visit. This was always a bit of a dance because when the Reverend was home, Momma Helen believed he needed to rest, but Reverend Jackson saw it differently and was always doing something in the community while there."

For Minyon, trips to Momma Helen's brought back childhood memories of visiting her grandparents' farm in Mississippi. She said, "It always reminded me of going back home to the South, where the doors were open, you always had the neighbors, they always came over to visit." When Reverend Jackson was coming to town, everybody knew it before the plane even landed. "Everybody was bringing food," Minyon says. "Momma Helen never had to overwork herself in the kitchen 'cause she knew some of the neighbors were going to bring dishes for Reverend Jackson."

But when Momma Helen did cook, if you didn't know, you had better ask somebody. She always made greens, chicken (baked and fried), sweet potatoes, peach cobbler—a feast in the great Southern tradition.

Minyon says, "She was a beautiful woman who had been a teenage mother. That's why he talked so much about teenage pregnancy, I expect. He had seen the challenges up close." But she overcame those challenges with the pure force of her positivity. Minyon adds, "She loved him so much, and at times, he would just stop and say, 'I got to go home and visit her.' Sometimes he would sit, but most of the time, he was busy on the phone till she'd just make him stop and eat. He was always working, but she didn't care. She knew that he was home. That's all that mattered to her. All that mattered."

After Paul Kirk won as the new DNC chair in 1985, he hired Yolanda as a senior advisor and executive director of the Fairness Commission, the group that would write the rules for the '88 presidential primaries. After the commission finished its work and the rules were voted on, Yolanda left the DNC and went to work for the Rainbow.

The 1986 political cycle was a unique moment for us. It was, as Donna remembers, "a cycle in which we were able to harvest the fruits of our labor. There was a revival of the Democratic Party following the campaign of Jackson '84. I went home to the South. I was helping a lot of races down in Alabama and Georgia. But in '86, I was looking ahead to help out candidates in the '87 cycle. I helped Mary Landrieu, daughter of onetime New Orleans mayor Moon Landrieu. Ann Richards had convinced her to run for her first statewide office, state treasurer. I went home to run her campaign. She was only thirty-three. I was twenty-seven."

Although she also worked while there on local campaigns, going back home to New Orleans allowed a moment of reflection for Donna. She was thinking about moving back there permanently and was considering applying to law school. While she was at home, she received a call from Reverend Jackson, who was bringing the '84 team back together. "He wanted to know what my plans were," she says. "I promised that I would come back up to Memphis and talk to him."

Reverend Jackson "took us back to our roots," Donna says. "Back south—back to Georgia, Alabama, Florida, Tennessee, North Carolina, Mississippi, Virginia—to raise hope. They went back to the places where Reverend Jackson had opened doors to encourage black folks and progressives to run and had registered hundreds of thousands of new voters. To continue to challenge the Democratic Party to reform. Nineteen eighty-six was going to be a year of action." After the November elections,

Democrats gained a net of eight seats, recapturing control of the U.S. Senate with a 55–45 majority, and picked up five seats in the House of Representatives, including John Lewis and Mike Espy.

Soon after, Donna drove the six hours from New Orleans to Memphis to join Jackson's campaign. She says, "I told him that I was going to stay home and work on Mary Landrieu's campaign, but that I wanted to see some of my other options for '88. And he wanted to know what my other options would look like. And I said, 'Well, I have received a call from Paul Simon. I have received a call from Joe Biden. I have received a call from Michael Dukakis, Al Gore, and Dick Gephardt.' And Reverend was almost—I don't know if you know how Reverend looked at me. His eyes widened when I mentioned those five white men.

"The Reverend said, 'Well, what's wrong with you coming back to work for me?'"

Donna says she replied, "'Not a thing. I will always support you. But this is what you wanted us to do. You wanted us to learn so that we may grow. You wanted us to find our seats at the table. If I'm going to be successful as a political strategist'—and my long-term goal, at the time, was to be a campaign manager—'the opportunity to go to one of these other campaigns will eventually put me on that track to be a campaign manager.' I explained all of that to him. And the Reverend looked at me and said, 'You're going to become a branch without a tree. You're not going to feel rooted. You're not going to grow and develop into the kind of person that you want to be, unless you come back.'

"I thought long and hard when I drove from Memphis back down to New Orleans, about what Reverend said to me. But eventually I made my decision to move forward and go ahead and work with one of the other candidates. And that was Dick Gephardt." Gephardt offered Donna not just a seat at the table, but a chance to build a new table.

"The summer of 1987 transformed me," Donna remembers. "I found my seat at a different table, in another house but in the same neighborhood. It was a tough decision—to go over the proverbial train track to work for Gephardt over Jackson."

Reverend Jackson was not happy with Donna's decision. As Minyon puts it, "He never wanted to lose any of the 'kids' he raised." But Donna, who had the ambition to run a political campaign, felt she couldn't pass up the opportunity. And Gephardt didn't disappoint. "Dick Gephardt was the first white candidate that I felt I had a good rapport with," Donna recalls. "We could actually talk about life issues other than politics. He was the first white candidate to ask my views on topics that were not germane to my race or my gender. Reverend Jackson was my mentor. He will always be my friend. I love him like a brother. He is a very, very supportive human being. Up until that point in my career, I'd only ever been asked to talk the civil rights struggle, the women's movement, and of course, young people with student assistance became one of my cornerstone issues. But this was the first time an elected official wanted to know where I stood on health care, trade, foreign policy. The first time [Gephardt] asked me what I thought about the trade deficit with South Korea, I looked at him like 'Excuse me?' But I thought that was refreshing. It was also a challenge. I had never been challenged in such a way to come up with my views on such a broad spectrum of issues, because no one had ever put those kinds of questions before me."

At the Gephardt campaign, Donna felt she finally had what she had always been taught to prize: a seat at the table. "I never had to fight to be in the room. I was always welcome into the room. I was always part of the plan. Dick Gephardt didn't have just one black woman. He had several of us: Deborah Johns [Hayes] was the press secretary, and Jackie Forte [-MacKay] was the CFO. This was a milestone. This was what Reverend wanted us to become. He wanted us to become leaders in the Democratic Party. I had a profound respect for Dick, Jane, his family. And I still stay in touch with the Gephardts. The friends I met in the Gephardt campaign remain my friends to this day."

When Jackson ran his second, stronger campaign, we were the same age that millennials are now. Minyon was deputy field director for Jackson

'88. Leah's father was intimately involved in the Jackson '88 campaign. At the time, Leah was working for Congressional Black Caucus member Edolphus "Ed" Towns. She recalls, "I was living out the principles I learned on the Jackson campaign, this time from a policy perspective."

Most seasoned politicos will tell you that campaigns are a young person's game. In September 1988, Yolanda turned thirty-eight. She was always the big sister in our group. While she was still considered young by the candidates, she says, "there were others working and volunteering who were much younger than I. I think people tended to have respect for me because, one, I was the go-to person and I followed through, and two, I came from the DNC, so I guess I had the 'white folks' pedigree."

In February 1985, a new DNC chair was elected, Paul Kirk. A former DNC treasurer, Yolanda had encouraged Kirk to run for the position. She says, "Paul was a Kennedy guy. I had gotten to know him and his wife, Gail, and like them both." Yolanda went to work for Kirk as a senior advisor. At the 1984 convention, several concessions were made between Jackson and Mondale. The most significant was the creation of the "Fairness Commission," the group of individuals who would come together to review and make recommendations on the rules of engagement for the next Democratic primary, which would be 1988, Jackson's second run. But when Mondale lost, everything was null and void. Paul Kirk was the new DNC chair, and it was his decision on how he wanted to run things.

When the time came to appoint the chair of the Fairness Commission, Kirk wanted to meet with Reverend Jackson. Yolanda remembers that Paul "set up the meeting at his law firm. He didn't want the Reverend to come to the office because that would signal weakness on the side of the new DNC chair." Yolanda remembers that "After '84, these white men were so afraid of Jesse, it was almost like every decision they made had to have a 'Jesse clause.' They couldn't say or do anything that gave the appearance of giving in to the Jackson faction."

Yolanda, Kirk, and Jackson met in a "tiny little office" at the law firm of Sullivan and Worcester in Washington, DC. Yolanda remembers the meeting as tense. "They both spoke *at* each other and heard what they wanted to hear. The Reverend was very clear about Mondale keeping his commitment to form a Fairness Commission and wanted to engage former Atlanta mayor Maynard Jackson as the chair." Kirk said he would take the Reverend's suggestions "into consideration." Yolanda notes that "it was a short meeting—and not a good one." Also, she was concerned that she "was going to be caught up in the middle." She explains: "That's exactly what happened. Paul was uncomfortable with Maynard being chair and wanted someone he knew in the role, someone from his camp." Yolanda suggested that Kirk consider Ernest "Dutch" Morial, who was then mayor of New Orleans. Morial was a DNC member and head of the U.S. Conference of Mayors at the time. Yolanda believed that Morial was "someone everyone could rally around, including Jesse." Kirk told her he'd consider it.

"Next thing I knew, he called me into his office and said he'd decided to appoint Don Fowler as chair of the Fairness Commission," Yolanda explains. "I felt like someone had stuck a stake in my heart. I was so disappointed in Kirk."

Yolanda says she finished up the meeting with Kirk and walked out of the DNC offices "pissed." She continues: "I went home and for the first time since I'd went to work for the DNC, I cried. I'd bought the white boys Kool-Aid and I got punked. Later that evening, Jean Dunn, who was Paul's chief of staff, called me at home and said that Paul wanted me to be the executive director of the Fairness Commission and work along with Don Fowler. I told her I would think about it and get back to her."

Next, Yolanda reached out to Maynard Jackson, to let him know what had transpired. He returned her call that evening, and she explained what had happened. She says, "I told him about my suggestion about Dutch, and he said it was a great strategy and I'd fought a good fight." Jackson urged Yolanda not to walk away from the role she was being offered. He told her, "You should take that job. Make sure it's a fair process and that the rules are changed to be more inclusive to all." Yolanda took his advice. Once the Fairness Commission issued its report, Yolanda quit the DNC and went to work for the National Rainbow Coalition.

In 1985, Yolanda became the first political director of the National Rainbow Coalition. Her next job in the organization was as chief of staff of the Washington office, a vital position, as the Rainbow headquarters were still, at that point, in Chicago. Yolanda was the Reverend's liaison with the DNC and all the other Democratic organizations—which meant she was, more often than not, the only black person in the room. Her work had a sense of urgency to it because she knew that "the Reverend had every intention of running again in '88, and this time it was going to be for real."

On the '88 campaign, Minyon was a field organizer for Jackson, with the title of deputy field director. She traveled to various states and was either the lead or on a team organizing that state or city for the campaign. "I started in bitter-cold Burlington, Iowa. I set up shop in a small house that had been converted to work space. I am sure it had been donated. I remember having no staff, no infrastructure—just a list of key contacts, potential volunteers, and walk sheets, referring to the list of supporters who needed to be canvassed. Eventually word got out the Jackson campaign had an office in Burlington, Iowa. People began to drop by to get literature. Volunteers began to show up to canvass the neighborhood. Each weekend, carloads of PUSH volunteers would arrive to help canvass and door-knock. The running joke was I would [put] a walk sheet in one hand and a box lunch in the other."

She continues: "The day of the caucus, I remember like yesterday. Jackson supporters started flooding into the caucus site. If you were a caucus voter, you were required to sign in. There were so many Jackson supporters that showed up to caucus, the caucus coordinator had to get on the mic and ask people to calm down and take a seat. It was unprecedented, and the officials didn't know what to make of it. As the voting got under way, it was clear Jackson was doing well, but there was only one slight problem: the sign-in sheet was not matching the number of people who were voting for Reverend Jackson. There was one extra vote. So, they repeated the count. 'If you are caucusing for Reverend Jackson, stand up.' It soon became clear where the extra vote was coming from. One of the senior citizens from Chicago, Esther Thompson, who had been canvassing [for] Reverend Jackson, only heard one thing: 'If you are supporting Reverend Jackson, stand up.' Esther was a very short woman and could easily get lost in a crowd. One of our volunteers noticed that Esther was including herself in the count. When we had to break the news to Esther that she couldn't stand with the Iowans and that she had to come and stand with us on the side, she immediately quipped, 'They asked us to stand if we are here for Reverend Jackson. That's what we are here for, right?'"

Minyon then traveled to Texas, New York, Michigan, California, and states in between. "Our motto was we were a poor campaign with a rich message," she recalls. "We stayed in supporter housing in every state we went to. It was rare that we got to stay in hotels. In some states, if you were there longer than a few weeks, they subleased apartments."

In California, Minyon had her first interaction with the force of nature known as Maxine Waters. "The young people today call her Auntie Maxine, but to me she is known simply as 'the Boss.'" Minyon continues: "California was my first glimpse into what it was like to have a powerful African American woman running the Jackson campaign in a state. Maxine Waters was no-nonsense. She didn't take any crap off the young organizers that were dropped into the state. I remember her specifically asking a few of the young organizers to leave because they were not adhering to the way politics were done in the state. It was a wake-up call for all of us. We were outsiders and didn't have a clue what the politics were. We either followed instructions or you left."

For us, it was a big deal to just be in the room with heavyweights such as Maxine Waters. We had a seat at the table—or at least a folding chair in the corner. We shuffled papers, ran errands, but the people we worked with were more than mentors; they became family. There was a great weight on our shoulders, but, as Donna puts it, "you felt honored to even carry their luggage. It was a chance to be part of history. The people in power gave you a sense of trust and responsibility. They didn't know you, but they trusted you." For all of us who had spent time within the Rainbow Coalition, aka "the movement," there was also a faith-strengthening resolve. The movement never had money, but in the end, things always worked out.

When Minyon arrived in New York City, Eddie Wong, field director for Jackson '88, asked her to report to Local 1199, a division of the Service Employees International Union, which was run by Dennis Rivera, a well-known Puerto Rican labor leader. "My first point of contact was to be Bill Lynch," she says. "He was the person in charge of the campaign."

Bill Lynch grew up on the North Fork of Long Island, the son of a potato farmer. David Dinkins said of Lynch that he was "a country boy like Jesse [Jackson] is a country preacher." After serving in the air force, he moved to Harlem, where he ran his first successful local campaign in 1975. He then went on to work on the presidential campaigns of Senator Kennedy in 1980 and Jackson in '84 and '88. David Paterson, who would later become governor of New York, said of Lynch, "He impressed me because he was the first really dynamic political person I had met who wanted to be a mechanic, who wanted to be on the front line but who didn't want to be a star."

Lynch and Minyon would find a lot of common ground in their shared gift for strategy and in their ability to work seamlessly behind the scenes. But first, they'd have to work together, which was far from a given when Minyon arrived in New York. She says, "I remember sitting in the waiting area for him. I didn't know who was in the conference room or what was being discussed, but I was told to wait. Eventually he emerged from the conference room. His first question was 'So what do you think you are going to be doing in my city?' My response was 'I thought I was here to help organize votes for the Jackson campaign.' He basically said, 'If you are here to f*** things up, you can leave now or get shipped home in a body bag.' I was terrified. He told me to sit down and wait until his meeting was over."

Several hours later, Minyon was still sitting there. She was so afraid of missing something that she did not even get up to visit the restroom. Finally, the door opened and powerful leaders emerged, leaders who had been meeting all day to put together the strategy for the Jackson campaign in New York. For her, "it was reminiscent of the Harold Washington meeting, except this time I was sitting on the outside. Basil Paterson, David Dinkins, Carl McCall, Percy Sutton, Harold Ickes, Dennis Rivera, and several others filed out one by one. They were all the faces of people I had only seen on TV or heard about."

When Lynch finally walked out of the meeting room, he took one look at Minyon and asked, "What are *you* still doing here?"

Her response: "You told me to wait until your meeting was over."

He shook his head in disbelief. Then he asked her to follow him as he walked and talked. "You know, you might work out," he said, looking down at Minyon. "You sure do know how to follow instructions."

From that day forward, Bill Lynch became a lifelong friend and mentor to Minyon, and a trusted advisor to several presidential campaigns. "To know Bill was to fear Bill," Minyon says. "But if you got past the rough exterior, he was a gentle giant. He had that rare instinct for politics and people, and knew how to win a campaign. I learned a great deal from him about mobilizing people and getting people to the polls."

Leah fondly called him "the Godfather." He always seemed to be able to move the pieces, make the connections, and push the levers of power that got things done. You never knew exactly who Bill knew. He was an invaluable advisor and confidant and someone you wanted on your side. And when he was in your corner, he was there until the end.

Jackson won the popular vote in Michigan's Democratic primary in March of '88. It was a significant blow to Dick Gephardt and Michael Dukakis. Joel Ferguson, Jackson's campaign chair, had plotted out this victory with such precision. Not only did he have Jackson visiting the big cities in Michigan, but he also had him on a bus going to smaller cities such as Lansing, Kalamazoo, Battle Creek, and Flint. He made sure organizers were in unexpected places, taking nothing and no one for granted. There was a feeling of excitement in the state. They called it "Jackson Action," a play on *Action Jackson*, the popular '88 film starring Carl Weathers. Powerful clergy and organizers were lending their talent and expertise. When the state was called for Jackson, it was a great feeling, but that feeling certainly didn't translate to front-runner status. Looking back, Minyon says, "I was too naïve and green to understand the significance of winning the popular vote in the Michigan caucuses. When I saw the headlines of several papers the next day, Jackson was considered the 'front-runner' because he had amassed more delegates. I thought to myself, I could be working for the first black president, something that I had dreamed about since his run in 1984."

A few months out from the convention, Jackson held an all-hands-on-deck meeting in a private room of a restaurant in Georgetown. He called his top supporters from across the country and delivered a heartfelt speech about how far they had come; Jackson won Super Tuesday and the Michigan caucuses, and Yolanda remembers "the white folks were getting *very* nervous. All of the big publications, *Time*, *Newsweek*, *Black Enterprise*, the *New York Times*, the *Washington Post*, were running cover stories with the same headline: 'What Does Jesse Want?'"

Yolanda remembers: "It was my idea that Ron join Jesse's campaign as convention manager. Jerry Austin was the campaign manager, but it wasn't unusual to bring on another operative to run the convention process. Ron's dream was always to be DNC chair—very few people knew that. Jesse had asked him to be his campaign manager, but he didn't feel he could leave his partnership at Patton Boggs and Blow, which was one of the most powerful law firms in the country. But we stayed in touch, and he was eager to help when he could."

Nineteen eighty-eight was a quantum leap for both Jackson and the power dynamic of African American politicians in the Democratic Party. As Yolanda puts it, "We weren't the little engine chugging along singing 'I think I can, I think can' anymore. We were a real, professional campaign with experienced professionals running it and [we] had damn near every black elected official in the country supporting us. We had a whole new mind-set—we really had a shot at winning this thing or at least being on the ticket. As Jesse was wrapping up his speech that evening—he stood behind Ron Brown and put his hands on his shoulders. He went into this football analogy—where I was pretty much lost because I don't know jack about football, but what I did get was, as he was standing there with his hands on Ron Brown's shoulders, he stated very clearly, 'I've gotten this far on faith and now I need my A team with me on the field.'"

The next day, Ron called Yolanda. He'd been moved by the meeting with Jackson and he wanted to help, but he didn't know what to do so late in the game. Yolanda said it was then that she and Brown discussed his serving as convention manager. "We needed someone who understood the party and knew the players to serve as chief negotiator for the campaign with the DNC and whoever won the nomination. I convinced him that this was a perfect segue for him to run for DNC chair after the November election. He had been away from the DNC for several years since his general counsel days, but this would be just the right high-profile position that would bring him back into the fold—and it was. At the end of the convention, he went to Boston to be a deputy campaign manager, along with Minyon, who joined the field team. Donna left Gephardt earlier on and joined the Dukakis campaign."

Looking back, we see that we did more than help Jackson create a campaign that had powerful momentum, though we certainly did that. By earning more than 1,400 delegates, Jackson and his supporters won a real *voice* in the Democratic Party. In doing so, we were responding to the times, to all the people who were hurting, and to our desire to help people of all colors make a living wage. Through Jackson's campaign, we helped introduce concepts (such as universal health care) that no longer seem as radical as they did in the 1980s.

We were coming of age politically. Our work with Jackson '88, by placing us in close proximity to the great black leaders in whose footsteps we were following, showed us both the values that had shaped us and what we might be able to accomplish once we got our own shot. At the 1988 convention, Minyon's first assignment was to set up the trailer for the candidate and senior staff and a boiler room where staff could work. "It was my first convention, so everything was new to me," Minyon recalls. "Talking about being baptized by fire, it definitely felt like that. It was also a very sensitive convention in terms of negotiating the role of Jackson and his allies. Ron Brown was key to making sure that Jackson felt included and was treated with the respect he had earned. Even then, Ron Brown's presence and support was extremely important. He mainstreamed Reverend Jackson in a way that [the Reverend] could not have done for himself."

After the '88 convention, Yolanda returned to the DNC as deputy chair to Paul Kirk. She recalls proudly, "Once again, I was in charge of all things black. I was the liaison to the Congressional Black Caucus, the DNC Black Caucus, and all organizations."

Yolanda remembers that although Maxine Waters was a huge support in the '88 campaign, "my first interaction with 'Auntie Maxine' was not a good one." It was 1985, and Paul Kirk had just won the chairmanship of the DNC. Yolanda was appointed his senior advisor, which she explains meant "I was the liaison with the black political establishment. He was going to California, his first visit since becoming chair. I was working on a list of people he should meet with, and I added Willie Brown, who was then Speaker of the California Assembly. Maxine was a member of the Assembly as well, and people trying to get to Willie generally went through Maxine. Well, I was still young and trying to make a name for myself, so I skipped over that little detail. I had a good friend who used to work at the DNC, Shelley Bates, who went to work for then-Speaker Brown in Sacramento. So, I reached out to her to get the meeting with the Speaker. Done. Maxine found out about it and was apparently a bit miffed. She mentioned the incident to Reverend Jackson, and he told me I needed to clean it up. So, he set up a conference call with Maxine and we discussed it." Yolanda says she "apologized for being a 'millennial' before they existed. Looking back, I probably did a lot of millennial-style things during those years. But I was finding my sea legs. For a long time after that, I felt like I was walking on eggs around Maxine, but I think those were my own insecurities. When I look back over the years, Maxine has always had my back, even when I didn't know it. During the '88 campaign, she was there. When I was under attack at the DNC, she always stood up for me. When I moved to LA in 2000, to work on the convention, she was a huge support for me. Maxine was a Colored Girl way before we were."

In 1988, Reverend Jackson was being considered for vice president on the ticket with Michael Dukakis. The Jackson legal team set about pulling together all the documents needed for the vetting process. They were about halfway through when Ron Brown got a call that the Dukakis campaign was about to announce Lloyd Bentsen as the VP candidate. Jesse Jackson was en route to DC via a chartered plane. As Yolanda remembers it, "Ron called and told me to go out to the airport and get on the plane and let Jackson know the news, before he got off the plane, so he wouldn't be blindsided. We put together a press conference that afternoon, and Reverend Jackson nailed it, one of the many times I was extremely proud to be a part of that campaign. But needless to say, it made for some rough patches throughout the rest of that election."

Once again, through Jackson's campaign, we came to see that winning could encompass a multiplicity of definitions. And that in the end, as Leah puts it, "Reverend Jackson did win: He registered record numbers of people to vote, which had a tremendous impact on the policies of Reaganism, and is *still* having an impact on the way that the Democratic Party's demographic is configured. He won because through his influence, he changed the way the Democratic Party operated."

Prior to Jackson, the Democratic Party did winner-take-all primaries. For example, if you won Michigan by one vote, you got all the delegates. After Jackson, and because of him, one of the things he required was that the party change its rules to proportional delegate allocation.

"The Republicans still have winner-take-all," notes Minyon, "but the Democrats don't, because of the Jackson campaign. Imagine how different things would be if we were still doing winner-take-all. He changed all of that, and it still has an impact. Reverend Jackson said, 'You've got to change the composition of the DNC. The only way to do that is add additional at-large delegates.' He called for the addition of twenty-five at-large members who would be from diverse communities, to ensure the DNC was more diverse. State parties were not electing diverse people. In the 1980s, it was a pretty lily-white, male DNC. The Reverend brought in women, people of color, labor." This was how Yolanda; Rev. Willie Barrow, Minyon's mentor; Jim Zogby, from the Arab American Institute; Ron; Harold Ickes; and others were appointed at-large members of the DNC. Richard Trumka, president of the United Mine Workers and an avid Jackson supporter (and now president of the AFL-CIO), was appointed, too.

"The result," Minyon says, "was that people who had always been on the outside of Beltway politics, but [who] had worked tirelessly and helped to deliver election after election, now had a seat at the table. They could help determine the party's direction." She continues: "He didn't win the presidency, but he won by changing hearts, ushering in a new generation of political leaders at every level, and by changing the party rules to be more inclusive. We got a seat at the table because of the Reverend. He opened the door for many of us in national politics."

7

We Are the Colored Girls, and
We Shall Not Be Moved

What It Takes: The Way to the White House, by Richard Ben Cramer, has been called one of the greatest books ever written about a single presidential campaign. In the book, Cramer chooses six candidates to follow in their quest to become forty-first president of the United States: then–Vice President George H. W. Bush, Senate Republican leader Bob Dole of Kansas, former senator Gary Hart of Colorado, Congressman Dick Gephardt of Missouri, Senator Joe Biden of Delaware, and Massachusetts governor Michael Dukakis. The book's author made a conscious decision not to cover Jesse Jackson. About that decision, Cramer would write, "The omission I most regret is Jesse Jackson, whose story is truly as fascinating as that of any man who has ever campaigned for the White House." Cramer claims to have discovered Jackson "late," but in his few mentions of Jackson in the book, he quotes other candidates as saying what Cramer himself surely felt: that Jackson could not win because Jackson was black.

The "woman question" is another matter. The *New York Times* proclaimed that Geraldine Ferraro's historic nomination for vice president in 1984 had "ended the men's club of national politics." But the men's club of national politics was still very much in effect in 1988, even when

Susan Estrich, as Dukakis's campaign manager, became the first woman to run a presidential campaign, taking the position following John Sasso's resignation. Estrich had roots in the Ted Kennedy campaigns and knew Ron Brown.

As for black women, we are virtually nonexistent in Cramer's *What It Takes*. When "minorities" are discussed, it's in terms of the Black Caucus and the Women's Caucus, with no reference to intersectionality. Most of the references to "women" in the book are about Gary Hart. We were not yet the Colored Girls, and three of our names don't appear in Cramer's book at all. The exception is Donna Brazile, who is mentioned only as being present as field director at a Gephardt meeting. That's it: one sentence, with no distinguishing characteristics given for her. Even more surprising, there are no quotable quotes from Donna. It must have been hard for Cramer and his peers to imagine that in only six election cycles, she would become chair of the Democratic National Committee.

With the Dukakis nomination sewn up, Donna went to Boston in April, and Minyon joined her postconvention to work on his campaign. Donna was coming in as deputy political director from Gephardt's team. Minyon joined the Dukakis campaign headquarters as a Jackson representative in the field department. As an additional deputy field director, she had as her principal job making sure the Jackson '88 campaign organizers felt integrated into the Dukakis campaign. She worked for the field director, Charlie Baker, of whom she says, "He's since become one of my dearest friends and a friend for life. Charlie was not just the head of the department, but he was a supporter and always went out of his way to make sure I had what I needed. Things weren't always easy because above both of our pay grades, Ron Brown was dealing with the leadership of the campaign to make sure Jackson would give his full-throttle support to Governor Dukakis. Before that could happen, however, certain conditions had to be met." She adds diplomatically, "It was an interesting experience, to say the least."

There were three black women on the executive floor of the Dukakis campaign. In addition to Minyon and Donna was Susan Rice. Rice was just twenty-four, a Rhodes scholar, and a recent Stanford graduate. She joined Dukakis's team as a foreign policy aide. Donna and Minyon knew of each other from Jackson '84 but hadn't had the chance to work together yet. As Minyon was settling in, she called Donna. Her first question was "Where are you?" Donna's response? "I'm on strike."

Minyon had grown up with a stepfather and uncle who were big in the Chicago postal workers' union. She understood the importance and power of a strike. She had never heard of campaign workers going on strike, though. She remembers looking at the phone and asking, confused, "Strike? For what?" Donna explained that the campaign was refusing to support the Congressional Black Caucus Foundation dinner, an annual event that raised money to bring black student interns to Capitol Hill.

Minyon knew the dinner was important. She also knew that she and Donna had a lot of work to do. So, she asked, "Well, are you coming back?" Donna said, "When they give me my money." Minyon remembers telling Donna, whom she hadn't even met in person yet, "Girl, you've got to get back up in here."

When Minyon hung up the phone, she thought, "Oh boy, what the heck have I gotten myself into?" Donna's request didn't seem unreasonable. But the fact that members of Dukakis's campaign didn't see the importance of the Congressional Black Caucus Foundation dinner was a problem. If the campaign knew that black folks would support Dukakis without any organizing in the community or support for black institutions, the community's value would be lost.

In the days that followed, Donna and Minyon forged a friendship: they were united over the principle of Donna's strike but also had an increasing awareness that their two very different styles complemented each other. Minyon was solid and hard-core. She had another gift: she was calm under fire and known for her open-door policy. She was a consensus builder and could reach almost any black leader in the country. She wanted to make sure that people knew they were seen and heard.

Donna says that her "great gift in politics was organizing. When someone called me to pull together an event, I delivered: crowds, equipment, media, celebrities, volunteers, or the votes. Along the way, I might have inadvertently ruffled a few feathers and cussed a few people out, moved someone out of my way literally and told the rest to simply go to hell." Feelings didn't matter. There was work to do.

Once the CBCF's funds were approved, the strike ended, and Donna returned to work, and she and Minyon began setting up their office. They were learning how to wield their growing influence. Minyon puts it this way: "The challenge for people of color when we take these unprecedented positions is that there's an expectation that we should carry the ball for everyone. You have to figure out how you are going to involve all people of color, all women, all disenfranchised groups. You become that voice and representative whether you want to be or not. Every time you go in a room, you have to ask yourself who isn't at the table, who isn't being represented, and how do you get them to the table when you are in a room? And yes, the other Colored Girls would say that's my kumbaya-ness. But to me it is more than that. It is a basic set of principles that you learn in the movement: you must see other people even if they aren't in the room."

One afternoon, Donna and Minyon were given the news that they were being relocated to another floor because their office space was needed. The request to move wasn't a total surprise: the field department was never given priority or prominence over other parts of the campaign. At the same time, the women were confident that if they moved to a lower floor, they would find themselves out of the loop. It would be an uphill battle for position, resources, and access going forward. As Minyon explained, "Being on the floor with the top leadership of the campaign wasn't about power; it was about proximity to decision makers and making sure we were a constant reminder of the constituencies we represented."

Their friend Charlie Baker was the field director, but they knew that when resources got tight in campaigns, field was usually the first cut, and it wasn't given the prominence it should have. Late that evening, inspiration struck them. The two women relocated to an empty office, set up camp, and moved in a big conference table. Donna wrote on a piece of paper, "COLORED GIRLS . . . WE SHALL NOT BE MOVED," and Minyon taped it to the door for all to see. "I am not sure what the campaign thought about our refusal to move. I don't think anyone ever asked us to move after that, to be honest."

For Minyon, the Dukakis campaign was a big learning experience: "Going from the Jackson '88 campaign to the Dukakis campaign was a transition. Working to make sure Jackson allies weren't left out also took some work. Developing relationships with new people and, frankly, with a new train of political thought was a challenge. Learning to do it their way while not compromising your values was a challenge. But I also think we were value added as well. There were times when having our voice, our organizing skills, and our connections helped the campaign tremendously. One big plus was having more resources. That was refreshing and a welcome change."

It was while working with Dukakis that Minyon got to really know Charlie Baker, Michael Whouley, and Chuck Campion. "Our friendship endured even over a somewhat testy and trying campaign."

The other rising star in the campaign was Susan Rice. Minyon recalls, "Susan Rice was in the policy shop. She was definitely smart as a whip. In fact, I would say she was brilliant. She also had a courage and fearlessness about herself that wasn't evident until you tested her. She stood her ground. She, along with several other black women (Janice and Davida Mathis)—they would hang out in our office late at night. We were a close-knit group of women who would soon be tested by the firing of Donna and the treatment of Jesse Jackson."

The Dukakis campaign did not handle the subject of race well, and on October 21, 1988, Donna said something that once again made her notable and quotable. She said, "When we started out in New Haven, Dukakis had been told that being seen with black people would weaken his campaign. That it would turn off whites, as if white people weren't turned off already. By October, although I didn't know it yet, I was ready to explode. So, I went to the back of the bus to brief the press on the day's itinerary."

There, she alluded to something that had never been spoken of by a major candidate in the mainstream press: the rumor that George H. W. Bush had had an extramarital affair. She told the press, "Let me just say this; if you guys want to ask all of these questions, why don't you ask George Bush if he intends to take Barbara to the White House?"

The reporters shouted back, "What did you say?"

By Donna's own admission, "I didn't know how to stop." So, she continued: "They talk about family values, they talk about all these family issues, but tonight on CBS News, no one is going to report that George Bush has a mistress and her initials are J.F."

A *Boston Globe* reporter named Michael Frisby gave Donna a chance to retract the statement, asking, "Donna, are you on the record?"

Donna replied: "I'm on the record, but I'm not speaking for the campaign."

By the time the bus arrived at the Waldorf Astoria in New York City, Susan Estrich had asked for Donna's resignation. She gave it. Michael Dukakis didn't want to see her again. Kitty Dukakis called and suggested that Donna go see a friend of hers, Ruthie Goldmuntz, who lived nearby, on Fifth Avenue. Donna said, "If you're going to get fired, get fired at the Waldorf and then get invited to a Fifth Avenue apartment for a drink." Debra Johns, one of the black women on the campaign, offered to join Donna for that drink.

"I got a call from Donna sometime that afternoon when the news began to break," Minyon says. "She was crying, and I asked where was she? I wanted to know above all else that she was okay. All I could hear her say was 'I got fired. I got fired.' I asked her if she did what was being reported. It was a horrible day for us at the campaign. We wanted to make sure we were a support system for Donna, but we also knew she had really stepped way out there with those comments."

Once she arrived at Kitty Dukakis's friend Ruth's apartment, Donna remembers "the Reverend had warned me that I would one day be a branch without a tree, and that's how I felt—utterly rootless and tired. I needed his advice, too. So, I went to Ms. Ruthie's bedroom to sob and call the Reverend. Debra fixed me a cocktail, and I started dialing home."

Donna has said that breaking up "with Reverend Jackson was one of the most painful things you could do." Minyon notes that when Donna left the Jackson camp, "it was like a divorce. But at the same time, when Donna was fired from the Dukakis campaign, the person who kept her spirits up was Reverend Jackson." Donna concurs: "He was the first leader to tell me it was going to be all right. Don't worry about it. Emotionally and spiritually, Reverend Jackson helped me develop wings."

"Looking back on the Dukakis campaign, it is probably easy to figure out things we could have done differently," Minyon says. "I think the campaign certainly had its fair set of challenges. But Dukakis's pick for vice president, Senator Lloyd Bentsen, was met with substantial praise. He was a steady hand in an uncertain environment. Dan Quayle was no match for Lloyd Bentsen at all. Senator Bentsen just felt presidential. He looked presidential. Governor Dukakis, while a fine and decent person, didn't seem to connect with the voters very well. He didn't pass what I call the Senator Chris Dodd test with voters, meaning if people don't like you, they will not vote for you."

Leah remembers her own impression of Dukakis: "I was on the Hill, watching the campaign flounder. That picture of him riding a tank, and his answer to the debate question about what he would do if his wife, Kitty, were raped . . . I knew he was going to lose. I was on the Hill, working for Congressman Towns, when Bush was first elected in November 1988. I was still very much connected to my Brooklyn community at that time. So, besides my parents, many of the people whom I held in esteem were the community activists who were in my orbit . . . Baba Jitu Weusi, Sam Pinn, Assemblyman Al Vann were key leaders in our movement and were like icons to me."

Dukakis lost a presidential bid that was tarnished by race-baiting and a concentrated smear campaign. While Donna would pay the price for speaking about racism, rumors of infidelity, and the Iran-Contra scandal, the Democrats would suffer for not fighting dirty. Doug Wead, who worked on Bush's team, described the Bush headquarters as divided in half. On one side, there was the candidate and his executive team. On the other, code-protected half of the office, staffers were tasked with digging up dirt on the opposition. "It was the degree and the success of it," Wead told the *Boston Globe*, referring to the Bush camp's attacks on Dukakis. "[For example,] the two words were 'Willie Horton,' so hundreds of people and hours of work and many polls and lots of research was able to reduce it all to a few words that could go on the back of a business card." In the face of the attacks, Dukakis, who insisted on staying "positive," seemed weak and incapable to the electorate, losing an election that many thought was his to win.

After the loss of the Dukakis-Bentsen campaign, Minyon returned to Chicago and began working for Rainbow PUSH. A few months later, Reverend Jackson decided he was going to move the Rainbow Coalition to DC, the seat of power. He felt that he needed to have his office where laws were being made. He wanted to be a constant reminder to the lawmakers that "laws are made to serve the people, not the powerful."

As Jackson's right hand, Minyon had a decision to make: she had to either leave Chicago, her family, and all that was familiar to her or stay behind. "The person who helped me make the decision was Reverend Barrow," Minyon says. "She told me I was ready. I was grounded in my faith, and the work must continue. She convinced me that it was time to spread my wings." Whether Minyon decided to go to Washington, DC, or stay in Chicago, Reverend Barrow gave her a piece of advice that would stay with her: "Don't get wedded to a seat; stay focused on the mission and the work."

When Minyon finally arrived in DC, the Jackson network provided a softer landing than she expected. Acquaintances became friends, and the unfamiliar became familiar very quickly. It was the end of the 1980s, and all of Jackson's hard work in the decade before had begun to pay off. The Rainbow Coalition established itself as a force to be reckoned with for many years to come. As for Minyon, she would eventually meet up with all the women who became part of the Colored Girls, but when she first arrived in Washington, only Donna was working on the Hill.

And of course, there was the Rev. Jesse Jackson. "I learned many lessons from Reverend Jackson," says Minyon, "but one of the greatest was to never underestimate the value of my relationship and closeness to the community I came from. He needed me, he explained, to mind his core constituency, his base—and by that, he meant he wanted me to be his point person with African American activists and leaders. And I told him I could do more than just black people. It was, after all, the Rainbow PUSH organization." She adds, "I'll never forget the Reverend sitting me down and saying, 'You know, when I was coming up under Dr. King, I said the same thing to him. You know what he said to me? He said, "Jesse, I will tell you this. What the other community needs from you, is they need to know that you understand your people and that you are connected to your people." Minyon, you have a unique ability to get to know leaders around the country, you would have access to them. Get to know them and build relationships with them.' I took that mission very seriously, and serving our people became my calling. It wasn't until much later in life that I realized just how valuable that lesson was. I got to know almost every leader in the country on a first-name basis and could pick up the phone and call them when I needed assistance, and they would call me if they needed to reach Reverend or needed help."

Leah knew of the future Colored Girls before they were the Colored Girls and long before she actually met them through her work at the DNC in 1989. Her father, Reverend Daughtry, had high praise for Donna, Minyon, and Yolanda. He saw them as worthy role models for Leah, describing the women at various times as "smart," "powerful," "conscious," "doing something," "going somewhere." And his highest praise: "They love the people." As Leah had been marked as an inside woman, her father wanted her to know that she would not be alone on the inside: there were other strong black women in the world of electoral politics. Leah assumed that Donna, Minyon, and Yolanda were already a collective, that they all knew one another and worked together. But that wasn't yet the case.

After graduating from college, Leah moved to Washington to work for her hometown congressman, Ed Towns. She loved the job but hated Washington. Unlike Minyon, who acclimated quickly to Washington, Leah struggled, feeling worlds away from the activist community in Brooklyn that had raised her. Minyon's years in the corporate world would serve her well within the corridors of Washington, but Leah found DC to be far too establishment for her liking. For an international city, for a city with a significant African American population, it seemed way too white-bread and whitewashed. "Where are the people with African names?" she wondered. "Where are the people wearing traditional African clothing? Where are the people talking about liberation and freedom and self-determination? Where are the women with natural hair? Or short hair, like mine? Where are the churches with the black Jesus?"

She had little interest in the social heartbeat of the Hill. She didn't want to network, she wasn't into meeting up for happy hour, and she didn't particularly want to rub elbows with lobbyists. She was, and is, the youngest of us, and she was our version of a millennial—bucking the rules, uninterested in the symbols of status and power, yet eager to make a difference and carve her own path. "Everyone, I mean, everyone, was always talking money," Leah remembers. "Money and politics. In New York, there are artists, activists, entertainers, government workers, politicians, teachers, some of everything. But in Washington, it seemed that, no matter where you went, everyone was connected in some way, shape, or form to politics, and that's all anybody wanted to talk about."

The thing that saved her, and soothed her, was that her job required her to spend weekends in the congressional district back in Brooklyn.

So, she spent her first four years in DC commuting to Brooklyn with Congressman Towns every Thursday after the voting had ended, and coming back on Tuesday in time for him to vote again.

That commuter life meant that, for a long time, Leah didn't develop any real roots in DC. She was also aware that she didn't have any deep friendships in the city. Still, her career was on the rise. When Congressman Towns accepted his assignment to chair the Congressional Black Caucus Foundation Weekend, Leah stepped up and served as his liaison for the event planning. Together, they made a few changes to the usual schedule, and what seemed like minor tweaks resulted in a hugely successful weekend. The fund-raiser cleared one million dollars for the first time in the CBC's history. For Leah, there was more than pride in the accomplishment. She realized that she had caught the event-planning bug.

Recognizing Leah's role in making the CBC fund-raiser a success, Amelia Parker, then executive director of the Caucus, urged her to consider a job at the Democratic National Committee. Ron Brown had been elected chair of the DNC in February 1989, and the site selection process for the 1992 convention was beginning. They were looking for a staff assistant to help with the convention planning, so Leah went over to interview with Yolanda Caraway, to whom the assistant would report. She remembered seeing Yolanda earlier, at the inaugural Rainbow PUSH convention in DC, and thinking that she "was very pretty and very well dressed. She seemed polished, professional, and poised. I noticed that she had on nice shoes—always a plus in my book—and a good handbag. She was also carrying a notebook that contained all the papers about the conference. She seemed so organized, and I remember saying to myself, 'So this is the famous Yolanda that I've heard so much about.' And I felt a little bit awed."

She had not seen Yolanda again, until now. They met at DNC headquarters in spring of 1989. Determined to win the job on her own merits, Leah didn't mention her father, but found out later that Yolanda "knew exactly who I was and that, unless I grew two heads in front of her, the job was mine before I even walked in the door." Not privy to that particular piece of information, Leah was a self-described "nervous wreck" during the interview. "I don't like talking about myself, and unfortunately, you *have* to talk about yourself in a job interview," she says. Yolanda asked Leah if she knew how to work an IBM Selectric or a Xerox Memorywriter, the kind of "typewriters with memories" that they used back then. There were no desktop computers at the DNC in 1989.

In May 1989, Leah was offered the job, and in July, she started at the DNC, sitting at an intern desk inside Yolanda's small office. The two women quickly discovered that they were both Virgos, which, as Leah explains it, "meant that we were both neurotic about details," one of the qualities both women brought with them to their work with the DNC.

Later, Leah would come to believe that "my upbringing as a church girl, and my time on the Hill, made me understand the ins and outs and the importance of being a good support staffer. Support staff do well when they know they are meant to be seen and not heard. You support your principal and make sure they have everything they need to get through their day. You're always three steps ahead of them. You are more than prepared, so that you can prepare them. You do whatever needs to be done so that your principal can function at maximum capacity—make coffee, fax papers, Xerox copies, make briefing books, memorize key phone numbers, run interference. Fix it, solve it, make it go away. And you never sit at the table unless you're saving the seat for them."

The job at the DNC soon became Leah's PhD in national politics. She learned how to deal with high-level donors; the importance of a good communications apparatus; and, as she puts it, "how to deal with white people in the workplace and still be black."

While working for Congressman Towns, Leah had found it hard to acclimate to Washington's social scene. Yolanda took her under her wing. Decades later, Leah is still a little bit awed by it all: "Yolanda took me to the best parties, where only the best champagne was served. She shopped at Neiman Marcus—gasp!—and bought gowns, real gowns. It was all a very different world than the ninety-nine-dollar sale rack at

Alexander's Department Store, where I was accustomed to shopping. And she wore Manolo Blahnik shoes, which I'd never heard of."

Yolanda's reputation as the black Martha Stewart continued to grow. She was always impeccably dressed, but she was also the consummate entertainer. For Leah, it was an education. She says, "I remember one brunch Yo hosted at her home in Northeast Washington. The menu was simple: quiche and salad. But Yolanda had made almost a dozen quiches, from scratch, all varieties and all flavors, and set them out buffet style on her dining room table. Now, I loved quiche; I ate tons of it when I was at Dartmouth. But I'd never met another black person who also liked quiche—and liked it enough to serve it to other black people. Especially serving it alone, without the safety foods of chicken wings, Swedish meatballs, or potato salad."

Yolanda was the first woman Leah had met who "seemed to have significant disposable income and wasn't shy about using it." During Leah's first Christmas working for her, Yolanda gave her a black leather Fendi wallet. Leah was shocked when she opened the box. She could hardly imagine how much such a gift cost. Yolanda simply smiled and said, "You did a good job this year."

It was one of those gifts that meant so much more than the actual item. "I still have that wallet," Leah says. "I don't use it anymore, but I'll *never* throw it away. That was such a validating experience for me—to know that I'd done a good job, that my boss was pleased with my work, and that my hard work had been rewarded."

In July 1989, Leah made another important friendship. While combing through the DNC senior staff roster, an unusual name jumped out at her: Hartina Flournoy, who goes by "Tina," was executive director of the DNC's Rules Committee. Leah laughs at the memory of it, admitting, "With a name like Hartina Flournoy, it didn't cross my mind that she'd be black. But with a name like Leah Daughtry, I should have known better than to presume."

When Tina came across the street to headquarters for a meeting and was introduced to Leah, Leah's first thought was "Oh, she's black!" Her second thought was "Her hair is short, too!" She clarifies this: "Short hair is popular now, but it wasn't so much back then, so it took great confidence and fortitude [for a black woman] to have short hair in DC in those days."

Style is always a moving target for women in the workplace. What's appropriate? What rules can you break? What is outdated and what will make you stand out, but in a good way? Leah admired what she called Tina's "stylish minimalism. I rarely saw her in a suit; she tended more toward dresses or separates with a good jacket. And no flashy gold jewelry for her. Just always a really good watch, maybe a bracelet, and some small, tasteful earrings. I thought of her style as unforced elegance. And it worked so well for her, I forgave her lack of interest in stilettos. Tina's heels tended more toward the two-inch height. Not nearly high enough for a shoe queen like me."

More important than Tina's style, though, was how much Leah liked her as a person. She remembers that when she met Tina, she felt "an instant bond," one that was intensified as they traveled across the country together on DNC business. As they got to know each other better, they found they had much in common. Both had roots in Savannah—Leah's father was from the city—both had been educated at predominantly white colleges, and both had excelled at those schools, overcoming the challenges of being black in a white academic world. On a more personal level, Leah remembers with affection that "we both loved to read and had eclectic tastes in music and books. And we thought the same things funny and found the same people annoying."

The year was 1992, and just as Minyon and Donna had been first on the ground in Boston, Tina and Leah were now first on the ground in New York. It was an epic year. The candidate was Bill Clinton, the DNC convention chair was the phenomenal Ann Richards, and two Colored Girls were opening the New York convention office.

At the dawn of a new decade, the 1990s, we began to grow in political experience and figure out how to navigate the parameters of our unprecedented roles. We were all, to use Reverend Daughtry's term, inside women now. This meant that our primary working relationships weren't just with one another, but also with (mostly white) men in power. Over the course of the next twenty years, we worked closely with every Democratic president, presidential candidate, executive cabinet members, and leaders of the national Democratic Party: people like President Bill Clinton, Vice President Al Gore, Senator Chris Dodd, Governor Howard Dean, Terry McAuliffe, and all their various deputies.

We were intelligent and capable. We were also nurturing, so much so that occasionally one or two of us wondered, out loud but only among ourselves, "Do the men in power think of us as mammies? Are we the C-suite version of *The Help*?" Donna offers, "Well, we're not butlers. That's for sure. I do believe they rely on our faith, they rely on our resilience; they know we don't break easily. And they know that we have been through so many storms." Leah adds, "And we're going to outwork anybody."

This last point is not to be underestimated. It is not just a critical plot point in the DC-centered television show *Scandal*. For generations, young black men and women have been told by their parents, grandparents, teachers, and other mentors that they need to work twice as hard to get half as far. It was a truth that we had all metabolized early on, so much so that it hardly came up in conversation. When the hours were long and the hurdles were mighty, we focused on our common goal to be, as Donna so poetically puts it, "workers in the vineyard of justice."

Politics may be the through line, but friendship is at the heart of our story. Minyon points out that when she loses focus, Leah is able to draw her back in. Tina, by contrast, is "very, very structured." Minyon says, "I talk to Tina two or three times a day." Sometimes the calls are short:

"You'd better get the *Daily Mail*."

"It has the whole story?"

Other times, the calls are shorter still:

"What the hell?"

"Okay, bye."

Tina concurs that "Minyon is the one I talk to every day. Sometimes that's cracking up on people. Sometimes it's like 'Do you believe how f***** up this is? I mean, we can be on the phone for five minutes or two hours, just talking about everything. Laughing about things. Talking about the news, talking about people's craziness, talking about our families. Talking about what she should be taking on a trip. Asking her why she overpacks everywhere she goes."

"Tina is incredibly loyal," says Minyon, "but she's also fiercely smart and, personality-wise, she's the opposite of me. We're all opposite of each other. I get along better with Donna than the rest of them. I get along with all of them better than they do each other. I just do."

We all agree, with a great deal of affection and admiration, that Minyon is the one who is the most willing to embrace outsiders. As Leah puts it, "Minyon always tends to draw the circle bigger." This is not always appreciated among the inner circle: "We'll say, 'Okay, *why* did Minyon invite that person? Or why is Minyon including this person? Doesn't Minyon know she or he is a knucklehead?'"

"Leah and I are the most alike," says Minyon. "On almost any issue, we will probably end up in the same place closer than any of the others will. And our experiences are somewhat alike. And we tend to like some of the same shows. Like *Game of Thrones*. I only watched the first season, but Leah is addicted to it."

Minyon is the glue—she's the connective tissue that keeps us together. To the outside world, we are a group of powerful black women who have become history makers, king and queen makers. But among ourselves, we are strong-willed, grown women who don't always see eye to eye. Minyon can always bring us back to the loving place, though. For any colored girls—or anyone, for that matter, who forms a group with the intent of wielding some kind of political power—having "a Minyon" to keep them together is the most important thing, especially when the going gets rough.

This ability to mediate among the powerful is a quality Minyon says she learned from watching leaders and seeing them up close and personal.

"Some had the ability to fail, fuss, and fight, but they could rise above the friction for the greater good. I'm always trying to, as Betty Shabazz used to say, find the good and praise it."

We are far from a monolith. We are as diverse as our backgrounds, our upbringings. "The truth is we really are pretty different," Minyon says, but notes, "We are united around a core belief that what's right is right; what's fair is fair. So simple, and yet that truth is one we've had to stand up for—for ourselves and often for others—to make it real."

Yolanda adds, "Like people who have spent their career in public service, we view our lives in four-year waves: presidential campaigns and elections have been a common thread."

It never truly abates, the struggle to do good and make a difference—even when there was a black president in the White House. Our determination to fight/maneuver/strategize for what is right and what is fair continues. We consider our story rich with history, but this is not a history book. It is a playbook about how to live and work with integrity, how to nurture and build deep, soul-sustaining friendships, and how to have the courage to use your voice to make a difference, even when the world is telling you, "Hush." (This last piece is some *very* valuable advice when one considers Donna, who for a while was known for being "notable but *not* quotable.")

We all have other friendships, men and women each of us sees more often and to whom we are just as close. But after so many years in the halls of power, after so many trials (public and private), after countless state funerals and state dinners, we four gradually "saw in each other and lived in many different ways with each other," and developed "a knowingness we could count on. We trust one another. We defend one another. We feel strong and sure in counting on one another."

8

Clinton '92

In 1989, Ron Brown was elected chair of the Democratic National Committee. Tina Flournoy had worked for Paul Kirk, the previous chair, and was director of the now-named Rules and Bylaws Committee when Brown began his chairmanship. Leah was on the Hill working for Congressman Ed Towns; Donna was home in Louisiana, dealing with the death of her mother; Minyon was at the Rainbow Coalition; and Yolanda was at the DNC.

When Brown decided to run for chair of the party, it was a historic race, and a controversial one. There wasn't so much as one main competitor to Brown but, rather, a faction, the Democratic Leadership Council. The centrist wing of the party, the DLC was not supportive of Brown's campaign, feeling the party needed to court more Southern white men.

Everyone knew that Brown had great relationships, but many felt it would be hard to resolve the Southern states problem with an African American chair, especially one who had worked for Jesse Jackson. The Colored Girls remember that among the party leadership, there was a feeling of "We can't have this."

Yet Brown lived to defy expectations. Leah remembers that whenever he entered the DNC headquarters, he always seemed "completely at ease. He was so polished and aware and strategic. He understood what was needed to win. He went after it. He hired the best people he could get."

After he was elected chair, Brown decided to hold a party fund-raiser in Alabama—to prove he could raise money, *and in the South*. The state party chair, John Baker, said that Ron Brown was not welcome in the state of Alabama because a black man should not be chair of the Democratic Party.

Brown's chief of staff, Alexis Herman, sent Leah to Alabama to organize the fund-raiser. There she had two clear hurdles to overcome: "I had never organized a fund-raiser, and I'd never been to Alabama. I said, 'You want me to do what?' Then I said, 'Okay, well, she's the chief of staff; she's the boss. This is what she wants me to do. I can do this. This will be fine.'"

The one upside, Leah reasoned, was that she would get to spend three weeks in a hotel. "It'll be fine," she remembers. "I'm going to stay at a hotel. I love a hotel. I'll make the best of it. I'm going to learn how to do this. Never did it before, but I'm going to learn." Herman, who was from Mobile, quickly burst her bubble; the DNC was on a budget. "You're going to stay with my mother." Leah's reaction? "Help me, Lord." Leah stayed with Herman's mother for three weeks.

As for the job at hand, her first task was to find someone *brave* enough to host the fund-raiser. "The state party chair had scared everybody. I'm from Brooklyn. I'm in Mobile, Alabama, trying to figure out who's going to host the fund-raiser. It was a mess." In the end, though, Leah, in typical Colored Girls fashion, got it done. Brown flew in; the venue—the beautiful home of businessman Donald Briskman—was packed, and they raised well over their target.

The event was slated to last from 6 p.m. to 9 p.m. And at 8:45 p.m. on the dot, Leah remembers, John Baker strolled in to make amends. Leah and Brown had done what had seemed impossible. As Leah says, "Baker had to fall on his sword."

It is notable that Brown never mentioned the hurdles of racism he encountered with the fund-raiser. "He didn't address it," Leah says. "He didn't comment on it. All Ron did was walk in and be gracious." Everyone knew that Brown was angry that Baker had thrown up roadblock after roadblock to his becoming chair, but it was not his way ever to let his frustration show. Outsiders to Ron Brown's inner circle were never privileged to his inner emotions. Leah says, "He was always, as the saying used to go, cool, calm, and collected. The only way you knew he might be a little upset was that he'd start shaking his leg and bouncing his knee. Just slightly, so if you knew him well, you knew 'This is not going the way he intended.'"

The controversy around Brown's becoming the first African American chair of the party proved to be a tremendous motivating force for his entire team. "He *had* to be successful," Leah remembers. "A man with Ron's ability, experience, and talent would have been a shoo-in if it wasn't for race. But his election as party chair was not inevitable; it was hard-won. There were so many people who didn't want to support him. We had to do whatever we could. We worked harder, and when we thought we were so exhausted that we might just fall over, we did more. We did whatever we had to do, because it was all on the line. If he wasn't successful, there'd never be another black party chair in our lifetime."

It was during this time that Leah's reputation in the DNC began to grow. Alexis Herman, who became her mentor, noted that Leah had "an unusual ability to manage people, politics, processes, and policy equally well." Leah says, "The spiritual side of me acknowledges this as a gift. The practical side of me just knows that I am the best manager you'll ever meet. It's that reputation that's gotten me every project and position I've ever had. Regardless of where and what I'm working on, I stay grounded through prayer and my relationship to God—I rarely miss a Sunday in church—and by remembering who sent me and who I represent. The folks in my community who are striving and struggling every day to realize the American dream in their own lives—I ask myself,

'What would *they* do? What would *they* want? How will this impact *them*?' And that keeps me focused."

After his election as chair, Brown played a pivotal role in the 1992 election of President Bill Clinton, as did Yolanda, who was Brown's senior advisor and his deputy when he chaired the Presidential Inaugural Committee.

Most of us were centered on, or moving toward, the DNC during the Ron Brown years. Donna, however, was on a different trajectory. She says, "Every other year, when I wasn't involved in a campaign, I'd go out and do movements. After I left the Dukakis campaign, going into '89, when Ron Brown became chair, I was working with Mitch Snyder and a couple other people on this campaign for housing. It was called Housing Now! It was a campaign for decent, affordable housing for others and to raise the issue of homelessness, which was a growing problem, still is, in our country, and how we would fight that as a society. In off years, I wanted to go off and change the world. In even years, I got even by getting involved in politics."

Ron's tenure as DNC chair involved a lot of "swinging people through," just as Jackson did before him. One example was Margo Briggs, an African American woman Brown hired to supervise security at the DNC headquarters. She had that contract for almost thirty years.

At the Clinton Foundation, they have a measure they call the "But for" test. It's meant to measure the impact and worthiness of a project. Tina Flournoy, President Clinton's chief of staff, described it this way: "We lean in and talk about things we might do and we say, 'Okay, this or that would not have happened *but for* our work.' I put Ron Brown in the category of 'But for.' *But for* Ron Brown, a lot of what we know about American leadership and opportunity would not be the same today."

The chief administrator Ron brought in, an African American woman named LaJuan Johnson, was charged with organizing the DNC chair's office to a level that had not been done before: from supply ordering to scheduling. Tina, who worked with Brown at the DNC, noted, "Ron was very 'Things have to look right.' They couldn't just *be* right, they had to *look* right. He cared about appearances in all the best ways."

Along with Brown, Alexis Herman would become a key figure in our political trajectory. Just a decade older than most of us, she'd amassed a wealth of experience that we knew would be valuable to our growth and development.

Herman was born in 1947 in Mobile, Alabama. Her father was the first African American elected to any office in the state of Alabama post-Reconstruction, and from him she learned early on the importance and challenges of coming together in support of her community. As she told one reporter, "He believed very much in the power of the political system to make a difference, and even though we couldn't vote in the 1940s, he never let that discourage him. He was always very steady, very focused. He was a gentle soul and when everyone else was going crazy and raising their voices around him, my father was the voice of reason, [the one] who always said, 'We have to keep going forward.'"

Herman learned the hard way the risks in becoming involved, having watched her father beaten at the hands of the Ku Klux Klan. Despite her youth at the time, the experience became for her an important bridge between the American past of segregation, and all that that involved, and the modern era: "We think of the ways of the Ku Klux Klan and the lynchings and things like that as things that happened in the past, and while it is a part of our past, for me it was very much a part of us growing up. The fact that I saw, as a young girl, my father beaten at the hands of the Klan—I didn't have an appreciation for the danger that he would put himself in when he would go to those small, backcountry off-road meetings and way-off places just to talk about what we had to do to get the right for our people to vote. And just how dangerous it was even to have the conversation about voting, let alone to be organizing in a room with other people about how you go out and do that. We take so much of that for granted now. He used to tell me stories about when they would take folks down to the polls to get them to vote and they had poll taxes, and literacy tests that they had to pass. We don't think about those kinds of things. I remember they would talk about Old Papa Joe, they used to call him, who went repeatedly, *repeatedly*, to try and vote. They asked him the same question over and over and over again, and he could never answer it. 'How many bubbles in a bar of soap?' And because he couldn't answer that question, they wouldn't let him vote. We have so much to be grateful for and to be thankful for and certainly never to take for granted the blood that was spilled, the lives that were put on the line, just for us to be able to do and claim the right and privilege we have today."

Her father's dedication fostered something powerful inside her. It also inspired her steel magnolia working style: "He was a very humble and a very gentle soul. He was the first African American elected to any office in the Deep South. This was back in the 1940s. There was only one ward where black people could vote, and it was Ward 10, in my hometown of Mobile, Alabama, and my father was the wardsman for that district in Mobile. He believed very much in the power of the political system to make a difference, and even though in the 1940s we couldn't vote—it was always about poll taxes or some other reason why we couldn't vote— he never let that discourage him. As I said, he was a gentle soul, and when everyone else was going crazy and raising their voices around him, my father was always very steady, very focused. That's sort of my picture of him."

It wasn't until her sophomore year of university, when she left Wisconsin to attend Xavier University in New Orleans, that Herman joined the movement more fully. As she told NPR, "Xavier was wonderful. It was the height of the movement to be back in the South. I transferred back to Xavier in my sophomore year because my father had become very ill. I started my first year in Wisconsin, so to come back to Xavier, to come back to the South, to come back to New Orleans at that point in time was very good for me. I was able to relate to a struggle and a people at a time when, quite frankly, if I had stayed in Wisconsin, I might have chosen a very different path. So, to be back at a historically black college, to be in New Orleans, to be able to relate to the struggles of my day in that environment, where we were encouraged to be a part of the movement, to be a part of the fight—I think it helped to make me what I am today."

Herman began advocating for minority women's employment immediately after college, and had a chance encounter with Democratic nominee Jimmy Carter. After winning the White House in 1977, Carter appointed Herman director of the Labor Department's Women's Bureau—at age twenty-nine, she became the youngest person ever to serve in that position.

During the 1988 convention, Herman was brought in as Brown's deputy. Then she joined him as chief of staff at the DNC, a signal to DNC members of the level of professionalism Brown aspired to. Herman was a corporate woman, and her hiring sent the message that the DNC was not just a political operation; it was a professional operation. "Alexis helped elevate the game," Minyon remembers. "And you knew that if you spoke to Alexis, you were essentially speaking to Ron. He made that clear."

Brown's trust in Alexis "freed him up to be able to do what he needed to do," Yolanda says. "If he needed to be on the road raising money or up on the Hill dealing with members, there was never a moment of 'Ron's not here; we can't get a decision.' Because Alexis was there and we all knew that."

It wasn't so much that it was unusual for someone in Brown's position to give a woman so much power, but the Colored Girls all agree that "it was factually unusual in that it hadn't happened."

The questions over Ron's ability to raise money as the first African American DNC chair continued even after he'd won the post. Yolanda remembers, "The DNC used to hold a big gala in DC every year. It was their largest annual fund-raiser. Everybody said that Ron wouldn't be able to raise money. So, we had this event. We had it at the National Building Museum in DC, and it was a great event; we sold it out. We raised more money than the party had ever raised before at the annual gala."

The entertainment that night was Dionne Warwick. "I stood to the side of the stage with Brown and Melissa Moss, who was the finance director at the time," says Yolanda. "When Warwick began singing 'That's What Friends Are For,' I whispered, 'Ron, go up there.' He kind of hesitated a bit, and I said, 'This is the end of her set. This is how she's going to end it.' I mean I just instinctively knew it, and said again, 'Go up there with her.'"

Warwick was famous for grabbing ahold of people's hands and swinging them in the air when she sang the song, and Yolanda said with a smile, "I am very good at orchestrating a memorable moment, and once again, I told him, 'Go up there.' He looked at Moss and asked, 'What do you think?' and she just shrugged. Well, at this point, I was so annoyed, I just said in a loud voice, *'Go up there!'* Just like that," she recalled. "I talked to him like that, as a sibling would. *'Go up there!'* So, he went. It turned out to be the most perfect moment. Dionne grabbed his hand, and they were swaying back and forth, along with the entire audience, and it was just perfect. Afterward, he came backstage and he hugged me. And I said to him, 'Don't you *ever* think I'm not going tell you the right thing to do. Don't ever doubt it. And don't double-check with the white girl after I've told you what to do.'"

And Ron Brown said, "I'm sorry. I'll never doubt you again."

In 1991, when Bill Clinton's campaign was heating up, Donna wasn't quite ready to spend "an odd year getting even." She had just turned thirty, and she remembered what Reverend Jackson had said about her being a "branch without a tree." It was time, she thought, to put down roots. "I developed my roots by doing two things," Donna says. "One, I finally decided I would have a job, J-O-B. I finally decided, after all of my on-again, off-again, on-again experience of being on Capitol Hill, I would actually start working for these people. I hosted a radio show, and I also started teaching at the University of Maryland, College Park."

The second thing Donna did, in an effort to put down roots, was to start looking for a house. So, when Mayor Lottie Shackelford, who was organizing a team to move to Arkansas, called, Donna told her, "'Lottie, I'm putting up curtains. I am going to buy myself a house. I'm going to start living a little. I've got to have a job now. I cannot just keep going,'" because, as Donna says, "I had spent almost a decade of my life living out of a suitcase."

Buying a house had been a longtime goal for Donna. The Louisiana home her family lived in belonged to her grandmother. But after her grandmother's death, "there was no real deed to the property for the line of succession. My own family experienced a little bit of homelessness," she remembers. Campaign work was far from lucrative. And in those days, we were rich in experience but not wealthy. "There was an attempt to, basically, buy the house from underneath us, and my family was forced to depart because we didn't have the money. I didn't have the money. I had not yet made any real money. I was twenty-four years old and I had all of five hundred dollars to my name. I used that five hundred dollars to help my mother get a down payment on a house back in New Orleans."

Donna's first home was on Capitol Hill. She wanted to be close to where Frederick Douglass called home when he lived there back in the nineteenth century. She paid $165,000 for the house. "To me, being able to have a home you can live in, one that you experience life and families— having a house is a very important thing to me because of my own personal experience." The house was "small, only about nine hundred square feet, but I loved it. It was a great house."

At the same time that Ron Brown became chair of the DNC, Lee Atwater, architect of the Willie Horton ads and campaign strategy, became chair of the Republican Party. It's long been a tradition for the DNC and the RNC to play each other in an annual baseball game, and the DNC hadn't won a game in forty years. Yolanda remembers proudly, "The first year that we played the RNC with Ron as our chair, the DNC won."

During his term as chair, Atwater was diagnosed with a brain tumor, which spread quickly. He knew he was going to die—his face was distorted, and his body was bloated; he had become unrecognizable—and when Ron went to see him in the hospital, Atwater apologized for everything he had done. Yolanda says, "The way [Atwater] used race in that campaign was deplorable." Yet Brown was that kind of person: "The man's dying. We're adversaries—still, he felt he needed to go and sit with him. Just to be decent. It was a very sad way to see somebody go out."

Minyon recalled that the first time she heard Bill Clinton speak in earnest was during a campaign stop he made in Chicago, Illinois, in June 1992. She had been tasked with the Rainbow PUSH Coalition and Citizenship Education Fund Conference. Jackson, who had known Clinton for years, dating back to his tenure as governor of Arkansas, had invited Clinton to the conference, and it was considered a big deal that he decided to attend. Minyon says, "I distinctly remember Reverend Jackson giving the staff this lecture before the conference. He said, 'This could be the next president of the United States.' He wanted us to make sure we showed every courtesy and professionalism to [Clinton] and his team."

Minyon remembers feeling that "it was an honor for us to have Clinton at the Rainbow, 'in our house.' It was an exciting time for the organization, and it was certainly a great thing that we would have a presidential candidate."

Clinton began speaking, and all was going well, but then his remarks took a controversial turn. After he had lauded the work of Jackson, he began to criticize one of the speakers from the night before, a rapper and activist named Sister Souljah. In an interview she gave after the Los Angeles riots following the beating of black motorist Rodney King, during which whites were wounded, Souljah had stated, "I mean, if black people kill black people every day, why not have a week and kill white people?" Clinton, in response, told the crowd at the conference, "If you took the words *white* and *black* and you reversed them, you might think David Duke was giving that speech."

At that moment, the room fell silent. The remarks seemed to be tone-deaf to the feelings, language, and experience of the young hip-hop community. Unfortunately, what then–presidential candidate Bill Clinton didn't realize, what his aides hadn't conveyed to him, was that Reverend Jackson had organized the forum of the night before to speak to the younger members of the black community about, as Minyon puts it, "responsibility and making sure they use their platforms for the greater good. Sister Souljah at the time was one of the most popular and provocative rappers on the scene. She was beloved by young people. Reverend knew she had a platform, and he had hoped to convince her and the other young folks to be responsible when they have a platform." Then Clinton said what he said.

Minyon and the Rainbow PUSH staff gathered to do damage control: "It was me, Carol Willis, and Rodney Slater," Minyon says. "We began to huddle, trying to figure out what [had] got into him. Why would he say that?"

The press soon took hold of the story and—well, things escalated quickly. Jackson issued a statement reminding Clinton and his supporters that it was important not to pull particular lines from a rap song, and to look at the music and the message as emblematic of something much more powerful. "Sister Souljah represents the feelings and hopes of a whole generation of people," Jackson said.

Souljah, for her part, criticized Clinton, accusing him of having been (right up until he announced his candidacy) a member of a golf club that wouldn't admit African Americans. Clinton admitted that this was true, and publicly apologized, but by then, the press had gotten involved, and all three parties, Jackson, Clinton, and Souljah, were criticized by pundits and pols across the political spectrum.

On that day when Clinton and Souljah tussled, Minyon saw a different Clinton emerge, one never reported in the press. She says, "One point that is never conveyed about that moment was once Bill Clinton heard the context of why Sister Souljah was on the panel, from Reverend Jackson, he hung around the hotel waiting for her to return, to speak to her directly. Unfortunately, she didn't return for several hours, and by that time the news media had taken the story and run with it."

Minyon remembers that "it also was a lesson for me in, when you have a presidential candidate attending your conferences, you have to take all types of precautions. I learned how quickly these situations can spin out of control if you don't get the facts out. It was a high-level lesson in politics, crisis management, and being very disciplined in your message. I certainly learned that day and at that moment, it's very hard to get back to a civil place when the media is driving the story."

It was there, in that moment, that Minyon began to gain a reputation as someone who could keep a cool head in a crisis, and build bridges between the black and white political leadership. During his second term, when he was looking to fill a deputy director position in the White House, Clinton would call on Minyon. And when Hillary Rodham Clinton made both her historic presidential runs, Minyon was by her side. Minyon didn't know then that it was a career-defining moment, but it was: "Politics dictates that you've got to be calm in the midst of a fire. You have to think through very complex issues and strategies very quickly, and you can't do it under hysteria. You just can't. At least, I can't. The calmer I am, the better I can assess the situation and figure out a game plan. It doesn't always work out the way you want, but for the most part, I try very hard to be value-added when hysteria is all around. When it gets crazy, I pull back a little bit."

Leah and Tina both worked for Clinton's transition team, helping to staff the new administration. It was, as it always is, a challenging timeline. The election takes place in November. The candidate takes office in

January, and in between, the transition team works tirelessly to staff the government. As Tina explains it, "you know that you have civil service people. The government was not going to shut down, because you had people to keep the trains running. But [the president-elect] has to have a cabinet identified. All the White House staff identified. The people running these big agencies—because they're in the hands of, at that point, the Republicans, who were there for four years under Bush, but some of them had been there under Reagan. So, you had twelve years of Republicans in positions that you now get to fill. You've got to think about who your ambassadors are going to be. It's a marathon. You've got to find a big office, and you've got to [hire] all of these people. Then you've got to put a process in place to identify people for jobs. You have to have a vetting operation. That was my operation, in which you vet all these people who are being proposed for jobs. You have to do all these background checks on people."

Vetting involves different levels. As Tina explains, it begins with "Does anybody know this person? What do they think of her? What do people say about her? As you move up the chain, then you have the FBI do some vetting. And then another level, you look at their financials and all that kind of stuff. And so, my team was over forty people."

Typically, a transition team is staffed by volunteers. What made the Clinton transition team unique was that its staff was paid. "Let me assure you," Tina explains, "I could have gotten a team of eighty and not paid them. Because they all saw that as their way to get jobs in the White House." But this would also have meant, she says, that her team would have been "all white, from affluent families," people "working in prominent law firms, or what have you." But, as she made clear at the time, "I can't go down like that. I said, 'Somebody's got to find money to pay people. People who don't need to get paid, we won't pay them. And if they're fine with not getting paid, that's fine. But people that need to get paid should get paid.'" It was an illuminating conversation. As Tina asked at the time, "Suppose there wasn't a black woman heading this operation? I expect that there are white people who would think about [doing the job for free]." But she wasn't going to settle for that.

In the end, Tina notes with pride, "Leah, Val, and I ended up getting a pretty diverse transition team. Some of them went over to the White House. Some were in the counsel's office. One of them is an author and professor at Georgetown Law. They went [on] to prominent law firms. One became deputy chief of staff at Treasury. A friend at Education then became chief of staff of Education. One of them went on to become the cabinet secretary at the White House. He's the liaison for all the cabinet members."

It helped that the newly elected president was on board. "Clinton was clear. He said, 'I'm going to have an administration that looks like America.' Having that coming from the top made it easier. But you have to watch every day," she adds. "The usual line is 'Oh, we couldn't find anybody.' But you can if you look hard enough. If you make the path open and wide enough. You have to be willing to go outside your comfort zone and look for people who are different than you. This doesn't just ever happen for us. Anybody who believes it does is just wrong."

Following Bill Clinton's election, Minyon held a variety of White House posts, eventually becoming the first African American to serve as assistant to the president of the United States and director of White House political affairs. In this role, she served as the principal advisor to President Bill Clinton, Vice President Al Gore, First Lady Hillary Rodham Clinton, and the senior White House staff. Her primary responsibility was planning outreach and directing the political activities of the White House. *Washingtonian* magazine selected her as one of the most powerful women in DC.

President Bill Clinton made many historic appointments throughout the government, asking people of color—especially women of color—to serve in positions that had only ever been held by white men. These appointments gave people of color a sense of pride. We believed that President Bill Clinton's choice to put people in strategic positions that didn't have anything to do with the color of their skin but everything to do with their qualifications was a game changer. When Clinton, with a push by his friend, civil rights icon and lawyer, Vernon Jordan, gave District of Columbia's Delegate to Congress Eleanor Holmes Norton senatorial courtesy (i.e., the right to nominate people to federal judgeships, U.S. marshal, and U.S. attorney) and made Eric Holder U.S. Attorney for the District of Columbia, we took advantage of this and found qualified people of color, including women, to apply for these positions. The Clinton African American cabinet appointees included:

- Jesse Brown, Secretary of Veterans Affairs
- Ron Brown, Secretary of Commerce
- Mike Espy, Secretary of Agriculture
- Alexis Herman, Secretary of Labor
- Hazel O'Leary, Secretary of Energy
- Rodney Slater, Secretary of Transportation
- Togo West, Secretary of the Army and later Secretary of Veterans Affairs

All of them served in roles traditionally not held by African Americans. President Clinton also made unprecedented senior-level appointments in the White House. To this day, he holds the record for White House appointments of African Americans, especially when it comes to appointing the assistant to the president, the highest rank within the White House.

During Clinton's first inaugural, in 1993 (an event Ron chaired), Yolanda remembers walking down the hall of the inaugural headquarters, at the Navy Yard, with Brown. He mentioned that Clinton had suggested the possibility of his serving as chief of staff. She told Brown, only half-jokingly, "Trust me, you don't want to work that hard."

When Brown got the call offering him the post of U.S. ambassador to the United Nations, Yolanda was at his house. He told the president-elect that he would think about it and get back to him. Brown's wife and son, Alma and Michael, were there as well, along with Bill Morton, his traveling aide and Yolanda's mentee. No one there was very excited about the prospect of Brown's being UN ambassador. "But none of us had any thoughts on what he should ask for; everything was happening very quickly," Yolanda says. The next day, Clinton called Brown and asked about serving as commerce secretary. Now, *that* had some meat on it, although we didn't quite know what that looked like yet. "What does the secretary of commerce do, really?" Brown wondered aloud. Yolanda told him, "I don't know, but I'll find out by tomorrow." And she did. The job was tailor-made for him.

Yet, there was no role for Rev. Jesse Jackson in the Clinton administration. In his book *Jesse: The Life and Pilgrimage of Jesse Jackson*, journalist Marshall Frady shares an interaction between Harold Ickes and Jackson during the Clinton campaign:

"You have such a gift," Ickes told him. "You've just got this gift."

To which Jackson replied, "Well, why don't you use that gift? Why don't you just bring me on in? You can keep trying to cut me out if you want, but I'm not going away. You can try to go around me, try to go under me—you sure can't go over me, you know that. So why don't you just bring me in?"

The 1992 Inaugural

The day after Clinton won the election, Yolanda called Ron and said, "I want to come back and work on the inaugural." He said, "Can you come back tomorrow?" Yolanda remembers, "I had stayed in New York after the convention to work on a new venture, an event management company with my late friend Caroline Jones and Stuart White. But I said, 'Okay, I'll get there.' I went back to DC the next day."

Ron was going to be chair of the inaugural, and Yolanda his deputy. She needed an assistant, so Amelia Parker, who ran the Congressional Black Caucus, lent her one of her staffers, a woman named Comelia Sanford. Yolanda remembers that she had "this little teeny tiny office, and Comelia sat right outside. We had to be there every day at seven in the morning. I've never worked so hard in my entire life. We worked ninety days straight. We had Thanksgiving off and Christmas Day off. That was it. Worked through New Year's, worked through everything."

From Election Day to the inauguration, she told herself, "You get ninety days. Ninety days to put together this humongous event. Nobody remembered exactly what to do, because we hadn't been in power for so long. None of us knew what we were doing. We had to go to the National Archives to pull up old files to see what you're supposed to do for a presidential inaugural. Fortunately, the military handles a lot, including the actual swearing-in ceremony. So, we didn't have to worry about that. But all these other events that were going on (the balls, the HBO special, other ancillary events for the general public) we had to do. We had to plan it and raise the money to pay for it. Rahm Emanuel was the executive director. Yes, that same Rahm from the [DNC training workshops]. He was head fund-raiser for the Clinton campaign, so it would make sense that he would run the inaugural."

One morning, Yolanda came in to find her assistant, Comelia Sanford, crying at her desk. "So I called her in my office. I said, 'What's the matter?' Keep in mind, back in those days, Comelia, admittedly, used to cry *a lot*. My attitude was 'What now?'"

Comelia explained, "I just saw that a friend of mine died."

"Back in those days, she called *everybody* her friend," Yolanda remembers, "so I didn't know if it was a close friend or an acquaintance."

Then Yolanda looked at Comelia and said, "'I'm very sorry about your friend, but we don't have time for this right now. You're going to have to grieve later.' And she snapped out of it. But she called me the Ice Queen after that." She adds, "'Girl, call me what you want. We have a job to do.' We still laugh about it to this day."

Yolanda attributes a lot of what she was able to accomplish in those ninety days to her work with Reverend Jackson. "We learned how to do things with no money and no time," she says. "It was not unusual for him to call me up at five o'clock in the morning and say, 'I want to have a press conference at eleven.' I had to get my ass up—I lived way out in

Maryland, so [it] took me almost an hour to get to work. But you just learn how to do something with nothing. Like the saying goes, 'We have done so much for so long with so little that we are now qualified to do anything with nothing.'"

Yolanda adds that planning an inaugural with the Republicans still in office presented unique challenges. "Everything was so intense. It was very frustrating." VIPs were allotted a certain number of tickets to various events, depending on their status. Most people could buy only two per event. But, as Yolanda remembers, "every day there was somebody who wanted more than two tickets. We had people who wanted to buy whole tables and multiple tickets for events." Every day, Comelia would go to the huge room that housed all of the computers used to handle ticket sales, to add people, change the numbers, and every morning—it never failed—when the staff came back, the numbers had been changed. "We just knew we were being sabotaged by the Republicans, because we were in the Navy Yard, in a navy building that was still under their control. So, they still had control over everything. It was horrible. It was the worst thing. Looking back, I can see that was my first experience with hacking."

Yolanda had planned a tribute event for Ron Brown, to be held at the Kennedy Center. Brown was the DNC chair and the chair of the inaugural. "The [inaugural] would be his swan song as he left the DNC," Yolanda explains. The tribute was going to be a spectacular event. "We had raised the money as needed and were about to send out invitations. Then we started getting calls from these reporters asking, 'Where was the money coming from?' All these crazy questions. Everything was totally aboveboard. We'd raised the money from friends at corporations who had budgets for this sort of thing. The [tribute] event started to overshadow the actual inaugural. Ron called me over to his office at the DNC. He just said, 'I'm not going to do it.' He really wanted it; Ron loved stuff like that. He loved to be loved. That's when I cried. That's the one time I broke down and cried. We had to call it off. We had raised the money. We bought this beautiful Maasai warrior sculpture, by the renowned sculptor Ed Dwight. I just felt like 'This is stupid. Stupid and unfair.' But that was my one cry time."

One afternoon, Yolanda had just landed in DC from New York when she ran into a friend from South Africa, Lindiwe Mabuza. She had met Mabuza through Jackson and their work with the African National Congress.

Yolanda remembers asking her, "How can we get Mr. Mandela to come to the inaugural?" Nelson Mandela had been released from prison in 1990 but hadn't yet been elected president of South Africa. Mabuza said, "I'll work on it."

What Yolanda didn't know then was that there's a protocol for who gets an official invitation to a U.S. presidential inaugural: Mandela's case was complicated, as he was not technically the head of state in South Africa. Yolanda and Mabuza worked tirelessly to clear this roadblock, and finally were able to work it out so that the Congressional Black Caucus invited Mandela to the inaugural and hosted him while he was in the United States.

One afternoon before the big event, Lauri Fitz-Pegado, an old friend of Ron's who was helping out on the inaugural, and Yolanda had lunch with Mabuza. The two women were exhausted, and as Yolanda remembers, "all we did was complain, complain, complain. Complain about this. Complain about that."

Mabuza said, "I want you ladies to stop and pay attention to this moment. You are the descendants of slaves, and you are orchestrating the peaceful transition of power in the most powerful country in the world. You are in a place that we never believed we could be."

"We all started crying," Yolanda says. "She reminded us that we were the daughters of slaves, planning the peaceful transition of power, and in that instant, we had a totally different attitude. Totally different. Never thought of it that way. You know, sometimes we're so entitled and spoiled, we had just never thought about it from that perspective. It transformed the entire experience for me."

The impact of what had happened with Clinton, with Brown, with all the Colored Girls, didn't fully hit Yolanda, she says, until the first event of the inauguration, the kickoff at the Lincoln Memorial. Quincy Jones produced the special for HBO. As Yolanda remembers it, "It was mid-January and the sun was shining. It wasn't that cold. I was walking through the crowd with Comelia, and we found Ron. We were standing together and we watched the flyby with the military jets. LL Cool J was rapping, and I turned around and . . . *there was a sea of people*, all the way back as far as the Washington Monument. Everybody's hands were going back and forth in the air. I started crying . . . Oh, Jesus. It was an amazing sight."

When Bill Clinton was sworn into office, Yolanda was onstage, seated next to David Dinkins, then mayor of New York City. The chairman of the Joint Chiefs of Staff was seated next to them, as were the heads of the four military branches. They stood in unison and saluted Clinton. "It just took my breath away, completely took my breath away," Yolanda says. "It's history. We had made history. We helped make history."

9

The Bank of Justice: Giving Back After You've Been Given So Much

When Bill Clinton won the presidency in 1992, there hadn't been a Democrat in the office since Jimmy Carter. As Minyon remembers it, "Bill Clinton was elected by being a self-described 'New Democrat.' He wanted to bring new policies and fresh thinking to the White House and the Democratic Party. His ideas were not readily accepted by some members of Congress nor the liberal wing of the party. Looking back, the ideological and political strain in the first year of Clinton's presidency was tough. For those of us who worked at the DNC, we constantly felt the tug-of-war."

She continues: "It certainly put a strain on David Wilhelm, who was the new [DNC] chair. He was fresh off of running Bill Clinton's campaign. He had liberals and the centrist Democrats pulling at him. He had the Democrats on the Hill yelling at him, saying you've got to spend more time raising money to help elect Democrats. And you had the White House saying, 'You've got to spend more time helping the president promote his policies.'"

The DNC would often find itself at odds with the White House and the various Democratic Party committees. Ultimately, our job was to help elect Democrats, to ensure the president was able to pass his legislative agenda. It wasn't to set policy. The White House was the big dog, and the DNC was the underdog. And the president, as titular head of the Democratic Party, was the DNC's greatest fund-raiser. So, if you get a call from the White House asking you to do something, what do you do? You do whatever the White House asks you to do.

Minyon joined the DNC right after Clinton won his first term, taking the job of director of constituency outreach. Leaving the Rainbow PUSH Coalition at that time was, she says, "a big, big deal. In fact, David Wilhelm, the [DNC] chairman, had to go to Reverend Jackson and ask his permission to hire me." Wilhelm was surprised when Minyon asked him to call Reverend Jackson, but she saw it as a show of respect. When Wilhelm placed the call, Jackson told him, "We teach them, we train them, and you all steal them. You are taking the motor out of my computer."

"It wasn't quite stealing," Minyon says, "but I understood Reverend's point, and so did David. A generation of young black and brown campaign operatives were able to gain public policy and political experience at the highest level because of his two presidential runs. We were able to compete with our white contemporaries without being told, 'You don't have the experience.' So, in his eyes, as soon as we get the experience, then we are hired away."

Minyon was ready to make this leap in her career, but "I still wanted it to be respectful. I also thought I could be a valued voice for the Rainbow Coalition, especially since the president was elected on policies that were promoted by the Democratic Leadership Council. I believed, since the two organizations were at odds with each other on big public policy questions, maybe this could be a bridge and potentially lead to a better understanding of where we all stood on issues."

She goes on: "Shortly after arriving at the DNC, I met Kiki Moore, who [had been] a top official at the Democratic Leadership Council. She was hired as the communications director for the DNC. We soon became known as the 'Moore Sisters.' I think we first bonded over having the same last name."

Their unique friendship became the bridge between the Rainbow PUSH Coalition and the DLC, with the two women able to quell some of the friction between the two groups. Minyon says, "I met Al From, the head of the DLC, through [Kiki]. And she met Reverend Jackson. We both gained a greater appreciation for the leaders. Amazingly, their portrayals in the media were very different from the actual people. Al cared about public policy, and so did Reverend. Like Clinton, they both believed we needed some new ideas and fresh thinking but getting to that consensus and finding common ground was the tough part."

Minyon goes on: "Kiki and I grew closer as we found ourselves on the same side—defending the party and Chairman Wilhelm. We would often think, 'What would Ron Brown do?' Ron was so skilled at navigating all the factions in the party. David was such a good person. He was a delight to work with and for. He certainly didn't get half the credit he deserved for trying to keep the party together. He brought the best of everything out in people and could always find a silver lining, even when no one else could find it. Eventually, David returned to private life. And as fate would have it for Kiki and me, a friendship was born. The DLC and the Rainbow were finally not at odds with each other, at least not from our perspective. Years later, [Kiki and I] both ended up working at the Dewey Square Group in our post-administration lives."

We often talk about roles as being "inside" and "outside." As a trusted member of Jackson's leadership core, Minyon had spent most of her career as an outside woman. On the outside, her role was clear: to let the Democratic establishment know that "Yes, we might be part of the party, but it doesn't mean we're not going to fight vigorously on behalf of our core constituents: black and brown people, women, seniors, the LGBT community, and people with disabilities. We were a constant reminder that change doesn't always come from the top down; it also comes from the bottom up." Joining the DNC was her first taste of being completely on the inside: "It was different coming inside, because now the very people you were pushing are your colleagues. The very people that you pushed are now the ones who are sitting at the desk next to you. The question was 'Okay, so how do I balance this?' I made a decision very early on in my career that while I wanted my colleagues to understand my values, I also wanted to be open to hearing opposing viewpoints and finding common ground where we could. I knew instinctively that I could represent a viewpoint that might be different without being disagreeable. I wanted to use that position to build bridges of understanding for people that the party or the White House wasn't dealing with on a regular basis."

We had all experienced, on a personal level, on a community level, fights to expand rights. We had been raised in a world where our equality wasn't a given. We had known since we were children that we lived in an America where being black, being female, did not entitle us fully, not yet, to the freedoms of democracy. As Tina explains, "So much of our work was big picture. But we were always very focused on how *we* fit in that picture. When I say 'we,' I don't mean a collective we. I mean the broader we: black people. 'Okay, so the Democratic Party is saying that there are going to be ten delegates out of Virginia?' We always had an eye out. How many of them are black? 'Oh, so you're hiring staff for the communications department? How many of them are black?' We all had a chip that, for us, those were immediate questions. Because you were on guard against it not being right."

At the White House, Minyon worked hard to adhere to a piece of advice that Vernon Jordan gave her before she started. He told her, "You will have the opportunity to advise the most powerful person in the world. You must be prepared, you must make sure you do your best research before giving that advice. But remember, it is only your advice. Don't become enamored with your advice. Give it and walk away from it even if he doesn't take it. In the end, the responsibility will rest with the president and he will have the right to determine the final direction. Words to live by: your advice is just that, your advice."

Another piece of advice she got was from Reverend Jackson: "Your dignity level must always match your insult level." That basically meant that you can't be afraid to speak up when you know what is being said should be challenged or an alternative position should be voiced. Of course, there is a right way and a wrong way to do anything, but the real point is that you must summon the courage to speak up when you know what is being said is flat-out wrong. So, if you are satisfied sitting in a room listening to people talk nonsense, or you're sitting in a room and they're talking about diverse issues that require more people and thinking, and you're the only person of color and you're afraid to speak up, then your dignity level has not matched your insult level. You have one of two choices: you can either speak up or help expand the table. Being silent or on the sidelines shouldn't be the option. I made a decision when I went to the White House: I would try to be as candid and as truthful as possible, even when it wasn't always the popular thing to do. I also set out to hire diverse voices in my department so that the White House and the president would hear from people with different sets of experiences."

There were some people in power, even in a Democratic administration, who did not like being pushed by liberals or the progressive community. Minyon says of the latter, simply, "They pushed us. They pushed us to be better. Sometimes they pushed us in the right direction; sometimes they pushed us in the wrong direction. These constituency groups were always fighting for more inclusion and for policies that they believed would make us stronger as a nation. That would make some people in the White House uncomfortable."

She continues: "On some days, you had to make a decision that you side with the groups because you knew it was the right thing to do. And there were other days when you had to be the bearer of bad news and you would have to let the groups know the White House is going in a different direction. It was always a balancing act, but the most important thing was you had to make sure their views were reflected in the debate. The good news was, as you got to know your colleagues in different departments, it became easier to convince the most rigid person that they weren't thinking broadly enough about a particular policy. You were able to show them where it could hurt a particular community or constituency. Ironically, building relationships of trust help shed some of the labels. You were no longer seen as the person from the left or the center of the party. When you are in meetings with people day in and day out, you get to know them and they get to know you. They understand your character and value system. They will understand when you say, 'I can't go there with you. Now, you might be able to take that to somebody else, but I can't go there. I can't sell that policy with a straight face.'"

By the end of her four years at the White House, Minyon felt confident that many in the administration had gotten to know, through her, a different version of the Rainbow and the progressive community. "I've learned this over the years," she says. "And I certainly learned this when I left the Rainbow to go [into] Democratic politics: part of the challenge in politics is [that] people who come from different political backgrounds, be it liberal, progressive, or centrist—they don't spend nearly enough time building relationships of trust. Not knowing each other is a big drawback to finding common ground in politics. You know, for us at the Rainbow, we didn't know what we didn't know. We didn't know how the party operated, or the White House. We didn't know the rules. And until you can learn the rules, you can't change them."

Bill Clinton's election prompted the creation of what we called the Bank of Justice. The Bank of Justice was a concept built on a promise: once you get to a position of influence, you pay it forward. We started consciously creating opportunities for qualified people who might otherwise have been shut out, especially women and people of color.

Minyon notes, "Clinton was a great advocate of this. President Clinton was adamant about having a White House that looked like America." He wanted to make sure his team was open and accessible to everyone. We took the mission seriously and made it a priority to help those people who wouldn't ordinarily have gotten the chance to attend conventions, inaugurations, White House policy briefings/events, or even to tour the White House. We not only went around collecting goodies (such as inauguration tickets) and opportunities, but we got everyone we worked with to invest in the Bank of Justice, too.

Minyon says, "We encouraged everyone to give us their résumé, and we worked the phones. We had both an inside and an outside strategy. We had eyes all over town." It became a regular part of our conversation: "What do you have in the Bank of Justice?" "What are you depositing in the Bank of Justice?"

She adds, "In theory, it comes as a result of the grassroots folks who do all of the hard work during an election cycle trying to help get a presidential candidate elected. Then you look up, and they say, 'Oh, I want to come to the convention,' but they don't know how to get a credential or access to the events."

We knew it was important to create opportunities for American citizens who didn't have fancy titles or access to power in the traditional ways. We felt it was our personal responsibility to make sure the hardworking activist had an opportunity to enjoy the convention just like everyone else.

Minyon remembers that "the first time we opened up the Bank of Justice, I never saw the convention hall at all, because I was stuck in a little room trying to give out convention passes, or to make sure that everyone who was trying to get a pass got in." She adds, "The question was simple: 'Can we get them in?' That's the selfless part of public service, and that's where I will say all of us succeeded to varying degrees. Because we all believe that we have an obligation to swing the door wide open, as Leah says. That's primarily the reason people, especially black people, felt like they had such unprecedented access to President Clinton, and to Hillary Clinton, and to the White House, Vice President Gore, and Tipper Gore. Because we willed it so. We used ourselves as that connection point, along with many others, of course, to make sure that people always felt that they could get into these places. It didn't matter if it was a White House holiday party, a briefing, or the chance to shake the president's hand on the tarmac. They weren't all celebrities or important people, which makes it so beautiful. I still meet people today who come up to me and say, 'I remember when you got my family that tour,' or 'I remember when I was able to come see President Clinton on the tarmac. I remember.' And sometimes I don't remember them at all, but *they* remember. And that's all that matters."

She continues: "Bill Clinton, in particular, was a huge supporter of making sure that we always had an eye toward inclusion. He was notorious for looking at an event list and noticing who was missing. He would say, 'Well, where is this person? Where is that? Don't you see that this list doesn't represent the nation?'"

We call Clinton "the best constituency president we ever knew." Minyon notes, "He did constituency politics all day, every day. He cared about what was happening with his friends, and he tried to keep up with them even as president. He was constantly writing personal notes." She adds, "We made sure to include [his friends] in events, especially when he was in their state. He would see things in the press and say, 'I need to give this person a call.' He would show up at funerals of longtime friends." To this day, Clinton still has friends around the country because he tried to remain connected to them while he was president.

Back home in Chicago, Minyon's parents were proud that their daughter, who'd given up her good corporate job with benefits, had made it all the way to the executive offices of the White House. Nevertheless, Minyon says, "My mother kept the real in the real. I'll never forget when we were in Chicago and we went to this event where they were honoring me—the 'Hometown Girl Made Good' type of event. You know how people overdo your résumé when they're introducing you? They have a tendency to make you out to be so much more than you are. You can't even recognize yourself. Well, surely my mother couldn't recognize that person, and she leaned over and she said to me, 'Are they talking about you?' So I said, 'No, I don't think so, but they might attach my name to it.' But she wasn't playing that 'Saint Minyon' game. She rolled her eyes and said, 'Lordy.' I don't think my family ever really knew *what* I did.

They just knew I worked for a president of the United States, and they knew I worked at the White House. They knew that my church was proud of me. They knew that some of my hometown friends, former schoolmates, were proud of me."

Minyon took to heart her mother's advice to keep the "real in the real." She says, "This is the thing that you know I've learned about living a quasi-public life. You really have to find your own moral center and compass, and then you have to anchor down, because people love looking up to people. They just do. It's the thing that I find the most fascinating about celebrities—how we admire them, we put them on pedestals, and we make them feel like they are untouchable. Then they make us feel like they are untouchable. I never wanted to get comfortable with the notion that people believe you are untouchable. I have been the most deliberate high- and low-profile person you will get to know. I've been very deliberate about it because I've never wanted to ever get to a place where the applause became what I was seeking."

Once, a group of older women from Operation PUSH in Chicago came to Washington for a visit. Esther Thompson, Betty Magnus, and Hazel Thomas were part of a long line of black women who worked tirelessly at Operation PUSH to make lives better for people in the black community. Those women epitomized public service without accolades. "The best part of my job was to be able to bring them to the White House. I could treat them to lunch in the White House Mess. Or when their families came to town, we could make sure they got tours of the White House. I always wanted to make sure they understood that 'I am you and you are me, and I hope that you know that you can experience this just like I can.' That, to me, was the joy of working in the White House. You were able to expose ordinary people to extraordinary things."

We believe that the Bank of Justice will always exist because it is a mind-set. There will always be people who don't appear on anyone's list or who simply don't know how to navigate political conventions or political campaigns. It is our hope that the next generation of Colored Girls will also see this as their mandate and their responsibility as they rise in power.

10

Clinton/Gore '96

In 1996, chief of staff Erskine Bowles called Minyon Moore and offered her a job at the White House. She politely declined. She says, "As I look back on it, it was out of fear. I didn't want to move out of my comfort zone. I probably didn't think I could do the job, so I said no." After four short years, the DNC was just beginning to feel like home. She didn't think she was ready to make the leap from there to the White House.

A few days later, she received another call. This one was from Vice President Al Gore. Minyon smiles. "Of course, it was harder to say no to him. I didn't really know what to say, other than 'Thank you for calling' and 'Sir, I will give it very serious thought.'"

Gore told Minyon he would have Erskine Bowles call her back before the end of the week. She began to get the sense that she was not just being offered the kind of job that most DC staffers dream about; she was being courted. "When I hung up, I remember thinking to myself, 'Girl, what is wrong with you?'"

Bowles called again. This time, Minyon said yes. He asked for her current salary. When she told him, he said, "Oh, you might have to take a pay cut." She said, "I can't take a pay cut. I just bought a house. And I didn't ask to go to the White House."

Erskine's response? "Let me get back to you."

A few days later, he returned with a better offer. Minyon recalls, "I took a thousand-dollar pay cut, but that was okay."

Before moving into her coveted office in the West Wing of the White House, Minyon had worked out of the Old Executive Office Building. She was shocked at how huge that office was. It had floor-to-ceiling windows, a fireplace, and even a balcony. "I had this huge office that was connected to my counterpart, Craig Smith. Ironically, Craig Smith was the political director when I joined the DNC. So, I became one of the deputies in his department, and then Karen Skelton, Vice President Al Gore's political director, soon joined as the other deputy. Karen and I would spend many days and nights in each other's office comparing notes, laughing, and just trying to figure out the job. We supported each other and helped each other navigate the halls of the White House." Minyon's new title: deputy assistant to the president and deputy director of political affairs.

Minyon was promoted twice during her tenure at the White House, first to assistant to the president and director of the Office of Public Liaison, and then to assistant to the president and director of political affairs for the White House. She was the first African American to serve as a director of political affairs, and she served Clinton's entire second term. Everything about the job was different, she says. "I can tell you that. It was different." She recalls, in the early days, opening the door to her office, taking a deep breath, and saying a small prayer: "Dear God, help me do this job."

First, she had to figure out what exactly the job entailed. "You get thrown in the fire," she says. "My first day on the job I found out that President Clinton was doing a political trip to Chicago. I had to help organize the trip—I suppose because I was from Chicago. I was introduced to a young lady by the name of Laura Graham. She was one of the new schedulers (working for dear friend Stephanie Streett). It was her first day on the job as well, and she handled the Midwest. Neither one of us knew exactly what we were doing. How do you organize a trip for the president of the United States? What if something went wrong?

"We found ourselves learning pretty quickly. My first trip with the president on Air Force One was heading back home to my hometown of Chicago. That was pretty sweet. But I was still terrified something would go wrong. We would forget someone, someone [had gotten] left off the meet-and-greet list. The good news: my first trip was a success. I even got an added bonus because my nieces and nephew were able to meet the president. And I got the chance to see some of my friends and mentors, which also made this trip even more meaningful."

Now, imagine what it must have been like for a young girl from the South Side of Chicago, never, ever dreaming she would hold such a position—imagine her sitting in the Oval Office or the prestigious Roosevelt Room, participating in meetings with the president and vice president of the United States, where they are debating tough policy positions and you are expected to give advice and know your topics.

Imagine making the first historic trip to Africa with the president, the vice president, First Lady Hillary Rodham Clinton, and cabinet and congressional members on Air Force One.

Imagine stepping off the plane in Ghana and as far as the eye can see, there are thousands of people who've shown up to meet this president and his delegation. Then imagine meeting, up close and personal, *President Nelson Mandela*, your lifelong hero. And then having the opportunity to brief President Mandela; his wife, Graça Machel; President Clinton; and Hillary Clinton on [Clinton's] first historic event with clergy from around the country at the White House for President Mandela. Imagine attending the state dinner given in President Mandela's honor and being in total awe the entire time.

Or just imagine riding on Air Force One and Marine One, not on one occasion but *several occasions*. Imagine the audaciousness of this plane—as we've often stated, "your office in the air." Imagine celebrating your birthday on Air Force One because "duty calls." Or just imagine the lighter moments, when playing cards (hearts) with the president and your colleagues was the only way to unwind and relax.

Imagine, years later, taking another sojourn to Africa with President Clinton and his delegation and having the opportunity to have lunch with President Mandela in a private room at the beautiful Saxon Hotel in South Africa. "I listened to him talk about his years of imprisonment," Minyon says. "He spoke about the difficulty of his time in jail and how he kept his mental strength and dignity. Yet he emerged unbowed and unbroken. It was the greatest testament of grace and forgiveness I had ever witnessed."

Then, just imagine: a girl from the South Side of Chicago did this, *and so can you*. Nothing is impossible if you work hard and get out of your own way.

It's helpful to remember that the office of the First Lady has experienced a slow-moving evolution. It starts with the geography of the White House. The First Lady's office, traditionally, was in the East Wing. It's largely disconnected from the main artery of the West Wing, unless you are very deliberate about including the staff of the East Wing in the day-to-day work of the West Wing.

Hillary Clinton was considered a nontraditional First Lady. Hillary mixed things up. First, she took an office in the West Wing, the first signal that she would be using her perch to help promote the president's agenda. Second, she advocated for her chief of staff, Maggie Williams, to hold the title "assistant to the president and chief of staff to the First Lady." It was an unprecedented move, but one that would fully incorporate Maggie into the day-to-day issues of the West Wing. As Minyon explains it, "it put her on the same level with all the assistants in the White House, and it gave her a seat at the table in the West Wing. She became a peer among peers. Once Maggie had that title, she became a bridge between the East Wing staff and the West Wing staff. She became a powerful advocate for the First Lady's office."

Another woman who worked for Hillary was Capricia Marshall, one of Hillary's first aides on the campaign trail. Capricia was one of the most likable members of Hillary's staff. She had such a radiant personality. She was always trying to be helpful to the West Wing. While people knew how close she was to Hillary, she never used that closeness to do anything other than help us understand Hillary and "Hillaryland." Capricia soon became the social secretary of the White House, and her popularity rose even further. She was the gatekeeper to all events held in the West Wing. Whether it was a party, a state dinner, or an East Wing briefing, Capricia's office was on point. Minyon and Marshall became close, along with Stephanie Streett, the president's director of scheduling. Stephanie controlled what went on the president's schedule, and if you thought about going around her, you were guaranteed to have your request slow-walked. The three of us became the best of friends. We looked out for each other. We made sure that we shared information. We formed a sisterhood and bond that was unbreakable. And because we all held very important positions in the White House, working together made us even more powerful.

"My first impression of Hillary was she was brilliant," Minyon says. "I was used to seeing that level of intellect displayed by men in politics, but it was refreshing to see a woman command a room with that level of intelligence." And while previous First Ladies had taken on less controversial issues, such as Nancy Reagan's "Just Say No" campaign against drug abuse, or Lady Bird Johnson's campaign to inspire communities "to clean up neighborhoods and highways," or Barbara Bush's important efforts around literacy, Hillary, Minyon says, "had an insatiable appetite for policy. [She] had the ability to absorb a lot of detail and retain information like nothing I had ever seen. She had been a strong advocate for children and families dating back to her days at the Children's Defense Fund. It was no surprise to anyone that she would continue advocating for children and families in the White House."

Hillary wasn't afraid to take on tough issues—especially if she believed it would help children and families. She had always been passionate about health care and believed our health care system was broken and in desperate need of reform. President Clinton had campaigned vigorously on the need for health reform. Once he was elected, he appointed Hillary to chair the Task Force on National Health Care Reform for the White House. This was yet another unconventional move for a First Lady. That became a defining moment for her and the White House, especially when the legislation didn't pass. We lost control of Congress. Some blame the loss on our health care plans.

Ironically, Hillary's fights, her bruises, and her battles against the powerful special interests didn't stop her. It gave her the fortitude to keep going. As First Lady, she worked with a bipartisan group of senators to help pass the Children's Health Insurance Program, which covers over eight million children. Senator Edward Kennedy would later say at a press conference, "Mrs. Clinton was of invaluable help, both in the fashioning and the shaping of the program and also as a clear advocate. . . . The Children's Health Program wouldn't be in existence today if we didn't have Hillary pushing for it from the other end of Pennsylvania Avenue." The bill was signed into law by President Clinton, as part of the Balanced Budget Act of 1997. While President Obama fought some of the same special interest groups, in 2010 he passed into law the Patient Protection and Affordable Care Act, known as "Obamacare," covering over twenty million people. One could argue that Hillary's health care fight, her scars, her battles, helped pave the way for President Obama's historic legislation.

Minyon's job, as it evolved, put her in both the political shop and the constituency shop, which meant she was constantly making sure her department and teams were bringing in the right constituents. She often asked, "Who are we briefing?" "Who are we talking to?" "Who should President Clinton be talking to?" On many occasions, we had to coordinate with the scheduling office, the First Lady's office, and the vice president's office. Having friends in these offices therefore became critical, especially when events were held in the East Wing.

Minyon remembers that there was "not a state dinner or a big event that went on in the White House that we did not have knowledge of and input in. That was due in large part to my relationship with Stephanie and Capricia. "It was also helpful that my office handled all of the political events for the White House," she adds.

One particular night—Minyon remembers it was extremely cold—after a fund-raiser that Hillary had attended, Minyon and a colleague were standing outside after the event, following the protocol of making sure the First Lady got in her car before securing their own ride back to the White House. Minyon remembers that the First Lady had gotten into her car and was about to be driven away when she rolled down the back window and peered out. She had noticed the weather and the two women standing out in the cold. "Well, where are you all going?" Hillary asked. "Are you getting ready to go home?"

Minyon told her, "Well, I'm going back to the White House to get my car."

Hillary said, "Well, why can't you just get in here with us?"

Minyon peered down into the limo and thought, "'Okay, it's already knee-deep with a bunch of chicks in here, and here we go, two more.' She just piled us all in her limo. That's the Hillary Clinton we got to know. She was the kind of person that was throwing wedding and baby showers for her staff. She held birthday parties for staff in the residence. If she found out somebody in the West Wing had sick family members, she would make it her business to make a call. She was always doing something unexpected and thoughtful—like asking two cold staffers to get in an already full limo."

Working in the White House can be challenging and exhilarating. If you're not careful, it can cause you to turn into a person who believes, because of her title and working in the White House, that she is more important than the people who pay her salary, the American people. As Minyon bluntly puts it, "You can become a fool in that White House. That is a choice, too. People sometimes mistake titles for something other than what they are, a title. It doesn't give you the right to talk down to people or treat people with disrespect. It just doesn't. But if you are fortunate enough to have the opportunity to work for the White House and get a big, grand title like 'assistant to the president and director of political affairs' or 'assistant to the president and director of public liaison,' you have to somehow remind yourself that this is just a title. You have to remain grounded and public service–minded. I would always tell my staff to be in the business of saying yes if we can. Don't say no just because you have the power to say no. Go out of your way to make this White House feel accessible. There are people who are not mature enough to understand how to handle the audaciousness of working for a president. They go down that path of self-importance, not fully understanding the White House has all the trappings of 'I'm better than you.' It has all the trappings of making you believe you are somebody you are not. But it also has all the trappings of having you become a fantastic public servant. But you have to choose your path."

Erskine Bowles, the White House chief of staff, was a good mentor. Minyon remembers that "Erskine was and is one of the finest human beings I have ever met and worked with during my professional career. In an environment that is known for competitiveness, chaos, and lack of discipline, Erskine's very presence invoked a different atmosphere and discipline. It could be that he had a strong business background and he brought a different type of leadership style and sensibility to the White House. Or that his character and integrity was above reproach. If he made a commitment, you could be assured he would hold to it. He exemplified 'your word is your bond.' He was widely liked and praised by both Republicans and Democrats on Capitol Hill. President Clinton had tremendous respect for him because he guided us through some of the most tumultuous times at the White House. He was very conscious of making sure women and people of color were in the room when big decisions were made. That was very important because the chief of staff controlled the manifest to big meetings with senior staff and the president. Erskine never made you feel like you were invited to the meeting just because you were black, brown, or a woman. If you did your job and did it well, you were treated like an equal, and your opinion mattered like the next person's."

The thrill of working at the White House was a daily inspiration for Minyon. She says, "Honestly, there was never a day that I thought it was an ordinary place to work. Now, there were ordinary days, but that White House will never, ever be ordinary. It is the only place in America where you can really change people's lives with the stroke of a pen. And if you are dedicated, hardworking, and conscientious, you can be a part of helping to change those lives. Every day that you walk into the White House you have an opportunity to make a difference, that is a fact."

The learning curve at the White House was steep. "I had enough organizational skills and knowledge about public policy, which gave me some framework," Minyon says, reflecting gratefully on her years with Rainbow PUSH and the DNC. "But I surely did not know how to apply these skills when I walked into the White House. I didn't even know what I didn't know. So, I humbled myself, and learned pretty fast."

She explains, "In a recent conversation, Maggie Williams said something very important: 'The greatest gift President Clinton gave me at the White House was to walk down the hallway and see someone who looks like me.' I so agree. Whether it was Capricia or Stephanie, Ben Johnson, Dawn Chirwa, Thurgood Marshall Jr., Maria Echaveste, Mark Lindsay, Bob Nash, Tanya Lombard, Cheryl Mills, or Betty Currie— my colleagues made my job easier, and serving with them and many more was one of the proudest moments of my career."

In 1999, Al Gore called Donna to join his team as the deputy manager and national political director and, later that year, asked Donna to step up and manage the entire campaign. Once in her new role, Donna found herself under relentless attacks from Republicans who wanted to smear Gore. This forced her, a person who would normally speak freely to the media, to guard everything she said, and she was right to do so. In the final months of the primary, Donna was quoted as saying that then-Governor Bush would rather take photos with black children than come up with policies to feed them. Boom. She went further, stating that the

Republicans' favorite tool was to always trot out a few tokens like J. C. Watts and Colin Powell to cover their despicable policies. Once again, Donna found herself in hot water with the vice president, who was fuming over her controversial remarks. With no place to turn, Donna sought out Minyon's counsel.

"I called Minyon—because Tina had already given me fair warning: everybody was out to try to slander and use this as an excuse to have me fired. I enjoyed stirring the pot, or as John Lewis would say, 'causing good trouble.' I ran over to the White House and hid inside the White House. I used the White House as a barrier."

Minyon remembers, "We called it the Bunker."

While the media went nuts, Donna went into the White House and hid out in the West Wing. She remembers, "I was just in there, eating M&M's all day long. Those presidential M&M's. I M&M'ed myself out." Ironically, it was another presidential cycle during which we were faced with yet another controversy surrounding our beloved Donna.

"I'm sitting at my desk," Minyon remembers, "and Donna is sitting on the couch. I'm like, 'Donna, we need to call General Powell.'"

"'We can't call Colin Powell.'"

"'Yes, we can call Colin Powell. We can call him from the White House.'"

Minyon called Signal, the White House switchboard, and asked if they'd place the call. General Powell got on the phone.

Minyon said, "Hello, General Powell. This is Minyon Moore. I work for President Clinton. I have Donna Brazile here, and she would like to speak to you."

Without hesitation, he said, "Okay . . ."

"The general was the picture of grace," Donna says. "He gave me the best advice. He said, 'What were you thinking?' He said, 'You can't tell everybody what comes to your mind. *What* were you thinking? You can't talk like that.' And I asked him, 'What do you think?'"

Colin Powell told her, "I'm just going to say that you and I talked. You're going to be fine."

Later, Donna called Tina, and Tina gave her the all-clear. It could've cost Donna her job. But it didn't because we had each other's backs.

Yolanda started the Caraway Group, a boutique public relations firm, in 1987. One of her clients was Burger King, and once a month, she'd travel to their headquarters in Miami and stay for a week. On April 3, 1996, Yolanda was sitting at her desk at the Burger King headquarters when she got a phone call from her assistant, Comelia Sanford. Yolanda remembers, "She was crying and sniffling, and she said, 'Ron's plane . . . Ron is missing.'" Brown and a delegation of American corporate and government leaders had been on an economic development trip in the Balkans.

Yolanda asked Comelia, "What do you mean Ron is missing?"

Comelia said, "His plane is missing. They don't know where. They can't find him. They don't know where he is."

Yolanda, whom Comelia had called the Ice Queen a few years earlier, replied, "Comelia, what are you talking about? They'll find him!"

At this point, Comelia was sobbing.

Yolanda began to worry. She said, "Wait. Is there something you're not telling me?"

Comelia said, "No."

Yolanda said, "Just keep me posted."

She remembers, "I was just kind of done with the speculation. I thought, 'They'll find him.'" She remembered, years ago, when Mickey Leland's plane disappeared in Africa and how they held candlelight vigils at the Capitol each evening until they found the plane.

Yolanda was slated to brief Burger King's then CEO, Bob Lowes, on a diversity action committee meeting they had planned for the next day. She says, "Bob was a good guy. He was a really good guy, actually. We had become friendly, pretty close. It's not that often that you really work with the CEO at these companies, especially in the area of diversity. You rarely even meet with them. Bob was very serious about the company's diversity policies and practices, and I reported directly to him. So, he walked into his office and he said, 'Did you hear? Ron Brown is dead. They shot him down.'

"I almost fell on the floor. He didn't realize how this news would affect me. He knew I knew Ron, but he didn't realize that we were that close. I just couldn't catch my breath." She remembers thinking to herself that he was wrong. That wasn't what had happened. "They hadn't even found him at that point," she says. "I just went into the bathroom and broke down.

"When I returned, Bob said, 'Do you want me to call off the meeting?'

"I said, 'No, we'll do it. I can do it.'"

Yolanda got through the meeting, returned to her hotel room, and stayed up all night watching the news. "They were still looking for the plane. I don't think they found it till the next day."

Minyon was at the DNC when "we started getting reports that Ron's plane was missing. At first, we thought this had to be a mistake, and then, as the hours set in, we knew it was real. I remember distinctly staff members standing in the hallway looking lost. Phones were ringing off the hook. Friends were trying to determine if it was true. When we got the news that his plane had gone missing, it was surreal. Not only was Ron on the plane, but many of our friends lost their lives that day."

Leah recalls, "I was living in Brooklyn then, running a mentoring program for girls, and I'd come down to Washington for some meetings with Clinton/Gore '96, when the plane disappeared. For a while there was too little information. So, I just sat in my hotel room transfixed to the television. I was worried about Ron, but my heart was in my throat about Bill Morton. No one seemed to know if he was on the plane or not. All I could learn is that he was not supposed to be on that trip. But no one could confirm. I finally gave up, checked out of the hotel, and went home to Brooklyn. The next day, someone—I can't remember who—called to tell me that Bill *had* been on the plane. And my heart broke into a million pieces."

Yolanda says, "I had no idea that Bill was on the plane. Morris [Reed], who was supposed to go, stayed behind at Ron's instruction, and Bill went in his place. I didn't even know Bill was on the trip. Morris Reed was a young man who contacted me when Ron first became chair. He wanted to come and work for Ron, but he was still in college. I said, 'Call me when you graduate.' He finished school and went to work with Ron at Commerce. Four years later, Bill said, in the early stages of Clinton's first inaugural, 'Morris is back.' Bill wanted to talk to Morris about being Ron's road person. Bill said, 'I don't want to do this forever. I can train him.'"

Yolanda remembers having lunch with Bill a week before that fatal Croatia trip and Bill saying "he wasn't going to travel anymore. Morris was going to be the guy. Well, Bill wound up going on that trip along with Morris. It was in Croatia that they swapped places. When I found out Bill was on the plane, it tore at my gut. He wasn't supposed to even be there. And Morris, who was in his twenties at the time, went through terrible survivor's guilt."

These were the early days of the internet, and the conspiracy theories around Ron Brown's death took on an unprecedented fervor, something bound to happen when you combine political intrigue, death, race, and technology. As the *Washington Post* reported as time went on, "Web sites purporting to show bullet wounds to Brown's skull have popped up, as have conspiracy theories suggesting that he was assassinated because he knew too much about Clinton-era scandals or because, as a black man, he was too powerful." Many were afraid that he had the potential to become the first black president.

Yolanda remained close to Ron's wife, Alma. She says, "I remember talking to Alma about all of the conspiracy theories. I said, 'Did you see the body?' She said, 'No, I never saw the body.' (As I recall, they recommended that the family didn't look at the remains.) Maybe they didn't find him. Who knows what happened? Now, there's some stories that he had some powder at the back of his head, and some people said they shot him because they were so afraid he was going to be the first black president. Alma said, 'What do you think I should do?' I said, 'Alma, there's not a thing you can do about it now. If it's true, if they went through those lengths to get rid of him, what do you think they'll do to you and your kids?' Her kids were grown. She was living by herself. I was worried for her. I said, 'We can't bring him back.' But I didn't really believe in the theories. I think there was simply a terrible, terrible tragedy. Some people are always going to have a conspiracy theory about something. I visited Croatia last summer with Leah and Minyon, and I could definitely see how something like [that crash] could have happened in those mountains, in the fog. It was an awful tragedy."

Just four days after Brown's death, Stephen A. Holmes wrote in the *New York Times*, "Since the founding of the Republic, there have been very few people who, if they were of a mind, could walk into an Oval Office, look a President in the eye and say, 'If it wasn't for me, you wouldn't be here.' The late Richard J. Daley, who delivered Chicago to John F. Kennedy in 1960, was one. Alexander Hamilton, who threw the Federalists' support to Thomas Jefferson in 1800, was another. Mr. Brown, who refinanced, re-energized and unified the Democratic Party after its loss in 1988, was the only African-American who could make that claim."

It was alongside such a lion that we were trained to be more than just power brokers, but also bridge makers: crafting an unprecedented path between the embers of the modern civil rights movement and the rise of Reaganism to the twenty-first century, when America would elect its first black president. There would be many losses along the way, but for us, Ron Brown would always remain more than a symbol of promise and potential lost. He was our friend, our mentor, our big brother. All we could do after his death was to push forward. Minyon said that the unending gift of having served with Brown was the confidence he instilled in you. You could climb the ladder and swing the door wide open at the same time. "That was the beauty of having his wind behind you," she says. "You could walk in a meeting with a sense of boldness, a sense of intention. You were so sure you were supposed to be there that you had no fear of bringing other people with you."

11

Lunch with the Colored Girls

In 1996, Minyon was living in a swank loft apartment whose previous tenant had been reportedly another DC wunderkind, George Stephanopoulos. "Anyone that knows anything about me knows I don't like walls. I like openness," Minyon remembers. "A friend told me about a beautiful loft on Fourth Street Northwest. When I walked in, I knew I had found the place I could settle in for a while. It was so inviting, and it was a place to entertain. I held many Thanksgiving dinners there. My girlfriend meet-ups and just small get-togethers were held there." Then, one day, Minyon had the idea to throw a Colored Girls lunch to end all lunches.

She had been recently named political director of the Democratic National Committee, the first black woman to hold the post. Committee cochairs Senator Chris Dodd and Donald Fowler praised Minyon's ability to "forge coalitions and her tireless efforts to expand the party's base of support" in a formal press announcement. Minyon was thirty-eight now, with an affection for suits and what she called an "Anita Baker haircut." The suits were a legacy from her corporate days. "I equated how I dressed to whether I would be taken seriously or not. But I also knew that I didn't want to be flamboyant, because I saw that as a distraction.

Since there were so few of us at a high level in politics and in government, I was always conscious of the fact that I represented more than myself."

The pixie haircut was more of a nod to her own personal style. "I loved her look when she burst on the scene," Minyon says of Anita Baker. She remembers Anita being fiercely independent and one of the rare artists who understood what it meant to control her own destiny. Similar to the Colored Girls, she was paving the way for many new artists.

"I wished I could sing like her, but since I couldn't, the best I could do was try to copy her hairstyle. Most of my earlier pics were with the short Anita Baker haircut." In fact, the two women were such doppelgangers that eventually they were introduced and became friends.

Minyon said, "I don't know how the seed was planted in me, or how I had the nerve and/or audacity to follow up on the idea to call these women and ask them to host an event with me—little old me—but somewhere, I summoned the courage to do so. You see, I had this vision that I wanted to do an afternoon soiree with women icons and women from all walks of life. I was blessed to have access to some of the most incredible women in the world, and I thought it would be great to share an afternoon of good food, great conversation, and wonderful bonding among sister friends. Dr. Angelou, Dr. Shabazz, and Cicely Tyson were women we all greatly admired, and many women looked up to them."

Those three women—Angelou, Shabazz, and Tyson—were often in Washington for formal functions, but rarely at the same time or in a casual setting. Finally, Minyon remembers, "I worked up the nerve to ask Cicely. She signed on immediately and thought it was a great idea."

Cicely Tyson and Dr. Angelou had been friends since 1961, when they costarred in an avant-garde production of Jean Genet's *The Blacks*. The play ran for 1,408 performances at the St. Mark's Theater and made history as one of the longest-running Off-Broadway plays. The play's radical take on race troubled the waters of New York's polite veneer of racial acceptance and challenged the notion that the only work to be done around race was in the South. Dr. Angelou, who played the haughty and imperialist White Queen, would later recall, "Some whites got up and walked out. Some blacks got up and walked out." Cicely Tyson recalled that "it was quite interesting to see people jump up and run out. One man was running so fast, he fell down the stairs and broke his leg." *The Blacks* brought Dr. Angelou and Ms. Tyson together as artists, activists, and seekers, and their friendship would last a lifetime.

Minyon had gotten to know Tyson when she worked for Reverend Jackson. She remembers that "As I moved up the ranks in the organization, many of the African American leaders would reach out to me when they were trying to track down Reverend Jackson, or I would reach out to them when he was trying to reach them. At first my relationship with Cicely Tyson was more or less relegated to me being a young staff liaison for Reverend Jackson. But soon the relationship began to deepen, and when we spoke, our conversations would be longer and more meaningful. When I left the Rainbow, we stayed in touch. I don't recall exactly when our relationship went from staff to friend, but she is one of the greatest blessings I have in my life today. Twenty or so years later, many conversations and laughs around my kitchen table are still going strong."

For her part, Tyson came to think of Minyon's home as a refuge. "It gives me some kind of solace," the actress told a reporter from the *Washington Post*. "I was just saying this morning, I could come here and sleep for days. Nobody would know that I was here—no phones, no emails . . . no nothing!"

Minyon had gotten to know Dr. Angelou through the Skinner family retreats. "I visited her at home in Winston-Salem and she was always a phone call away," Minyon recalls. "She was one of Hillary's most ardent supporters in 2008. Dr. Angelou always made you feel like a lady, even when you didn't always live up to the properness. Although the formality didn't mean informality."

The original "phenomenal woman" not only agreed, but offered to pen the invitation:

PLEASE COME SHARE CORDIAL CONFIDENCES AND COPIOUS COLLATIONS WITH A COMPATIBLE COMPANY OF SISTER FRIENDS. CONVIVIALLY, MAYA ANGELOU, CICELY TYSON, MINYON MOORE

The invitation went out, and women flew in from all across the country to attend: from New York to Los Angeles and cities in between. They were congresswomen and businesswomen, entertainers and members of the ministry and the media. As one guest later wrote, "You can imagine the waves of shock, warmth, and excitement that went through me when I was invited to a lunch hosted by Maya Angelou, Cicely Tyson, and Minyon Moore." Of Minyon, the guest gushed, "She's big-time. She's the political director of the Democratic National Committee."

Cicely Tyson, whom Minyon affectionately refers to as Drama Queen, told the story of being turned down for an audition and going home in tears. Her mother, Frederica Tyson, a woman who had worked her entire career as a domestic and didn't know a thing about Hollywood, looked at her and said, "Let me tell you something: what is for you in this life you'll get; what is not for you, you will *never* get." Tyson said, "That piece of advice has carried me through my career." The Colored Girls got it right away. It was both the message and a lesson about the messenger: the importance of looking to *their* people, no titles necessary, for wisdom and sustenance.

Of course, few human beings in the world are like the great Maya Angelou. You can sit the Colored Girls down in a room and they can, without notes or the use of Google, dispense an apothecary's supply of Angelou's greatest sayings:

- "People will forget what you said, people will forget what you did, but people will never forget how you made them feel."

- "Nothing will work unless you do."
- "If you are always trying to be normal, you will never know how amazing you can be."
- "Never make someone a priority when all you are to them is an option."
- "Trust life a little bit."

We all remember a moment during Jackson '88 when the campaign was trailing and everyone was moping. Rev. Willie Barrow burst into the room, took one look at our depressed faces, and reminded us, "We ain't never been here before. What's wrong with all of you?" Everyone in the room burst into laughter, because they had all, as black women, had that moment when they were down and seemingly out for the count and then they remembered, or were reminded, that their very existence was a cause for celebration, that every door they burst through was a triumph. There were, and still are, so many places where a black woman could look around and say, "We ain't never been here before."

In her recent book *Democracy*, Condoleezza Rice wrote, "When I was secretary of state, I told my aides that it was appalling to me that I could go through an entire day of meetings and never see someone who looked like me. The president of the United States had selected two African Americans in a row, Colin Powell and me, to be the country's chief diplomats, and yet the Foreign Service was still just 6 percent black, a percentage virtually unchanged since the 1980s and half what one would expect based on the population."

Minyon's lunch with the icons was memorable for *years* in DC because black women in public service were starved for the kind of mirroring, affirmation, and encouragement that the gathering provided. The Colored Girls were well known and easy to identify because there were so few black women in the halls of power they traversed. We were called the Colored Girls because we *were* the Colored Girls.

Minyon remembers, "To say that I loved these women for lending their names and showing up is an understatement. The support they have given to us over the years—you just can't imagine or buy. The wisdom they shared with us that day still remains the highlight of my life, and for many of the women who attended. And the special bond these women shared with each other was also undeniable—in many ways, watching them, how they supported and loved each other, is a constant reminder to me of why the Colored Girls are so important."

12

Stepping Forward

At one point, we started to step forward in the way that women such as Maya Angelou encouraged us to. None of us would ever be someone's "option" again. We started to step forward, figuratively and, in Minyon's case, literally.

In 1998, Yolanda was cochair of the Site Selection Committee for the 2000 Democratic National Convention. The Dems selected LA, and Yolanda was in the running to be convention CEO. She recalls, "Initially, I was supposed to be CEO of that convention. I had been through all of the interviews, the last one being with VP Gore, at his residence. Everyone had signed off on it, and they wanted to make an announcement soon. I thought it was a done deal, but little did I know that when I was leaving the residence, Tony Coelho had just been named campaign chair and was coming in to meet with Gore. It was his decision that they should hire a Latina to run the convention because we were going to Los Angeles, and there was a large Hispanic population. They tried and tried to find someone who was willing to do it. I was told that Clinton advisor and deputy chief of staff Maria Echaveste said no, Aida Alvarez, who headed up the Small Business Administration, said no, and there were a couple of others. Finally, Bill Richardson, who was at the time secretary of energy, came up with a young Latina who worked for a voter registration organization in San Antonio and had never been to a Democratic convention in her life. (All of this searching going on without my knowledge, mind you.) It was her first encounter with the convention, and she had no real idea what she was signing up for. I knew the learning curve was going to be steep."

Once Yolanda finally figured out what was going on, she called Tina Flournoy for advice. Tina explained the situation, and Yolanda went to Joe Andrew, who was DNC chair at the time and the person who was pushing for her to be CEO.

She remembers, "He told me that they still wanted me to play a key role, and I said the only way I would do it would be if I could report directly to Joe, and I wanted two hundred thousand dollars. He said that would be more than the CEO was making, and I said, 'It should be. I have a lot more experience than she does. And if you want me to clean up her mess, you're going to have to pay me.' So I got everything I asked for, and moved out to LA. I wound up, yes, cleaning up a lot of poo, but I also got to work on a great project, so I was fine. Rod O'Connor, who was deputy, and Tom O'Donnell, an attorney, pretty much took over the day-to-day. Terry and I went back to the early DNC days, when he worked for Peter Kelly, the finance chair, and I worked for Ann Lewis, the political director. We really made a good team."

Donna Brazile tells her stepping-forward story, the story of how she became the first African American to run a major campaign, this way:

Knock, knock,
Who's there?
Al Gore.
What the hell do you want?
I need you to manage my campaign.

"WTF? Thank God for Tina Flournoy," Donna says. "Without Tina's calm, her sense of history, her sharp analytical skills, and grace, I would have lost my balance. Or slapped some white boy silly. Along with our daily calls, Tina's ability to read my thoughts ahead of time and help me write memos, communicate with my superiors—I would have simply been lost. You see, Tina taught me how to be powerful without alienating, to work in a diverse, complicated world where white men ruled, white women complained of being left out, black men whined of not being in charge of black women, and black women could actually lead if others left us the hell alone. I respected Tina's ability to be a bridge builder and navigate the powerful. She has gravitas. She is smart and was deeply loyal to our friendship through one of the most difficult chapters in my life."

Donna continues: "By the age of sixteen I knew exactly what I wanted to do with my life. I said to God—because I always talk to God: 'Dear God, when I turn forty, I want to be a campaign manager.' I thought it would take me until that time. I didn't say 'when I'm thirty, thirty-five, thirty-six.' I said 'by the age of forty,' and that was my marker, and I was on my mark. I think I only told maybe a handful of people that this is what I wanted to do, including Paul Tully and Ann Lewis, who were my mentors, who I really felt would give me wings. Paul Tully was one of the most incredible people in our lives because he was a visionary. He had worked for Bobby Kennedy, and he, too, believed that people of color and women should have a seat at the table. That's why I liked Tully, and Tully was someone I could invest my time in. Ann Lewis, who also helped advance the career of Yolanda, was always there pushing me."

Paul Tully, a legendary Democratic strategist, had worked on every presidential election since 1968. As the *Washington Post* said, Tully "cut his teeth on the old politics of coalition. But colleagues credited him with an equal mastery of the new politics of communication: polls, issues, focus groups, regional differences in the electorate, what it takes to get people interested, how to engage them in the process." Donna prized the fact that Tully—Long Island–raised and Yale-educated—was committed to the Jackson ideal of opening the door wide and swinging as many people as possible through. She says, "He mentored us in a way that gave us opportunities. I mean, back in the day, it was hard to give a woman the title of state director, and yet it was Tully who said, 'Yes. She can become state director. She knows what she's doing. I'll help her.' When I became campaign manager, the first thing I said is 'I want women and people of color to lead the state.' For example, my home state of Louisiana had a black man as campaign manager. New York State: Arthur Eve's son Eric Eve became the state director in New York. I wanted to help change the face of black politics one state at a time. Out in California, I appointed a Latina. When you set out in life to achieve your goals, and you try to lead by example, ultimately you are challenged by the example you set. When I became campaign manager I had to go back to the lessons of those who had trained me, and Tully was one of them."

The aspiration Donna had written about in her diary when she was just a teenager was finally coming true. "I was a little more polished. Most of my rough edges had disappeared, not because of age, but I had finally reached a place of respect inside the political world and didn't need to cuss my way through the gripers, whiners, and others who'd slept their way into the war room," she says, with her trademark candor and Louisiana color. "I got in by destroying the door or building a new room where colored girls and colored boys could thrive. Jackson taught us that there are two kinds of people on this earth: tree shakers and jelly makers. I was a tall, round, black tree shaker."

In March 2000, President Clinton was scheduled to march across the Edmund Pettus Bridge for the thirty-fifth anniversary of the 1965 Voting Rights Act. He would be the first American president to take that historic walk that had been hailed as Bloody Sunday. Minyon was a member of the White House team assigned to make the moment happen. She remembers, "It was organized chaos at its finest. It wasn't enough to have leaders from around the country descending on Selma, Alabama, but to also have an American president—that brought it to another level of chaos."

Still, at the end of the day, there they were: Coretta Scott King, arms linked with President Bill Clinton to her left and Reverend Jackson to her right. John Lewis was on Clinton's other side. It was more than a photo op; it was a looking back and a pressing forward. It spoke of a vigilance and a determination not to undo the gains made after a history of loss and sacrifice that is the African American story at the heart of our commitment.

13

The Troubles

In 2000, a number of us were working in and around the seat of Democratic Party power. Tina Flournoy was cochair of the DNC Rules and Bylaws Committee, and had been instrumental in Donna's joining that committee. When Tina stepped down as chair to become Al Gore's finance director, Donna replaced her as cochair. (The other cochair was James Roosevelt, grandson of President Franklin D. Roosevelt.) Then Donna joined the Gore team and, in the process, became the first African American to manage a major presidential campaign. Leah was at the Labor Department with Alexis Herman. After the Supreme Court gave the presidency to Bush, Leah stayed on at Labor, as the transition official, and worked in the Bush administration for the first four or five months. Little did we know that the Troubles were dead ahead . . .

Here's what happened: At the DNC, we chose to support Terry McAuliffe as DNC chair over Maynard Jackson, although Donna was initially reluctant. It was the first time we were crossing the line racially, and all hell broke loose, literally and figuratively. Donna remembers, "I was ambivalent because I wasn't sure where Terry stood on the number one issue for me: voting rights. I wasn't ready. I thought that I might have to cause a disturbance. Raw. My emotions were very, very raw."

"We all had various interactions with Terry but as chair," says Minyon, "I believe I signed up first to help him out. I knew and had worked with Terry as chair of Bill Clinton's finance committee. I loved his energy and his dedication to Democratic candidates. Amy Chapman signed on to help run his campaign for chair, and I served as an advisor. Terry works harder than anyone I know, and he doesn't have a sense of entitlement. I don't recall a day that Terry wasn't able to make a hard day seem better. His parents instilled something very special in him: confidence, optimism, and an infectious smile and sense of humor.

"Because most of the DNC members knew him as a finance guy, Terry had to prove to the members he would be an advocate for the state parties. I remember him calling all the DNC members, asking for their vote. He ran the election for chair like he was running for president, taking every member seriously and asking for their vote personally. As the campaign got under way, we started getting word that one of the African American community's icons and respected former mayor Maynard Jackson was thinking about entering the race.

"When Maynard Jackson entered the race," Minyon continues, "many blacks supporting Terry found themselves in a very difficult position. If I recall correctly, it was actually at the urging of Donna Brazile that Jackson entered the race, even though she was also supporting Terry. Maynard had thought it was time to continue the work of Ron Brown, and at the urging of Representative Maxine Waters, he jumped into a race he thought was wide open. The race got very contentious, and it was the first time many of us who were raised on movement politics broke with the established black leaders."

Maynard was considered a leader in the black community. He was revered because of the many historic things he had accomplished as mayor of Atlanta. Choosing whom to support was a very difficult decision for us. Maynard certainly had the gravitas, and no doubt would have been a great party chair, but there was one small problem: Terry had outmaneuvered him. He had secured the votes to win, and was elected DNC chair in 2001. And although we broke with tradition, Terry was smart enough to get Maynard's involvement after he won.

Yes, we were instrumental in helping Terry get elected. In many ways, embracing the more pragmatic choice signaled that we had reached a level of political maturity. That didn't mean it was easy; supporting Terry also meant breaking ranks with Maxine Waters, an iconic figure in the black community, and this would have repercussions later on. A year after Terry's victory, with Minyon as chief operating officer of the DNC and Leah as director of administration, it was time for the DNC Black Caucus to conduct its own elections and choose its chair. We felt there needed to be a change in the Black Caucus's leadership. At the time, Leah said, "We've got to let go of the old race-based model of 'you're either with us or against us.' We decided we've got to expand as a group, not contract."

Once again, we found ourselves butting heads with established political leaders. Al Edwards, a state representative from Houston, was the incumbent chair. Leah had known him for years because of his involvement with the Black United Front. Maxine was backing Edwards. At the conclusion of a preelection meeting, things between the parties got so tense that Donna and Maxine almost got into a heated confrontation over the deliberations. Al Edwards tried to get between them, and as Donna remembers it, he was none too careful where he put his hands. When Leah, who was halfway out of the room, heard Donna shout, "Let go of my breasts!" she sent a staffer to chase down Minyon, who'd left five minutes earlier. When the staffer moved too slow for Leah's taste, Leah took off running down the hall herself. She found Minyon and ran with her back to the conference room. The two helped defuse the fight, but everyone's hackles were up. In the end, we got the quorum we needed to hold elections, and a new DNC Black Caucus chair, Yvonne Atkinson-Gates, commissioner of Clark County, Nevada, was elected.

It was a time of change for all of us. In 2001, Minyon was CEO of the DNC, and Donna, still recovering from the Gore election, spent time at Harvard's Institute of Politics, where she coordinated a study group examining the 2000 election. Later that year, she returned to

DC and decided to get back to teaching once a week—and went back to the DNC to start all over again. She needed the health insurance, a place to recover and consider her next steps, and working for Minyon fit the bill. Yolanda was in California, and Tina had joined the American Federation of Teachers, as assistant to the president.

That summer, Leah went to the DNC as director of administration. In 2002, she became an ordained pastor, the fifth generation of Daughtrys to serve in the ministry. Faith has been a through line of her journey in politics. She remembers, while growing up as part of a faith activist community in Brooklyn, participating in marches and sit-ins. "That was an article of faith for me," she says. Today, she continues to find ways to let her spiritual and political experience work together: In addition to serving as chief of staff at the DNC under Howard Dean, she created Faith in Action, the Democratic Party's outreach to communities of faith. In 2006, the Religion News Service named her one of the twelve most influential Democrats in the nation on faith and values politics.

"I didn't know Terry before I started working for him at the DNC," says Leah. "I was working for the Bush administration Labor Department when he was elected chair in February 2001. When I decided to leave Labor, Alexis, who was running Terry's transition with Harold Ickes, called and asked me to come to the DNC. I went as a consultant in August 2001, and eventually accepted a job as director of administration. In 2002, I became chief of staff. Terry is one of a kind, and was exactly the chair the DNC needed post the theft of the 2001 election. He has that boundless, 'I'll sleep when I'm dead' energy and vision."

As for Minyon, she says, "I committed [to the DNC] a year, but I stayed a year and a couple of months. That was because I promised I would help get Terry elected and help transition him in. Leah moved up when I moved out. I'd met Charlie Baker, Michael Whouley, and Chuck Campion at Dukakis-Bentsen, and we'd all stayed friends. We all worked together on various campaigns, and had always said, 'Maybe we'll work together. You know, ha, ha, ha, ha, ha.' Before I left the White House, they were courting me, asking me to come work for the [public affairs firm] Dewey Square Group, and I didn't know really what I wanted to do. Then Michael and Chuck and Charlie got very serious about it, but then Terry started putting pressure on me: 'Come on, help me win this race. Help me. Help me.' I told Dewey Square I would have to put it on hold because I'd promised Terry that I would help him. As soon as I felt like I had my sea legs with Terry and the transition was up and running, and we were putting the right people in place and around Terry, then I resumed my conversations with them. Together we have been on the battlefield with more campaigns than I can remember. When I decided to leave the DNC for the second time, I was CEO to Chairman Terry McAuliffe, I joined the firm of Dewey Square Group as a partner, a company which they founded after the election of President Bill Clinton. Sixteen years later, I remain at the firm, and we are all still best of friends: the same people I'd worked with in 1988. Shows you that's just how small this world is."

Everything seemed like it was going great, but looking back, we call this period in our political career "the Troubles," after the turmoil that Northern Ireland experienced in the late twentieth century. After Minyon departed the DNC for the private sector, Leah began working as Terry's chief of staff, and that's when the Troubles began. There was a giant budget cut at the DNC, and when each manager came back with his or her recommended dismissals, the entire list turned out to be composed of black staffers. Coincidence? When word began to leak out that there was a list of all black staffers about to be dismissed from the DNC, Donna, Tina, and Minyon strategized about how to save those jobs.

Leah, as the inside person, was caught betwixt and between, and the rest of us sent her a huge bouquet of flowers once the media storm began. And when it did, three of us were right in the middle of it with her. Leah's father, the legendary Reverend Daughtry, sprang into action. He called up Minyon and Tina and asked, "Am I organizing the buses?" Then he called every black member of Congress he knew, alerting them that he would be bringing buses of people to picket Democratic headquarters. We reached out to Terry to request a meeting to discuss the proposed firings, and designated Tina as the lead spokesperson for the meeting, in part because of her legal background, her methodical nature, and her calm under pressure. Once the situation reached the chairman's desk, he was appalled that this could happen, and asked for a meeting with some of his key advisors. When the three of us stepped off the elevator, the DNC staffers began to applaud. When we heard that applause, we knew we were not just speaking up for those who were being let go, but for all the staff who needed a voice.

The applause wasn't lost on Leah, who says, "When I came to Washington and I went to work for the party, what people knew is that I had all these people behind me. You might not see them. It might not be obvious, but I could call, and a collection of electeds and ministers and nationalists and civil rights folks would show up because I called. Because they had raised me and birthed me, and I was part of that community. That's part of why, I think, people respected not just my work, but they knew I had—the Maya Angelou thing. You know: 'I come as one. I stand as ten thousand'—this army behind me. Those people and those buses will be down here in a minute, now. Don't mess with her."

Cooking with the Colored Girls

One winter afternoon, not too long ago, we gathered for brunch at Donna Brazile's home. We stood around the large kitchen island while Donna stirred the pots, thinking back to 2000, the things we did and the things that made us stick together.

The CGs recall the events of that period:

Minyon: We had just figured out that Gore had won, but they stole the election.

Leah: I was still at Labor, with the Republicans. I worked for Bush for his first six months.

M: Yeah, okay, Ms. Bipartisan.

L: Pff . . . I was certifiable. Then I came to the DNC that summer, and Terry and Minyon had been there for six months.

Donna: I had come from the Gore campaign. I'd spent a semester at the Harvard Institute of Politics and then I went over to the DNC and served as Minyon's intern. I had to start all over again. And what better place to start than with Minyon?

L: I didn't know Terry as well, and I had to deal with Josh Wachs [DNC COO]. I didn't know him, and he didn't know me. It was not the best match.

M: He was chief of staff before you were.

L: And then you left to join the Dewey Square Group, and his position was changed.

M: I think he wanted to be the CEO.

L: But he wasn't.

M: He'd worked as one of my deputies.

L: He was part of that gaggle of white boys who came into the DNC after the Gore campaign. A whole set of white boys and me. Thank God I went to Dartmouth and could speak white boy language.

D: All those white boys, I would've gotten in trouble. They would have cussed me out.

L: So, you know . . . people were accustomed to Minyon's style, and I have a different style.

At this, the whole group erupts into laughter. "We do! We have different styles. We end up in the same place; we just have different styles of doing it."

M: Leah is kind of matter-of-fact, direct. No kumbaya with that miss. I am a consensus builder; I try to make everyone feel like they've been heard. If I don't get a consensus, I at least want everyone to feel like they've been heard. And Leah does, too.

L: Minyon is much more kumbaya than I am. She had this wonderful open-door policy, and people would sail right in all day long and take a seat and talk about whatever. Which was great, except that, at the end of the day, Minyon had to spend three more hours at work! But we got to the same place. But I'm much more regimented. I need a schedule. "What is it that you want to talk about?" and "Let's get down to business!" Once we are done with business, we can chitchat. But I've got stuff to do! And I still carry my giant index cards.

M: You knew Leah meant business when she walked in with those big notecards! She came in to do *work*. She's here with those notecards. Here's the deal: There was nothing to worry about with Leah overseeing admin. She didn't ever have to come to my office, because everything was taken care of. And I didn't have to worry about anyone stabbing me in the back, because Donna was hearing everything.

The Colored Girls chuckle again.

M: Donna was the "palace guard." She was sitting right outside my door as if to signify that "she had my back."

L: So, you knew those white boys were bold to walk past Donna and pick a chair in Minyon's office. You could walk by anytime and there would just be people in there kicking back, talking about something. I just wanted to kick 'em out: "What are y'all doing in here? This woman's got work to do! Go back to your own office."

M: Yeah, you're right, I had to stay three extra hours as punishment, and we were trying to change rules.

L: We were trying to get a new chair in the Black Caucus, and I didn't know anything about how that worked. And then there was the state party stuff, which I didn't get. So, they were like coaches. And there were the white boys—who were nice—they were just the white boys. They were great guys, and I didn't have any problems with any of them.

M: You know the challenge with people of color, when they take on these unprecedented positions—although being CEO or COO wasn't new, because Alexis had held that position before—there's an expectation that we should move the ball. So, you almost always have to figure out "Okay, how are you going to involve people of color, women, all of those people that believe that they should have a voice?" How do you get them to the table? And that's my kumbaya-ness. Because, unfortunately, when you try to make these seismic shifts, you almost always have to figure out where your relationships lie. Counting your votes.

All the Colored Girls join in about "counting your votes." It's almost like a football cheer shouted in waves across the stadium.

D: That's basic politics!

L: Not that everyone in DC knows how to count! But you know the principle of counting . . .

Yolanda: Everybody doesn't know the strategy around counting votes, and how to do it, and why you do it.

M: Maxine would *never* walk into a meeting without knowing her audience. She just wouldn't do it. And if you're trying to make change, any smart person knows you can't just walk into the room without knowing who's on your side.

Y: Any politician knows about counting votes. Or any person that works for campaigns.

M: Or counting your relationships, in this instance. Who's going to be with you and who is going to undermine you? You have to judge the whole room the moment you walk in.

D: We have to see ourselves in the room. Then we have to say to ourselves, "Okay, if I respond like this, then I'm offending black women. If I respond like this, I might be offending black men." We can never go in a room with our own voice, because we always have to figure out, "Okay, what is the other person thinking?" We had to evolve.

One of our most consistent allies was Hillary Clinton. Growing up in Park Ridge, Illinois, Hillary had met Dr. Martin Luther King Jr. himself.

King left an impression on her mind and soul, and her reflections on the moment they met are inspiring:

Clinton said, "I stood in a long line to shake Dr. King's hand. His grace and piercing moral clarity left a lasting impression on me. . . . Now I was realizing that many Americans were still denied the rights I took for granted. This lesson and the power of Dr. King's words lit a fire in my heart, fueled by the social justice teachings of my church. I understood as I never had before the mission to express God's love through good works and social action." This mission would lead Hillary to Marian Wright Edelman, the first African American woman admitted to the Mississippi Bar. One of Hillary's first jobs was working for Marian at the Children's Defense Fund, where she investigated low-income children's attendance in school. After collecting enough data and sending it to Washington, Congress voted to give every child the opportunity to attend school. Hillary would continue pushing this kind of social justice as First Lady to "the first black president" and as a senator representing the state of New York.

One winter day in 2003, Minyon Moore received a call from Hillary. Minyon remembers, "She said, 'I need you to meet with Barack Obama. We want to get Barack Obama elected to the U.S. Senate. We need to diversify this Senate. Can you meet with him?' I had also gotten a call from [political advisor] Joe McLean, who was helping him with his campaign." Minyon agreed, and asked Donna to join the meeting. And so, one day, in a conference room at the Dewey Square offices on Tenth and G, Barack Obama discussed with Minyon, Donna, and Joe McLean his bid for the Senate. Obama told us who he was: the grandson of a Kenyan who had worked as a domestic for the British, the son of an African man who came to the United States on scholarship, and the beloved older child of a white woman from Kansas who had raised him in an intergenerational home with her parents. As he would in his Democratic National Convention keynote address, which we would help to promote a year later, he assured us that he believed as we did, that he owed a debt to those who came before him and had made his life and opportunities possible. Obama told Minyon and Donna that if he were elected to the U.S. Senate, he would not be merely a cog in the machine. He would ambitiously take on a scope of projects that went far beyond what might be expected of a first-time senator. He described his vision for labor, education, foreign policy, and homeland security—the last heavily a work in progress in those early years after 9/11. He was also opposed to the Iraq war. Donna and Minyon were impressed, and vowed their support.

Around this same time, Obama requested a meeting with the president of the American Federation of Teachers, Sandy Feldman. She was out of town, and in her absence, Tina met with him as the person who oversaw the union's political operation. He came with Joe McLean, and was determined to get the union's support for his campaign. Tina met with Obama and McLean for well over an hour. She says, "I left the meeting thinking I could have spent several more hours talking to him. Our union ended up supporting him."

All of us knew the power and value of a Senate seat. If elected, Obama would be only the fifth African American ever to serve in the Senate and only the third to serve in the twentieth century. (The first two African Americans, Hiram Rhodes Revels and Blanche Kelso Bruce, both men, were elected as Republicans, the party of Lincoln, shortly after the Civil War.) Inspired by Obama's intelligence, humility, and commitment to change, we began to bring others into the room where it was happening. We wanted to raise his profile. We called Alexis Herman and Bill Lynch, and they started to raise money. They also inquired about the possibility of who would be the keynote speaker at the Democratic Convention. In early 2004, Hillary Clinton hosted a fund-raiser for Obama at her home in Washington and attended another fund-raiser in Chicago. In November 2004, Obama won the Senate campaign with a sweeping 70 percent of the votes.

14

Hurricanes and Heartbreak,
2005–2006

Hurricane Katrina was a national tragedy, but for Donna, it was a personal tragedy, too. Nothing compares with waking up one day and not knowing if your entire family has been lost. When the storm made landfall on the Gulf Coast, hitting Donna's hometown of New Orleans, some of her family members just grabbed anything they could. Some of them were rescued, but what "rescue" meant in those first days was that the first responders basically took you wherever they could. Some of Donna's family landed in Mississippi, some were taken to Atlanta, and some stayed, thinking the storm would soon blow over. That last group included her father, Lionel, and two sisters, Zeola and Sheila, who lived at the time in an assisted-living facility in the New Orleans neighborhood of Mid-City. As Donna notes, "I thank God for the Colored Girls, who not only called me hourly and prayed for my family but also put me in touch with folks like Bill Clinton, who could help with the recovery."

By the time Donna's father, her sister Zeola, and other members of her family were rescued, thousands of people had been reported dead. Donna's family members were flown to San Antonio, where Minyon reminded Donna that their friend Andy Hernandez resided. Hernandez immediately went to work to get them out of a hot and crowded shelter and into a hotel near the airport.

Some of Donna's extended family landed in Arkansas. Donna recalls that in the first days of Katrina, "There was no plan, no strategy. They were treated like refugees—which everyone hated—told to keep moving. They were just dumped all over America. It was so painful. At one point, I was crying to Saint Anthony, the saint of miracles, or Saint Jude, the saint for hopeless causes. My dad taught me to believe in the power of prayer. I wanted them to all be alive. I prayed and searched for almost eight days before I found everybody. I pulled every string I could think of, large and small. I put in calls to FEMA, publicized my missing family members on CNN—thanks to Wolf Blitzer—called the governor of Louisiana, and got my brother, who was just outside the city in St. Charles Parish, and my cousin, who was a New Orleans policeman, to rescue my disabled sister Sheila once my contacts and networks figured out she was stranded in a YWCA, surrounded by eight feet of water."

Donna continues: "My father won four Bronze Stars for his service in the army, and he told me Katrina was worse than Korea. I was worried about all the kids in the family, the ones who had to see so much death. My niece, who is now in law school, said, 'Auntie Donna, we kept raising our hands. We kept trying to tell the helicopters, *Come and get us.*' I listened to all of those stories. I listened to how they got out. I listened to those stories of survival. I've spent a lot of time over the last eight years making sure they've had therapy. I put them in summer camps so that they learned how to swim, so that they wouldn't grow up terrified of drowning."

In order to get her family back on their feet, Donna "started working like a crazy woman. My life didn't matter. My life was fine. I started working four, five part-time jobs because I couldn't let my family go on like that. I knew I had to do it. At the height of Katrina's aftermath, I was probably spending anywhere upward of ten thousand to twelve thousand dollars a month to keep my family afloat. So, I had to bring in nearly twice that to both support my family and keep Brazile and Associates open for business. I told people I was available. I said, 'Here I am. Use me.' I was on the road three, four, five times a week traveling, making five hundred here or five thousand there. And then I took my entire savings and took all of the equity out of my house. I bought homes. I rented apartments. All to relocate my family. That was my sole focus."

We all pitched in and helped Donna gather an abundance of clothes, used furniture, and toiletries to spare. She remembers that "Terry McAuliffe and his wife went through their neighborhood with a truck saying, 'You all know you want a new flat-screen TV. Go ahead and give us [your used] TV.' The McAuliffes filled up a whole truck to send to Louisiana, and my friend Elaine Kamarck and close pal Marvin Turner and the other DNC staff helped to get trucks and staff to drive down supplies. Leah got the black churches to give. Minyon rallied her groups to give clothing and furniture. Tina lent us countless hours of legal expertise to review documents, and got organized labor groups to donate. They all had my back."

Some change is permanent. Donna lives with the scars of that disaster every day: "I'll never be pre-Katrina Donna again," she says. "I cannot put my body through what I put it through in those years ever again. I had to make the money, so I had to get on the road. I had to work more jobs. I had to put off sleeping, put off eating, to help my family.

"I did it all. I did political consulting. I took on Microsoft. I took on Verizon as clients. I did everything short of lobbying, but I needed to work—grassroots training, strategic communications. I started getting speaking gigs at colleges and universities, working with nonprofits, helping them put together training programs. Some of my friends called me and said, 'Hey, the labor union needs somebody to put together organizing camps.' I did that. If I could earn a few dollars, working a few hours, even if I had to fly two thousand miles, I did it, because I had to send the money back home. I had to keep them afloat."

By 2010, five years after Katrina, Donna says with pride, "I owned three houses and was renting another in Baton Rouge to help my family survive. Everyone in my family had a roof over their heads. I was pleased."

On October 25, 2005, Minyon received a call from a woman in Detroit named Elaine Steele. Steele had been the longtime aide to the civil rights icon Rosa Parks. Parks had died the day before, and along with a man named Willis Edwards, Steele had the idea that they would like to hold Mrs. Parks's homegoing in Washington, DC. She was wondering if Minyon could help make it happen.

Rosa Parks's story is as layered as it was well known. On December 1, 1955, Parks, a seamstress in Montgomery, Alabama, sat in the first row of what had been marked as the "colored" section of a city bus. As the bus began to fill, the driver, James F. Blake, moved the sign saying "Colored" farther back and ordered Parks to give up her seat. She refused. It was a lightning rod moment for the civil rights movement, one that became imbued with all the mythology of a movement not born in a twenty-four-hour news cycle and one that made the career of a young minister named Martin Luther King Jr. In his book *Stride Toward Freedom*, King would write, "Mrs. Parks's arrest was the precipitating factor rather than the cause of the protest. The cause lay deep in the record of similar injustices."

As the *New York Times* later reported, "Blacks had been arrested, and even killed, for disobeying bus drivers. They had begun to build a case around a 15-year-old girl's arrest for refusing to give up her seat, and Mrs. Parks had been among those raising money for the girl's defense. But when they learned that the girl was pregnant, they decided that she was an unsuitable symbol for their cause."

Rosa Parks was a suitable symbol: both educated and well trained in the movement. Born in 1913, the young Rosa McCauley had dropped out of school to care for her mother and grandmother. Later, in 1933, with her husband Raymond Parks's encouragement, Rosa completed her high school education. At that time, only 7 percent of blacks had a high school diploma. During the summer of 1955, Parks attended an interracial leadership conference in Monteagle, Tennessee. Both she and her husband were active members of the local branch of the NAACP. At the time of her arrest for refusing to give up her seat, she was forty-two years old, five feet three inches tall, well dressed, and well spoken. Her mug shot and the ongoing legal case against her, coupled with the yearlong bus boycott, led to her becoming an international symbol of what was wrong with Jim Crow.

Though blacks comprised more than 75 percent of Montgomery's bus riders, the segregated system required black people to give up their seat to any white person who needed one. Also, if whites were seated at the front of the bus, blacks boarding the bus were required to pay their fare and then exit the bus and reenter through the rear door. More than one bus driver would drive off after the black riders had paid but before they had time to reboard. As Parks famously said, "I did a lot of walking in Montgomery."

After Parks's arrest, the civil rights leaders sprang into action. The Women's Council printed more than thirty-five thousand flyers reading, "Don't ride the buses to work, to town, to school, or anywhere on Monday." On Sunday, clergy, including King, the newly minted pastor of the Dexter Avenue Baptist Church in Montgomery, urged their parishioners to carpool, take a black-owned taxi, or walk. Many walked, some more than twenty miles, on that cold winter day. The boycott lasted more than 381 days, crippling the city's economy and continuing despite threats and acts of violence, including the bombing of Dr. King's home.

Rosa Parks was awarded the Presidential Medal of Freedom and the Congressional Medal of Freedom, and always remained a sweet-faced symbol of the movement, but her life was never easy. Both she and her husband lost their jobs as a result of the case against her. They moved to Hampton, Virginia, and then, at the invitation of her younger brother, to Detroit. She worked as a seamstress for another ten years and then as an aide to Rep. John Conyers. She was widowed in 1977, when Raymond passed away. The years that followed were ones of constant personal and financial struggle for her. She was beaten during a house robbery in which a young man took all of fifty-three dollars. The local church helped to pay her rent until the very end.

It was with the full knowledge of how much Rosa Parks had given and how modestly she had lived that Minyon began to consider how the Rosa Parks memorial in DC could be configured. In addition to Elaine Steele, Minyon was also receiving calls from Willis Edwards, who was working with the Parks family.

Edwards was a colorful character we all knew well. Born in Texas in 1946 and raised in Palm Springs, he became the first African American president of Cal State–Los Angeles and would later become president of the Beverly Hills branch of the NAACP (where he famously convinced NBC president Brandon Tartikoff to air the NAACP Image Awards on the network). The recipient of a Bronze Star for his service in Vietnam, he worked on Robert F. Kennedy's presidential campaign and was with Kennedy in the Ambassador Hotel when he was assassinated. Edwards also assisted with the presidential campaigns of Jesse Jackson and the historic run of Tom Bradley, who became Los Angeles's first African American mayor. Diane Watson, then-Congresswoman from California, said of Edwards that he was "really a creative genius. He could gain access to the White House or any chamber he wanted. He could get doors open that others couldn't. He was a connector, a doer. There was nothing impossible for Willis."

Willis Edwards had gotten to know Rosa Parks in the 1990s, when she was attempting to start her own civil rights institute. He introduced her to the Clintons and walked her down the red carpet of the 1998 Academy Awards. Now he was on the phone, wondering if we could help him do what had never been done before: have the casket of an ordinary citizen lie in state at the Rotunda of the Capitol Building in Washington, DC.

Of Edwards, Minyon says, "To know Willis is to love him. He had this grand personality. Everything he wanted to do was always larger than his budget could accommodate, or larger than any organization could really put on. He was talking about this memorial and how 'We've got these family members that want to come in . . .'"

Minyon remembers doing the math: "I instantly started saying to myself, 'Okay, so this is going to require some money.'" She asked Edwards, "Well, what's your budget? Have you got a hotel? How are you going to get everybody here?" Neither Edwards nor Steele knew, but they felt confident we could help them figure it out.

As Minyon remembers it, "Nothing was in place. I just started praying, 'Lord Jesus, help me, Father, Holy Ghost.'" The other thing she did was call Leah, who was at the DNC. The DNC gave a donation, and then "we pressed her into service to help with the planning, and put Reverend Daughtry—Reverend Leah Daughtry—on the program." The two of them then called Tina Flournoy, who was at the American Federation of Teachers. The AFT donated some of the housing and hotel rooms for Parks's relatives. After that was accomplished, we talked Southwest into flying Rosa Parks's body in for the service. Donna began working the Hill. Minyon started working on the church.

Following the service in Alabama, Mrs. Parks's body was flown to Thurgood Marshall Airport, in Baltimore, where it was greeted by an honor guard. Secretary of State Condoleeza Rice arranged the transportation.

We pulled it off, and Rosa Parks became the first woman and the second African American—Jacob Chestnut, a Capitol Police officer killed during the line of duty in 1998, was the first—to lie in state at the Capitol Rotunda. Over the course of twenty-four hours, more than forty thousand people lined up to pay their respects to Parks in the Rotunda.

Minyon still remembers it as a sort of out-of-body experience: "I mean, people were lined up for miles to see her. We just kept looking at each other and saying, 'Oh my God. This is just incredible.' You couldn't even believe that you were a part of such majesty."

The church service was held at the Metropolitan African Methodist Episcopal Church, which could seat 2,500 people. Inside, luminaries such as Oprah Winfrey, Cicely Tyson, and Gwen Ifill waited to laud Parks, but as we stood outside the church, we realized there was a problem. When the body arrived from the Capitol, there was no one to take it into the church. The Capitol Police who were working Capitol Hill asked Minyon, "Do you have somebody to take the casket out of the hearse?" To which Minyon replied, "Aren't you all the people who put the casket in the hearse? Aren't you going to take it out?" But the Capitol Police could not "transfer the body. It was like a jurisdictional problem that we didn't even calculate. We had to scramble. We ran into the church, got the DC Honor Guard to come out and usher the body into the church. Oh, it was just a hot mess. Because if it had come down to us lifting the casket up and taking it into the church, trust me, we would've done it."

Inside, the old gender bias reared its head. Leah remembers "how dismissive the male clergy were of me and Mrs. Parks's pastor, who was also a woman. They even rearranged the order of the processional line so that we were out of the customary order of lineup. Very insulting. Once they learned that, besides being a pastor, I was also the DNC chief of staff, they were very embarrassed. But it was too late for me; the damage was done. I will never forget how they treated us just based on the fact of our gender." She adds, "And Cain Hope Felder, a legendary and venerated theologian, had forgotten his Bible and tried to, uh, appropriate mine. I didn't know whether to be insulted or honored."

Yolanda, Minyon, Tina, and Donna all served as ushers, with some of their younger mentees, such as Tanya Lombard and Jessica Briddle, helping them. Leah, in full clergy apparel, and Mrs. Parks's pastor were seated on the pulpit—albeit the lower pulpit, as the male clergy all took the prime upper-level pulpit seats. From her seat, Leah could see both the audience and the speakers, though she longed to be working the floor with the other Colored Girls. Oprah Winfrey told the crowd about how, as a child, she'd listened to her father tell her about Rosa Parks. And how, in her child's mind, she'd imagined a tall woman, a David who had been brave enough to take on the Goliaths of Jim Crow. When Winfrey, who was five foot seven, met the diminutive Parks years later, she said simply, "Thank you. For myself and for every colored girl and every colored boy. . . . I would not be standing here today, nor standing where I stand every day . . . had she not chosen to say we shall not—we shall *not*—be moved."

The crowd called out, "Well done, Rosa" and "Thank you, Rosa." For us, it would always remain a bonding moment, when we made a way out of no way in a matter of days for the homegoing of Rosa Parks. As Minyon puts it, "If only we had done more for her while she lived. The people of Detroit took her in. She became the favored daughter, but for the most part, there was no real thank-you for these people. People like Rosa Parks gave their lives not just for black Americans, but for all Americans, to understand that we can do better. We can do better, we can live better, and we can live peacefully together."

In 2006, when Yolanda's son died, tragically and unexpectedly, she was at work. Her sister called and told her employees, "Have her call me back and don't let her be alone." When Yolanda received the news, when all the world went blank, she remembers uttering these words to her chief of staff, Jason Llorenz: "Call Minyon. Minyon will know what to do."

"I remember so clearly that day," Minyon says. "I grabbed my purse and just headed for the door. I probably made it to Yolanda's house in three minutes. All the girls were notified. But on this day, all of Yolanda's extended family and girlfriends converged on her. Everyone wanted to be there. They wanted to show their love and support. When evening struck, Yolanda's apartment was full of her friends. We didn't want her to do anything but sit and be still."

In the weeks that followed, we took care of her, along with her nephew Wendell Phillips, and made all the arrangements. There is no true healing when a child dies. The natural order of life is forever off and out of whack, but there is survival.

Minyon says, "While I personally will never understand the feeling of losing a son, I do recall when my mother lost her oldest son. The pain, the agony, the questions that just linger. What is for certain, only time heals the broken heart, but their memories last."

When the worst happens politically, the power brokers call the Colored Girls. When the worst happens personally and privately, we do what we do best: lean on one another. Tina Flournoy, who was part of this circle from the very beginning, calls it having "someone to know on," and the knowing is powerful and deep.

15

The Room Where It Happens

There is an old Gaelic term, *anam cara*, that means "soul friend." A soul friend is one with whom you can reveal yourself, uncover all that is hidden, laying it bare and allowing them to accept you. The Irish poet John O'Donohue has said, "You are joined in an ancient and eternal union with humanity that cuts across all barriers of time, convention, philosophy and definition. When you are blessed with an *anam cara*, the Irish believe, you have arrived at that most sacred place: home." We Colored Girls were one another's *anam cara*. In Washington, a city known for its scheming, maneuvering, backstabbing, and friendships of convenience, we found in one another a true home.

The 2000 presidential campaign had literally ended in a tie. After numerous delays to have all votes counted in the state of Florida, the U.S. Supreme Court ruled in *Bush v. Gore* that the results would stand. Texas governor George W. Bush would be declared the winner of the Electoral College, though Al Gore had won the popular vote.

There were a lot of angry people who worried that our democracy was at risk. With the failure to "count every vote" and the incoming administration's pledge to reverse much of what Clinton/Gore had accomplished, we found ourselves at a major crossroads—not just in American politics, but also in our own lives.

The theft of the Gore campaign had just about left many broken hearts. As campaign manager, it was up to Donna to wind down the campaign, close field offices, and begin to turn to the recount efforts under way in Florida. Yolanda headed west, looking literally and figuratively for her place in the sun. Yolanda remembers, "I was so depressed after the election. I went to Tennessee for Election Night. I was hanging out in the Finance Lounge with all of the big donors, and by 9 p.m., everyone was pretty much trashed." She remembers, "The entire evening was so surreal. We all thought Gore had won; then everything went crazy. People waited for hours in the rain for him to come out and make some kind of statement. I was up most of the night, and had a 5:30 a.m. flight back to LA. There was no clear decision, and little did we know that we were about to go into new, foreign territory. That an election could actually be stolen, in the twenty-first century, was beyond the grasp of anyone's imagination. I moved to LA to work on the 2000 Democratic Convention and decided to stay. I couldn't bear the thought of being in DC with George Bush as president. I became bicoastal, opened up an LA office, and went back and forth for four years. I stayed out for his entire first term."

Leah was at the Department of Labor, serving as acting assistant secretary for administration and management. She'd been at Labor since 1997, holding various roles, including chief of staff, before taking up the assistant secretary role in late 2000. From her perch at Labor, she'd supported labor secretary Alexis Herman as a key advisor to Gore. Throughout the campaign, Leah was the designated staffer to travel with Secretary Herman to campaign-related events, taking personal and vacation time to do so. This was how she came to be part of the Gore debate camp team, traveling to each prep site several days before the actual debate, and then on to the debates themselves. "I remember when they brought in 'the real people' to help with debate prep. Those folks were brutally honest with the VP about his debate performances. While I think their candor was jarring for him, I believed they helped him trust his gut, and he liked having them around."

In the months preceding the 2000 convention, Leah went with Alexis to Los Angeles to help convention CEO Lydia Camarillo do a late assessment of convention readiness; Lydia had wanted an outside view of how the convention plans were shaping up. We gave the best advice we could, helping her determine how she and her team should focus their time and attention in the few remaining weeks. When we showed up for the actual convention a couple of days before gavel, Lydia gave us the grand tour of the convention facility. "My heart was in my throat for her because, just forty-eight hours before the convention, they were still installing carpet in the main hall," Leah remembers. "And wonder of wonders, she gave us the tour while wearing stilettos. Alexis and I had brought our flats; given our experience at the 1992 convention, when Alexis was CEO and I was managing director, we knew the drill. I still don't know how Lydia managed that amazing shoe feat—when I was managing the convention, by twenty-four hours out, I was in sneakers!"

Minyon was working at the White House during Gore 2000. "I was one of the principal liaisons to the campaign. As the convention neared, my department was in charge of all things convention-related. That included President Clinton's role and his participation during the convention."

Harry Thomason, a film producer and friend of the Clintons, came up with this idea: he would film the president's walk into the convention hall. He had been working on various production aspects of the convention. "When Harry explained the concept," Minyon says, "I thought to myself, 'Oh, that's interesting.' And why not? This was the president's swan song. Frankly, nothing jumped out at me, like 'Oh, be careful, you don't want to upstage the nominee.' But keep in mind, I was listening to this idea via phone."

Minyon agreed to the idea, and then Thomason said, "We probably want to keep it off the radar and just have this as an element of surprise." At that point, she admits, "Bells went off. But I still believed in my head it was only a little walk down a hallway—how much trouble could that cause?"

Minyon flew out ahead of the team and "finally caught up, in person, with Harry. I had to see for myself what was entailed in this walk. Well, not only was this the longest walk I could have ever imagined, but the way Harry had it staged, the cameras would be in front of him, and the president would be projected into the convention hall so that the momentum would continue to build with every step he took. 'Lord have mercy, I am going to get fired' was all I could say to myself. And what was even worse, I still hadn't told anyone about this entrance. It was no longer a walk; it was a dramatic entrance. I remember standing on the president's balcony at the headquarters hotel with my colleagues as the president was practicing his speech. John Podesta, our chief of staff at the time, asked me to walk through the logistics of the president's participation. I decided to downplay it. If I could describe to you the look on people's faces when I tried to describe this walk, you could have sold me for a nickel. In my heart, I knew I would not be going back to the White House if this backfired. Well, I can say this: the walk was executed perfectly. It did exactly what Harry anticipated—the convention hall was electric."

Leah was sitting in the hall. She remembers that as Clinton was walking down the hall, we could see him on the screen, and the achievements of his administration were flashing across the video screens . . . Twenty million new jobs! Record homeownership! Etc., etc. The crowd was going crazy. The noise was deafening. It was sheer pandemonium.

"The Clinton staff was elated," Minyon recalls. "The Gore staff, however, wasn't as pleased. The unintended consequence of that walk was that we upstaged the nominee. Sorry, Vice President Gore. I *really* didn't mean to do that. You know how much I adored you!"

Back at Labor, as the election neared, Alexis asked Leah to serve as the department's liaison to the transition team. Government regulation requires that each presidential campaign begin transition discussions months before the election, to help ensure a smooth transfer of power.

As the transition official, Leah met with both the Gore and Bush teams—separately, of course—answering their questions, gathering documents, etc., as they prepared to take over the government. As the Florida recount and the Supreme Court case moved along, the transition planning continued. Leah shuttled between their separate offices at the department, addressing various issues and setting up briefings.

Leah: "The difference between their approaches was, as my mother would say, like chalk and cheese. The Gore team was loosely organized and far more casual, including in their dress. They worked from yellow legal pads and would give me handwritten lists of documents they wanted. Their requests were varied, and I couldn't discern a clear focus. The Bush folks, on the other hand, came to work every day in suits. I was always addressed as 'Ms. Daughtry,' never by my first name. Each team member had a Bush transition notebook, containing documents, flow charts, etc. They asked very pointed questions about regulations, expiry dates, personnel, budgets. I knew from their questions that they had already done their homework, and that there were specific things they would focus on in their first one hundred days . . . regulations to be rolled back, personnel actions to be reversed, programs to be cut. I rationalized that the Gore team didn't have to be as specific because Gore had been part of the last eight years of government, so there was little to nothing to roll back or undo. Still, the difference was striking. When the Supreme Court sided with Bush, and he became president, I was heartbroken. But I didn't have time to be sad. I now had to shut down Alexis's office, help the political appointees transition to new lives, and stay connected to the Bush team as they prepared to move in. I had to ignore my sadness and dismay in order to get the work done. I stayed on at Labor to help the new secretary, Elaine Chao, get settled in once she was confirmed. It took a little while to get her sub-cabinet officers confirmed, so I stayed even longer. As their transition style predicted, [the Bush people] came in on day one with military precision. The process for stopping or repealing legislation, like the ergonomics rule"—which aimed at preventing carpal tunnel syndrome and other problems associated with repetitive motion—"for undoing personnel actions, and for revising the department's budget all began on day one, within the first hour of the workday."

Leah remembers that she "was surprised how different the department felt in the Bush administration. Everyone worked behind closed doors, and the career staff was not welcome or expected in most meetings. Very different from the Clinton administration, where every door was open and the career staff were considered part of the team. Some of my Republican friends tried to get me to stay at Labor, and I considered it for a while. I liked Elaine Chao, and I thought it might be an interesting experience to see how the other side functioned. But ultimately, their mind-set was too different for me, so I left. Plus, the stress had finally caught up with me, and my body was in constant pain. Once I decided to leave, and told Elaine, just like that, the pain in my body was gone. I went home and slept for a week, and then I went to the DNC in June 2001 as director of administration. My task was to try and bring some management and organizational systems to the institution, which meant I got to work with Minyon (who was the DNC CEO) very closely. When I arrived, there was Donna, with whom I'd spoken almost every day during the campaign, sitting outside Minyon's door." Leah remembers asking Donna, "'What are you doing here?' She said, 'I'm Minyon's intern.' I just stared; I was so confused."

About a year later, Minyon left the DNC for the Dewey Square Group. Leah had become chief of staff at the DNC, a huge job that would entail rebuilding the infrastructure, constructing a new headquarters, overseeing the technology updates, retooling the fund-raising apparatus after campaign finance laws were changed, and getting the institution ready for the presidential cycle—all after the changed environment precipitated by the terror of 9/11. She wanted and needed guidance, advice, and support, and asked the girls if we could set a regular dinner. "I hoped it would help me be successful at my job and help me give Terry the best political advice possible," Minyon says.

Minyon would call Donna: "Are you free Friday night, Donna B?" Donna says, "We were all hungry. Thirsty. And in need of each other's company." So, Donna, Minyon, Leah, and Tina got together for dinner as often as they could. And when the city started gearing up for the 2004 election, Yolanda joined them. "I came back in '04 because we had to take the White House back," she remembers.

At first, the dinners were never overly planned. "A lot of times, one of us would just say, 'We haven't had dinner in a while. What are y'all doing on Friday?'" Leah says. "Friday night was often the night since we didn't have anything to do the next day." They'd meet at Bobby Van's. Or the Tavern at the Henley Park Hotel.

"Me, Tina, and Yolanda were always on time," Leah says.

Minyon adds, "I was always emailing them telling them I was on my way—usually about thirty minutes late."

Yolanda laughs. "We'd wait for hours!"

"Not exactly true," Minyon says. "Well, at least I was letting you know!"

Those dinners would go on to become much more, but they started out as a respite from the political scene. They were personal, off-the-record, lay-my-burdens-down-by-the-river moments when we could speak frankly, laugh freely, and refill the well after a long, hard week. "The dinners were mainly about cementing friendship—and getting to know each other on other levels," Leah says. But before we could talk about anything, it was "What are we having for dinner?" and "What's on the wine list?"

"I used to have a scotch before we started eating," Donna says. Yolanda never ordered the same thing twice, while Leah always had a Coca-Cola. And on most occasions, the dinners started with a glass of champagne.

"Once, we got tossed out of a restaurant called Ceiba for complaining that their Veuve Clicquot was flat," Donna says.

"They brought us three bottles," Yolanda adds, "but if you take the champagne out of the refrigerator and let it get to room temperature and then you put it back in the fridge, it'll change the texture of the bubbles. The first bottle came, and Tina and I looked at each other and said, 'Ugh, this is flat.' So, they brought us another. And another. Next thing we know, the maître d' is coming over. He slammed the bottle down and said, '*This* I *know* is fine!' He got nasty, so we got nasty back. Finally, we said, 'We'll just go.'"

Leah laughs. "It was too bad because they had good food." Not long after that, Ceiba closed.

By this time, Yolanda was back in DC running her PR agency and working as a DNC member and superdelegate to the convention. Leah was at the DNC as Terry McAuliffe's chief of staff. Minyon was a partner at the Dewey Square Group. And Donna, after appearing as a political commentator and publishing her first book, *Cooking with Grease: Stirring the Pots in American Politics*, had started her own strategic communications consulting firm, Brazile and Associates, and was back teaching at the University of Maryland, College Park. She began teaching at Georgetown University in the spring of 2002. For her part, Tina was assistant to the president at the American Federation of Teachers.

Our dinners were a regular thing, but Tina and Minyon also started attending dinners organized by one of the DC strategists. It had long been a custom for power brokers to organize informal, off-the-record dinners for presidential hopefuls. "After one dinner, a lightbulb went off in our heads," Minyon says. "We thought to ourselves, 'Why aren't we doing these dinners?' None of them to date had addressed any of the issues we were concerned with—especially around the black community in general and black women in particular." She adds, "So, that night, a new idea was birthed. The Colored Girls would host the presidential hopefuls. We discussed the concept with the other CGs. Everyone signed on."

When we started talking about it seriously, we thought about the networks we'd need. We counted off the people most likely to be running for president in 2004 and realized that, between us, we knew all the players, the hurdles, and the opportunities in the election process. We knew we could pull it off.

Moreover, hosting our own dinners would do something critical: it would force candidates to think about and talk through the issues that mattered to the Colored Girls from the very beginning when considering a presidential run. At the other dinners, most guests and political hopefuls talked about current polling, or analysis from focus groups, or the donors' concerns. No one ever brought up women's rights and equal pay, gay rights, poverty, income inequality, mass incarceration, and education. It was time, past time, for presidential hopefuls to be asked to talk about race, culture, and economic development in diverse communities. We also thought we could be an invaluable resource for candidates because we all had multiple presidential elections under our belts, as well as state and local campaigns. So, we made up a list of potential candidates and began inviting them to dinner.

Minyon explains the rules for the dinners: "We only had three criteria: First, the presidential hopefuls would come alone. (We felt it would be easier for them to be candid, and we also wanted a more relaxed and informal setting. We wanted to get to know them.) The second rule was they would have to pay for the dinners; it was only fair. (We were providing them an audience with some of the smartest influencers in the country. Paying for the dinners was a small price to pay to have these smart women assembled in one room. Surprisingly, when we issued the invitations, I don't believe anyone declined.) Third, we didn't see these dinners as press events, so we encouraged their staffs to keep them off the record. (We wanted the participants to feel comfortable talking through issues and getting candid feedback.) The dinners proved to be interesting in themselves but a huge success in terms of getting to know [the candidates'] perspective." For once, black women were at the head of the table, not just taking a seat at it.

Donna says that for the first dinner, "[Iowa governor Tom] Vilsack missed the memo on rule number one and brought his wife, Christie, who technically isn't staff, so he probably thought it was okay." Leah adds: "We were at Ruth's Chris [Steak House], in the private room, and Tom and Christie sat side by side." We sat across from them and on the sides of the table, so it almost felt as if the candidate and his wife were at a group job interview. "His was the first dinner," Donna says, "so we really didn't have a set format or a plan for how the dinner would flow. We'd thought we'd just do some formal introductions, ask a couple of questions, and let the conversation flow." And that's exactly what happened. It was the Vilsacks and the five of us. Vilsack opened up by sharing that he was born in Pittsburgh to an unwed mother who put him up for adoption. I believe he shared this background with us to let us know he wasn't some privileged white man. He did miss a beat with one of his comments, but we understood his general sentiment. In essence, he had worked hard to make something of himself against amazing odds.

We thanked them for coming. Then we each introduced ourselves, and some of us gave a little statement about why we were having these dinners. Each of us would generally then follow the leader and talk a bit about herself, her experience, what she was working on now, and the issues that were important to her. One thing about elected officials: they are always eager to talk about policy and politics.

It wasn't all serious. With Vilsack being from Iowa, it was unavoidable that the conversation would eventually turn to that most Iowan of Iowa things: the Iowa State Fair. Leah had managed to avoid it all these years, so she was fascinated about stories of fried butter, pickles, Snickers bars, etc. Apparently, anything edible can be found fried at the Iowa State Fair. And of course, the turkey drumsticks, the ears of corn, and all the other regular county fair foods. If you're running for president, you have to attend the Iowa State Fair. Vilsack's being from Iowa made him an expert on how to navigate the fair, and Leah made a mental note for when she ever got there: take it slow, pace yourself, take a look at the cattle, and don't forget to see the Harry Potter sculpted from butter.

John Kerry had considered Vilsack for his VP in 2004, so Vilsack's stock was pretty high. "He knew he had to broaden his base and his appeal, so he was eager to sit down with us," Donna says. "He seemed overwhelmed already by the prospect. He understood the importance of the Iowa Caucuses, and he knew he could win there, but beyond that, I don't think he knew just how far his campaign could go. So, we tried to paint the broadest possible picture of what the campaign would look like beyond the Iowa Caucuses." Still, it was an early night. "Dinners were usually at seven. We were done around nine." As Leah remembers him, Vilsack "was a really nice guy, and we knew he'd make a great cabinet secretary."

"The most interesting part about all the dinners," Minyon says, "is to this day we are good friends with all of the former presidential candidates. The dinners were nonconfrontational. We said, 'Listen, we're an open book. These are some of the issues that impact our community, but these are some of the issues we know on a national level that have nothing to do with our community.' After the first dinner with the Vilsacks, we were like 'Okay, this is interesting. These dinners are a good idea.'"

We also wanted to offer ourselves as resources to the potential candidates, to help them connect with community leaders across the country. It was a way of helping our communities be in direct communication with the candidates, of having a seat at the table, and also helping the candidates have a direct connection with the leaders in local communities who could best speak to the communities' issues of concern.

In Lin-Manuel Miranda's landmark musical *Hamilton*, the jazzy, showstopping number "The Room Where It Happens" describes the famous Dinner Table Bargain (or the Compromise) of 1790. According to Thomas Jefferson, he ran into Alexander Hamilton one early summer afternoon outside George Washington's New York City office. Jefferson described Hamilton as looking "somber, haggard and dejected beyond comparison." Hamilton had been pouring energy into an ambitious plan to establish a centralized federal debt system, but his plan lacked support in Congress. He feared that without such a system, which would shore up the nation's rights of taxation and its ability to borrow funds from abroad, the new United States would fall into financial ruin. He had been to see Washington because he was considering resigning as the secretary of the treasury.

On June 20, 1790, Jefferson hosted a dinner to which he invited Hamilton and his bitter enemy James Madison. He allowed each to state his case and propose a compromise. At the end of the evening, a bargain was struck: Madison promised Hamilton that he would secure the necessary votes to pass his debt plan. In return, Hamilton agreed to support moving the nation's capital to the Potomac, a site that the Southern leaders believed would serve their interests both geographically and politically. In the musical, Aaron Burr, left out of the dinner, bristles at his lack of influence.

Something magical happens over meals that can't happen in a formal boardroom. The dinners we held were relaxed, and we created an environment where candidates could be thoughtful and engaging rather than trying to talk in sound bites or make a presentation. We never tried to trick or trap a candidate; we were just trying to get to know them. And whatever bits of knowledge we had, we tried to pass on. By 2004, the informal Friday night dinners we had begun as a means of friendship and support had grown to include off-the-record strategy with top members of Congress and presidential hopefuls. Everybody was trying to get invited to one of our dinners. The list was growing by the day. We were in demand.

Our dinners looked much different from those normally given by Washington insiders. With the exception of Hillary, the candidates were all men. With the exception of Obama, they were all white—which meant that, nine times out of ten, it was one white male candidate and as many as ten powerful professional black women at the table. "I doubt most of them had ever broken bread with that many black women," Yolanda recalls. "I also don't think they expected us to be as thoughtful as we were. They often expected us to talk about so-called black issues, such as drugs and crime. But they didn't expect us to ask tough questions about foreign policy or campaign finance reform."

Governor Howard Dean, who had dinner with the Colored Girls in 2004, has said, "If you're smart and you want to get ahead in politics, then if they ask you to dinner, you better go. They're very rare Washington insiders who understand the rest of the country. That's part of what makes them so valuable. These women have not lost their connections with where they came from."

At each dinner, Donna usually spoke first, and her first question was always "What's your 2168 strategy?"—meaning, how do you plan to get the 2,168 delegates you need to secure the Democratic Party nomination? (That was the magic number at the time.) Some of the candidates would look at her blankly. They didn't understand that the rules of delegate math had changed—or that the women at the table had helped to change them. We also wanted the candidates to understand that we understood electoral politics. First, you needed to secure the nomination and then you had to consider your prospects of winning the Electoral College.

We had just voted for new rules at the DNC that would force the state parties to do significant outreach to historically underrepresented groups. Under the new rules, half the convention delegates would be female, and African Americans, Latinos, women, labor, and the LGBT community would be better represented. We knew the rules inside and out, and were willing to advise the candidates on how the game had changed. Because we all played major roles in the party, we were doing these candidates a favor by freely offering our experience and know-how to them. The challenge, we learned early on, was to figure out which candidates we were going to support, either individually or as a group. Everyone on the short list of presidential candidates has outstanding qualifications. When you get to that point in your career, the question becomes are you headed for a presidential campaign, or should you set your sights on the vice presidency, or are you cabinet material?

In 2004, when Howard Dean ran for the chairmanship of the DNC, Tina brought him to a Colored Girls dinner. In his book *The Argument: Inside the Battle to Remake Democratic Politics*, Matt Bai writes, "It was an odd alliance—this pairing of a blue-blooded Vermonter with a group of black women." The Colored Girls didn't see it that way. Decades into our careers in Washington, we had forged many alliances with powerful white men. We had made real and lasting friendships with people who didn't share our color or our gender. But most important—and this is the part Bai seemed to have missed—the Colored Girls weren't a monolith. In his book, Bai is incredibly specific in his description of Dean as a "blue-blooded Vermonter," but he fails to point out that we were each very different: in lineage, in experience, in temperament. It was in the recognition of our differences and the sharing of our strengths that our power grew.

Yolanda notes that most of the dinners were held at Ruth's Chris Steak House on Ninth Street ("sometimes called Rufus Chris, because it's popular with black people"). Our dinner with Chris Dodd, at Bobby Van's, was an unexpectedly long affair. We didn't expect to find Dodd such good company. As Minyon explains, "To know him is to love him. Senator Dodd, as we all expected, would be forthright on all the issues we believed in. It was in his DNA. He was considered one of the most liberal members of the Senate. But frankly, it was more than that. Dodd understood politics and people. He had the heart, the passion, the fire in his belly. He understood race. He was fluent in Spanish. And was just a person you enjoyed being around. He had a strong command of the issues and how to navigate the politics. He would often say, 'If people don't like you, they won't elect you.' He was beloved in Connecticut, but unfortunately it didn't translate on a national level. I think the country was yearning for something different—which we eventually got." She adds of Dodd: "He was the only one we closed the restaurant down with. A man worthy of respect, in my opinion. He would have been a great president."

Leah agrees: "The Dodd dinner was absolutely the most fun. When we got through the serious stuff, we laughed the whole night. Toward the end of the night, we looked up and realized we were the only people in the restaurant, and the entire staff was waiting for us to leave so they could go home!" As they departed, Donna told the senator, "I will see you on Sunday at St. Joseph's Catholic Church." The two became pew buddies.

Evan Bayh also surprised us. Noted as a policy wonk, Bayh, Minyon says, "turned out to be very interesting and thoughtful. I think there was an anticipation going into these dinners that he would be the most conservative and, quite frankly, the most boring. He was everything but that. Bayh was one of these gentlemen who was born for this type of run. He had the looks, the family, the grooming/pedigree. But he was also considered very safe and not a risk taker. He was a pleasant surprise at dinner, very engaging. Of course, he was prepared, but he was also insightful. [He] wasn't sure he would make it through the primaries, but [he] could have made a good president."

Leah remembers, "I liked Bayh very much and thought he would be a very good candidate and a very good president. He struck me as thoughtful and steady. I was surprised and a little disappointed that his campaign did not take off."

She continues: "I went in with an affinity for Bayh. He was the son of a famous dad, so he moved with a kind of pedigree, born into public service, and groomed from birth for leadership—but also walking under an invisible cloak of expectation that guides your decisions and shapes your path. As with other daughters and sons of high-profile activists, I identified with that space—so I was partial to him, I think. He was an intense listener. Paying strict attention to whoever was speaking, watching you with a piercing stare, as if he was trying to imprint your words on his brain. He was not an interrupter. He waited until you were done talking, then took a moment—as if to process fully what you'd said—before responding. You had to catch the rhythm of this way of interacting, or you'd mistakenly take it for disinterest."

Generally, after the dinners, we'd say good-bye to our guest, walk him out of the restaurant, and then chat for a few minutes among ourselves. "So. Whatcha think?" And we'd dish very briefly.

"He was really good."

"Nice, but not going anywhere."

"What the hell was *that*?"

"I hope he runs."

"He ain't ready."

"I'd help him."

If it was a late night, we'd head home and call each other from our cars. Over the phone, as we drove home, we'd have the same conversations: "GIRL!" or *"Girl"*; "What the?"; "Help us, no, help him, Lord"; "Well, that was dull/fun/interesting." And then: "Who's up next?"

16

Hillary Clinton, Barack Obama, and the Colored Girls

We did not expect that four years after working with Hillary Clinton to get Barack Obama elected to the U.S. Senate, we would find Clinton and Obama running against each other for the Democratic nomination. But when that moment came, we invited both the candidates to dinner. Minyon notes that, as time went on, "Some of the dinners we would open to a larger group of black women. That was especially true for then-Senator Obama and Senator Clinton. Women like then-chairman and CEO of BET Debra Lee and prominent attorney Florence Prioleau were regulars." She adds, "We really wanted to bring other African American women to the dinners, not as much for our benefit as for the benefit of the potential candidates. Each of the women had her own sphere of influence: social, political, economic, and geographic. They could be an important resource for any candidate as the candidates moved around the country during their campaigns. We always made the point to the candidates that they should consider these women as resources and reach out to them for advice, suggestions, and connections to other folks."

Leah remembers that the Hillary dinner had so many guests that "We had to have the restaurant expand the usual table to accommodate the number. We were in a big square, with Hillary sitting between Maggie Williams and Minyon. The evening was light and enjoyable. There was no subject that Hillary couldn't discuss in depth. That night, she easily navigated between being a policy wonk and being a girlfriend. She was completely and totally at ease. In the after-dinner conversation, all the women agreed that they were wowed by her intellect and her ease. It was clear that she would be a great president and that many would have signed on to her campaign that night, if there'd been a campaign. She hadn't declared her candidacy yet."

Over dinner, Hillary drank a gin and tonic and ordered what the Colored Girls called "a big old steak." She also cut right to the chase and said, "I want your support, and I'll do what I need to do to get it." Minyon says of Clinton, "Make no mistake about it: she wowed us effortlessly. A true connection was made with the expanded group of black women. [Hillary] was, as they say, comfortable in her own skin. This type of setting wasn't new to her. She knew many of the women at the dinner. Maybe history was unbroken continuity: her mentors and friends were Marian Wright Edelman, Dorothy Height, and Dr. Maya Angelou. So many of us shared that bond. [Hillary's] longtime friend and chief of staff at the White House was Maggie Williams, our friend and colleague of many years. When she took her seat, she didn't feel like a stranger at the table. There was a round of drinks, laughs, and then down to business. I think what surprised many was [Hillary's] depth of knowledge and her command of the issues. Seriously smart. Eerily smart. Was she too smart? Was America ready for the first woman president? Well, you couldn't help but ask the question. We wondered how she would deal with the sexism and the misogynistic behavior. Unfortunately, being smart couldn't shield her from the deep-seated fears and hatred that were yet to come. Hillary was being touted as the front-runner. Maybe it was an idea whose time had come. I think, in many ways, the woman that sat with us at that dinner table was more hopeful and full of life. She had a certain confidence in her tone. While she wasn't born for this, she was certainly prepared to take on one of the great challenges of her life—at least we thought so. There is no doubt she would have been a superb and even phenomenal president. I would say after the dinner, many people were leaning toward Hillary. I remember one of the women pulling me aside and saying, 'I think I will go with Obama. I think we need to be in all camps.'"

As the race got under way, there was nothing in those dinners that prepared us for seeing young men standing up in audiences and yelling, "Hillary, will you iron my shirts?" or holding up vulgar, degrading signs. Nothing in those dinners would have told us that Hillary would be running against a young black man whose hopeful message was inspiring a new generation to get involved. At those dinners, we could not foresee history about to collide or race and gender being put on display in ways we could never have imagined. We had no road map to deal with these two historic and emotional touchpoints.

The Obama dinner was held in the private dining room at Ruth's Chris in Chinatown. It was one of the larger dinners, with a table expander brought in to accommodate all the guests. At that dinner, Leah, who sat next to Obama, remembers, "His expectation was that he was walking into a room of adorers and supporters." When the questions started, he didn't seem to like it. Donna asked him what his 2168 strategy was, and he bristled. Another participant asked him, "What's your race strategy?" And we all remember him saying, "Oh, race won't be an issue. America is past that." That left us all with our mouths slightly ajar. Obama's belief was that American families' problems were universal, and "to close the gap between minority and white workers may have little to do with race at all."

The Obama we met that night at dinner represented a kind of bargaining that made us uncomfortable. In the *Los Angeles Times*, conservative columnist Shelby Steele criticized Obama's "post-black" platform:

Obama's special charisma—since his famous 2004 convention speech—always came much more from the racial idealism he embodied than from his political ideas. In fact, this was his *only* true political originality. . . . This worked politically for Obama because it tapped into a deep longing in American life—the longing on the part of whites to escape the stigma of racism. In running for the presidency—and presenting himself to a majority white nation—Obama knew intuitively that he was dealing with a stigmatized people. He knew whites were stigmatized as being prejudiced, and that they hated this situation and literally longed for ways to disprove the stigma.

At those dinners, we shared a little of what we had learned over decades of work on presidential campaigns. Leah was DNC chief of staff at the time: "I was required to be neutral through the primary season. At the point of the dinners, there were no candidates at all, so it was really easy to be neutral. As candidates announced, I felt lucky that I didn't have to make the hard decision to choose any of them. But I was also really confident that any of the candidates would be a good choice."

The dinner with Obama was tough, tougher than any of us expected. Obama was reserved and a bit overconfident. As Leah remembers, "Some of it was, I think, black male bravado, and I don't mean that in a negative way. I have a father, a brother, and nephews. We know that this is a world where black men have learned, out of necessity and circumstance, how to mask their insecurity. He came in trying to be comfortable, but he didn't know us. He never asked for help. You didn't feel like he was genuinely interested in engaging with the group outside of the dinner conversation. I didn't leave that meeting thinking he was going to reach back to the group."

Of Obama, Minyon says, "Well, how should I say this? I found it no surprise he would go on to become president. First, he is a rule breaker." In defiance of the Colored Girls' first rule, he showed up with a staff person. Senator Obama was at the height of his popularity when word started surfacing that he might run for president, so next to Hillary's dinner, his dinner was by far the second most popular. She adds, "Then-Senator Obama was an incredibly confident person, so I am still not sure that this dinner ever rose to the level of importance in which he saw himself. Nonetheless, he came, and the women were eager to hear from the senator from Illinois. While he didn't have the relationships that Hillary had with many in the room, he displayed a certain comfortability—like he belonged. We were eager to hear his vision and eager to get to know more about him. We were also deeply concerned about how race would be handled with his candidacy. Some of that was born out of experience and fear. I remember when he said, 'Race won't be a problem.' Many saw that as naïve on the one hand, but others thought, 'Maybe he will be able to deal with America's greatest sin . . . race in America as a biracial American.' What stood out for me that night," she continues, was that "Obama, while he didn't have the knowledge base the others had, he had something that continues to carry him forward to this day: he believed in himself, and he believed in the American people, and sometimes that is enough. He was an idea whose time had come. For me personally, it was a decision point. I had worked for Senator Obama's 'Yes We Can' PAC, which was training a new generation of political operatives. I had also worked with Senator Clinton. I eventually had hopes of working for the first female president."

The dinner with Obama foreshadowed an issue that would later surface between political veterans and the new-school team that made up the Obama campaign. The veterans believed that history was unbroken continuity. We'd garnered extensive experience from eight successful years in the White House, in addition to so many presidential campaigns. This experience would be invaluable to any presidential candidate, and many wanted to put that to work for the Obama campaign. The new folks, on the other hand, seemed unaware of what had been accomplished or who had accomplished it. And in that, it felt like history had been erased, or at least overlooked.

So, after a season of dinners with the Democratic candidates, this was where we landed: Minyon, Yolanda, and Tina supported Hillary. Leah, as chief of staff of the DNC and convention CEO, was neutral, because she had to be. Donna was uncommitted.

During the South Carolina primaries, President Clinton was campaigning for Hillary at a polling station with two congressmen supporting her when a young man working from a local radio station came up to them to discuss the status of her race. They talked about the history of the South Carolina primaries and more specifically the history of Jackson's two races. The young man asked President Clinton if he thought Obama would do well. The president stated he thought he would because Jackson had won the state twice and he acknowledged that Obama's team had worked hard in the state. The comment was interpreted as President Clinton somehow race-baiting and belittling Senator Obama's campaign. Some of us saw it as merely a statement of fact. Even Reverend Jackson wondered what all the fuss was about. But it was an explosive moment in the campaign, and it had legs.

Minyon notes, "I know well the difference between the person at the podium and the person behind closed doors. My respect for President Clinton and my belief in his commitment to race relations as a critical component of moving our nation toward 'a more perfect union' was built on years of behind-the-scenes interaction. It was not reported in the newspapers, but just the night before the big toss-up, President Clinton was speaking at a rally when a minister stood up during the question-and-answer portion and said he liked both Obama and Hillary but had decided to support Hillary because he didn't think America would elect a black president. I distinctly remember Clinton thanking him for his support, but he disagreed with his assessment and told him why. He proceeded to tell the minister that Senator Obama had won in Iowa and might win the nomination. He then stated, he would do all he could to help elect him if he won the nomination. So much attention was given to his Jackson comments, but no attention was given to the fact that he was campaigning for his wife but vigorously defending Senator Obama.

"For the blacks working in the Hillary campaign and who had previously worked for President Clinton, we found ourselves trying to figure out, do we defend President Clinton over a black man without elevating this story? Do we say something in his defense, or do we just let this die down?

We knew that the characterizations that were being made about President Clinton were flat-out wrong. We chose not to respond. I had proudly worked for Reverend Jackson's campaigns, President Clinton's White House, and Senator Obama's PAC, but to suggest that Clinton had somehow become a racist was an unexpected low point in the campaign cycle."

Minyon and Cheryl Mills met and wrote an op-ed "that we were going to release, trying to put this back in perspective. Then as we sat there and as we talked to more of our colleagues, we just decided that it was probably a no-win situation for us, because we didn't want people to think we were insensitive to race. But we knew President Clinton personally, we had worked with him at the highest level, and we knew the stories being told weren't true."

Then President Clinton called in to Al Sharpton's radio show to say that the "fairy tale" comment he'd made about Barack Obama was being misconstrued. He wasn't calling Obama's bid for the presidency a fairy tale, he said; he had been talking about Obama's *take on the war*.

And Donna, appearing on Wolf Blitzer's CNN show the day after, responded, "There is nothing fairy-tale about Obama's campaign. It's real and strong, and he might win."

Here's what you need to know about Donna: when she says something, because she is so pithy, people listen. Her comments took the explosiveness of the situation from zero to a hundred. People's outrage over her remark was at a fever pitch, and we Colored Girls were all in new territory. It was difficult to balance our joy at having a black candidate with having black operatives in the other campaign on opposite sides on matters of race.

President Bill Clinton called Donna to discuss her comment. Donna knew she was in for a tough conversation as soon as an assistant came into her office and said, "Bill Clinton would like to speak to you." ("I said, 'What the hell?'" she remembers.) She had been on the other line with Eleanor Clift, from *Newsweek*, trying to do her usual spin. Donna still grimaces at the thought of what happened when she switched lines to talk with Clinton: "He read me the riot act. I could call it a heated exchange, but I was, for once, dumbfounded. I had infuriated him. When I was finished talking to him, I was aghast. It would take a long time for us to regain the trust and easy conversation that had been the hallmark of our acquaintance."

When we started out having dinners with candidates, we expected the presidential contest to be between white boys, the same as it had ever been. Then, when it turned out to be about a white woman and a black man, as Colored Girls, we appeared to be taking sides against ourselves. The situation mirrored that playing out in African American households across the country. Leah recalls that in her own family, some of the family were with Hillary and some were with Obama, cutting across gender and age. It made for too many heated conversations and family dinners. It was, she says, stressful and exhausting.

As Donna so vividly remembers, "In my mind, I was neutral. In my spirit, I was in flux. If someone criticized Hillary, I defended her—like I defended her when people thought that she was too emotional after losing the Iowa Caucuses when she was in New Hampshire and she broke down and basically said, 'I'm in this because I care about children, I care about families.' She was really, really good. I know what PMS is. That's not PMS.' But on the race stuff, I also had to stand up and speak out. When Bill Clinton said 'fairy tale,' I said something to the effect of 'Of all people, Bill Clinton knew that this was not a fairy-tale campaign.'"

Then came the date that would change everything: May 31, 2008. Tina and Donna were both on the Rules and Bylaws Committee, which was set to decide a dispute over the seating of the Florida and Michigan delegates. How did we get to this moment of truth? According to arcane but clear party rules, in 2008, only four states were allowed to hold election contests before February 5: Iowa, New Hampshire, South Carolina, and Nevada. In contravention of that rule, Michigan and Florida voted to move their primaries into January 2008. As punishment, both states were stripped of their pledged delegates, the people who would represent

Michigan and Florida at the nominating convention. At the RBC meeting in May, proposals were considered to end the dispute and, basically, find a way to allow the delegates from the two states to attend the convention.

Florida was easy to settle, at least as it related to the number of delegates awarded to the candidates. Each candidate's name had remained on the ballot (there was no real way to take them off), so there was a clear way to apportion delegates based on the Florida primary vote. Michigan, however, was a different kettle of fish. Hillary's name was on the Michigan ballot and Uncommitted was on the ballot, but Barack Obama's name was not. One hundred and twenty-eight delegates were at stake. Based on the primary results, Hillary Clinton earned seventy-three pledged delegates. Uncommitted earned fifty-five.

Three proposals were on the table to settle the dispute:

The Clinton campaign's position was that the delegates should be apportioned based on the primary vote: seventy-three pledged delegates for Clinton, fifty-five pledged delegates for Uncommitted, none to candidates who weren't on the ballot.

The Obama campaign's position was to the split the one hundred and twenty-eight delegates evenly, sixty-four for Clinton and sixty-four for Obama, even though Obama's name had not been on the ballot.

The Michigan Democratic Party's proposal was to give Clinton sixty-nine delegates (less than the seventy-three she'd won based on the vote) and to give Obama fifty-nine delegates (though his name had not been on the ballot) based on the primary results, exit polls, and a survey of uncommitted write-in votes.

The Michigan Democratic Party proposal was approved by the RBC. Tina voted against the proposal and Donna voted for it. It became the rift heard around the world. For Donna, this was a matter of fairness. She believed that Obama should not be penalized.

Now, as to the threshold question each candidate faced about staying on the ballot in Michigan, Tina said she could argue it square or round. But she didn't believe anyone should argue with the decision the voters made when they cast their ballots. Tina believed, and deeply, "that the RBC vote turned the Constitution upside down. You can't go inside the voter's brain and, after the fact, decide that a vote for uncommitted is a vote for someone not on the ballot. You've now substituted the judgment of the DNC for the judgment of the voter." After Iowa, this was a major loss for Hillary's campaign.

The 2008 election tried our friendship like no other. Those of us who were with Hillary (Minyon, Tina, and Yolanda) had to take Donna off our emails. We go "book, chapter, and verse" on email—going back and forth in messages that would zip as fast as a teenager's texts and could number a hundred messages in just a few hours. Donna missed the lifeline of friendship that the emails represented. She remembers that she "felt the chilliness. I felt the cold shoulder." So many people were telling us, "You're black; you've got to be for Obama." And then others, mostly white women, were saying, "You're a woman; you've got to be for Hillary." Donna remembers telling one person, "Yes, I'm black; yes, I'm a woman, but I'm getting old and grumpy, and I'm going to support John McCain if y'all don't stop."

"It was ugly," Minyon says.

Some of us who were supporting Hillary began getting vicious hate mail, threatening us and accusing us of disloyalty for not supporting Obama instead. Leah, who as convention CEO had been neutral throughout the primaries, was not exempt from some of the wrath; those from the Obama team who mistakenly believed that the Colored Girls were monolithic in thought assumed Leah was supporting Hillary, and that made for some very tense times in the last weeks of convention planning. We are tough; we had been through so much, but that summer, things got particularly ugly.

Eight years later, Hillary Clinton ran for president once again. The 2016 election would become stranger than fiction and challenge our friendship in new and unexpected ways. The Russian interference into the 2016 election would cause turmoil and division and sow discord not just in the election but between friends.

17

Real Power Whispers:
Dr. Dorothy Irene Height

Leah first met Dorothy Height a full decade before the Colored Girls dinners, when she went to work for Alexis Herman at the DNC. Herman was chief of staff at the time, and Leah worked as her executive assistant. One day, Herman sent Leah to the National Council of Negro Women to help organize their upcoming gala. Leah laughs as she remembers: "I'm afraid I wasn't much help, as the ladies had a *very* particular way they wanted to do things and they weren't inclined to a bunch of new ideas from a twenty-seven-year-old kid on the eve of their big event. When I walked into Dr. Height's office with Alexis, she didn't introduce me to her; she dived right into the work."

Dr. Height seemed to know who Leah was and referred to her, without introduction, as "Ms. Daughtry." This was not unusual: "She called everyone by their last name," Leah recalls. "And it was a habit of the entire team at the National Council of Negro Women. No one was called by their first name. As a matter of respect, it was 'Mrs.' or 'Ms.' or 'Miss.' Dr. Height occasionally called Alexis by her first name, but only when the two of them were alone. Dr. Height was part of Alexis's world, so as long as I worked for Alexis, Dr. Height was ever present. Because I worked for Alexis, I was admitted to Dr. Height's inner circle."

Dorothy Irene Height is known as a civil rights activist, a women's rights activist, and an educator. Those words seem hollow when you consider her life, her impact, and her reach. Height was a force of nature who blew through the twentieth century, making changes, and then picked up a little bit of a wind so she could set a few things straight in the twenty-first century before she was done.

She was born in Richmond, Virginia, in 1912 but was raised in Rankin, Pennsylvania, a steel town with integrated schools. She was accepted to Barnard College, only to be told upon her arrival that the college had an unwritten rule not to allow more than two black students to matriculate each year. So, she chose to attend New York University instead, where she earned her undergraduate degree and then went on to earn a master's in psychology. She did further course work at Columbia University and the then-named New York School of Social Work.

In her twenties, she became active in the civil rights movement and joined the National Council of Negro Women (also known as the NCNW). As an executive at the YWCA, she led the desegregation of that organization's facilities throughout the 1940s. In the 1950s, she started a program called "Wednesdays in Mississippi," in which groups of black and white women flew to the state for integrated lunches that promoted conversations between women across the racial divide.

In her forties, Height became president of the NCNW, a position she held for nearly forty years. James Farmer, founder of CORE, the Congress of Racial Equality, called Height one of the "Big Six" of the civil rights movement—along with himself, Martin Luther King Jr., John Lewis, and two others: Roy Wilkins of the NAACP and Whitney Young of the National Urban League. Farmer noted that it was only sexism that kept the press from acknowledging Height's power and influence in the movement. Still, she was a sought-after advisor to the greatest leaders of her time, including Eleanor Roosevelt and Presidents Eisenhower and Johnson. She once told the *New York Times*, "I don't know if 'counseled' is the right word, but I have known every president that has been in office since President Roosevelt."

Maya Angelou remembered that she first met Dr. Height at an event in 1959. Angelou, a dancer and calypso singer raised in St. Louis and San Francisco, was the daughter of a gun-toting card dealer and was bohemian through and through. At the event, she was snubbed by a group of what she called "black bougies." Dr. Height noticed the snub and invited Angelou to a private lunch. As Angelou told it, "She took my heart from that moment to this."

Coretta Scott King, whom no black bougie would ever dare to snub, felt the same elevating lift from her friendship with Dr. Height, of whom she said, "I love the woman, and love what she represents. She's a teacher. She's a healer. She's a redeemer."

For Leah, Dr. Height would be all those things and more, including friend and neighbor. When Leah returned to DC in 1997 to work for Alexis Herman at the Department of Labor, Herman arranged for her to live in Dr. Height's recently vacated apartment. The three women all lived in the same building, Height on the first floor, Leah on the second, and Herman on the sixth. Herman gave Leah a spare set of Dr. Height's keys so that she could go in if the elder woman became ill or needed something urgently. Leah remembers, "It was *years* before the magnitude of that hit me: I was walking around with Dorothy Irene Height's house keys. In case she needed something, in case she got sick—I had the keys!"

Over the years, Leah says, "I got used to being in her orbit and listening to her stories about Martin and the movement. If Dr. Height was looking for Alexis and couldn't find her, she would call me. At any hour. She was a woman of few words, so when I answered the phone, she'd say, 'Ms. Daughtry, would you please do such-and-such.' And then she'd hang up. I don't think I got two words in edgewise. Sometimes, rarely, we had a complete conversation."

If Dr. Height left anything out of their morning call, she would catch up with Leah in the building's lobby. Leah remembers, "I had a dog named Khola back then, and I'd throw on the first thing my hand touched to walk the dog in the morning: sweat suit, flip-flops, T-shirt.

Just whatever. I'd take Khola down, and without fail, Dr. Height would be in the lobby, full makeup, styled to the teeth, and magnificent hat, waiting for her driver to take her to work. She'd be dressed and on her way to work at seven or eight in the morning. Without fail, I'd groan and say to myself, 'Why is this old lady always in the lobby when I look a mess?' I'd try to slide out the back door, but it didn't matter. She'd say, 'Ms. Daughtry.' I'd slink over and say, 'Good morning, Dr. Height.' Sometimes that would be it, and other days, she'd proceed to give me my instructions for the day. And she always ended by saying, 'And how is Brother Herb?' Referencing my father. Be clear: this was every single day that she wasn't traveling, until she went into the hospital."

Leah remembers how she first knew Dr. Height was sick: "Because she wasn't in the lobby for several days. Then Alexis called me, asked where I was—I was on the road—and when I was coming home. I answered, and she told me Dorothy was sick and to come straight to the hospital."

Leah came home right away and went right away to Howard University Hospital, where she met Herman. The two women went to see Dr. Height in her hospital room, and Herman asked Leah to pray. "I prayed, and as I did, Dr. Height turned and looked at me, and then she squeezed my hand. I sat a little while, and when she dozed off, I left the room."

Herman asked Leah to set up a visitation system. So many were coming to see Dr. Height. It would've been an exhausting schedule for any elderly person in the hospital, but Dr. Height was ninety-eight, and the doctors were concerned. Leah worked with the hospital administration to come up with a system. She took Herman's phone and went through her voice mail, returning calls to everyone who had called about Dr. Height. From then on, Leah fielded calls from everyone who wanted updates and visiting hours. She remembers, "As Dr. Height became more frail and more ill, we had to restrict the visitors' list, and many were disappointed."

Leah goes on: "When she died, Alexis called me with the news. I shed a few tears, thanked God for her life and her witness, recalled our many conversations, and then I went to Alexis's house to check on her and sit with her for a while. I knew there was work to be done. When Alexis was ready, we started talking about the services for Dr. Height. Fortunately, and as an example to all of us, Dr. Height had left specific instructions about her service—the music, the speakers, the eulogist; very specific—and we just followed her instructions. This was a good thing, because so many wanted to honor her. We would still be in service now if we'd said yes to everyone."

Leah remembers that "To my surprise, Alexis asked me to serve as the national coordinator for the homegoing celebration, which turned out to be a multi-event celebration of life, six or seven events over three days, including a community celebration at Shiloh—which Dr. Height had not scripted—and a celebration of life at Washington National Cathedral. The cathedral service was the one that she left specific instructions for. We followed them to the letter, except that the eulogist she'd wanted had predeceased her. So, because the cathedral team was insistent, we acquiesced to their custom, and the dean of the cathedral gave the eulogy. The big unplanned thing was the president of the United States. Dr. Height hadn't accounted for him wanting to speak—but one does not say no to such an honor."

Leah quickly pulled together a team. And, as she puts it, "it required a team. This was no ordinary citizen, and this would be no ordinary funeral. We commandeered the third floor of NCNW, and that's where all the planning took place. I did not lack for volunteers, and of course I called in people I knew I could rely on. I needed this to be as flawless as I could make it. Minyon was with me from day one; she camped out in NCNW with me for the better part of two weeks, to manage all the VIPs. The outpouring of love and support for Dr. Height was present throughout the planning and through the execution of the services. From the members of Congress (including the Speaker of the House, Nancy

Pelosi) who boarded buses to NCNW, where Dr. Height lay in repose; to the everyday people who lined Pennsylvania Avenue to pay their respects; to the sisters of Delta Sigma Theta, who honored her with an Omega Omega service at Howard University; to the unbelievable crowds who waited to get into Shiloh Baptist Church for a near-five-hour community celebration; and finally, to those who lined up early in the morning, hoping to snag a seat at Washington National Cathedral."

"I remember going to the event at Shiloh, the evening before her funeral," Yolanda says. "I got there early, and all of the girls were there: Flo McAfee, Dana Shelley, both of whom I had worked with at the DNC and beyond. I asked Minyon what she wanted me to do. She said, 'Find a seat. You've earned the right to be a guest.' First time in my life being at one of these events [when] I didn't have to work but was able to enjoy a beautiful homegoing ceremony."

She continues: "At the funeral the next day, I remember I had on a purple dress—it was actually more maroon than purple, but it was the only thing I had that came close to purple, which was Dr. Height's favorite color. It was sleeveless, and it was April, and it was too damned cold to wear a sleeveless dress, even though the sun was shining brightly. I parked about four blocks away from the National Cathedral, which is where the service was held, and once I got there, a gazillion people were standing outside of the cathedral talking. I remember I was freezing my ass off asking myself, 'Why the hell didn't I wear a coat?'"

"Each event was moving in its own way, and each honored her beautifully," Leah remembers. "Since I was producing, I didn't really get to sit and appreciate any of it, until the cathedral service. Once the guests were in their seats, and the VIPs were comfortable, then the Speaker of the House, the vice president and Mrs. Biden, and the president and First Lady came in and took seats. I went to the back of the church and cued the processional to begin, and that was it. Like any church event I produce, once the service starts, it's pretty much on auto. I took a seat next to my dad, who'd come down for the occasion. I sat on the aisle, just in case I had to get up to attend to any details. And then I became a worshipper.

"It was a beautiful service. Beautiful," she remembers. "The highlights for me were Maya Angelou offering a poem in her longtime friend's honor; Jeff Majors, the harpist, playing Psalm 23—from that day to this, it has been one of my favorite devotional songs. Of course, BeBe Winans singing 'Stand.' Lawdhammercy! The capper was Alexis, giving the closing remarks, reflecting on her long relationship with Dorothy. It was an amazing few days, and I was honored and humbled to be part of it. Dr. Height remained, and remains, part of my life. . . . I helped pack her apartment after her death. Found her Spingarn Medal in a box under her bed. Oh, and a letter or two signed by 'Martin.' *That* was a total pearl clutch. I helped transition NCNW to new leadership. Four years later, I joined the board of directors. And now I live in her old apartment, which she sold to me a few years before her death, and I eat at the dining room table she gave to me because it wouldn't fit in her new apartment."

Dr. Dorothy Height once said, "I want to be remembered as someone who used herself and anything she could touch to work for justice and freedom. . . . I want to be remembered as one who tried." Spoken like a true Colored Girl.

18

Love Extravagantly

On a personal level, as we grew in our careers, the Colored Girls were constructing our own definitions about what a fulfilled life looked like. For almost all of us, being married with children was not as critical, or as necessary, as it had been for women in previous generations. Marriage did not seem a priority partly because it wasn't the preeminent model among the women whom we came up with. Leah remembers that "not many of the women in positions of power were married. By my observation, they all dated, but very, very few married."

In Brooklyn, Leah had seen examples of traditional marriages with a modern, feminist layer, in "women like Atchudta Barkr, an unbelievable community activist who was also a fierce traditional African dancer, and of course the women in my church. They each could sing, cook, praise, preach, teach, lead, follow, make picket signs, lead marches and rallies, jump over police barricades, and serve as security. They were Everywomen."

Alexis Herman was, Leah says, "this interesting mix. That's where I saw someone other than the women in my church do the holistic feminine thing: be a powerful force at work, then go home and cook your husband's dinner, and do the laundry. Make sure your husband had clean socks. In the other parts of my life, women didn't do that. They were just a strong, focused presence, and frankly, their men had to fend for themselves. They didn't do the 'Let me take care of my husband' thing."

Leah remembers that when Herman was secretary of labor and she was chief of staff for Labor, the two women lived in the same building. Leah would tell her boss, "You're going home to cook dinner after a day like today? Really?" She clarifies that when Alexis Herman said she was going to cook dinner, it wasn't "Let me go to the supermarket and pick up a roast chicken" dinner. No, for Alexis, cooking dinner meant "Let me go to the supermarket and buy some collard greens and some sweet potatoes and a raw chicken, and let me go home and cook a meal."

Leah remembers, "I would just look at her and say, 'Are you serious? Make dinner? From scratch? Girl, you better make some reservations.'"

But Alexis loved cooking for her husband: "Chuck likes to have his collards . . ."

Deep down, Leah and her friends had a deep admiration for women of Alexis's generation, who could stand so comfortably with one foot planted in traditional mores and one foot in the world of modern work. "My friend Pat Lattimore said, 'That's why she's married and we're not. She's willing to do this when I'd say, "Baby, you better get good with takeout."'"

That was simply how Alexis Herman moved in the world. Leah notes, "She was tough as nails, hard-driving, dealing with these union presidents during the day, and then, in the car at the end of the day, she'd say, 'We've got to stop at the store on the way home so I can get some sweet potatoes. I want to make Chuck some candied yams.'"

The Colored Girls observe that for many of their peers in the world of Washington politics who did get married, divorce was a common, and not unexpected, result. As for her own single status, Leah says, "I've dated my fair share, but I suppose the work consumed so much time. As I climbed the career ladder, I encountered fewer and fewer black men, and I definitely wanted a black man."

Minyon didn't feel exactly the same: "If I was to get married, I would certainly like to find a decent, good man, and if he was African American that would be great, but it wasn't a prerequisite. I think, the older I've gotten, the more open-minded I've gotten in terms of what love is and what it looks like. . . . The more diverse your world becomes and the more you see people in different venues and different lights, your mind just opens up and your heart opens up. I would say my heart is probably more open to difference than it has ever been."

With the exception of Yolanda, we Colored Girls consider ourselves PANKs, or "professional aunts, no kids." Similarly, marriage has largely not been in the picture. That said, we have all figured out, in our own way, how to make love a central focus of our lives.

Leah decided "years ago that I wouldn't have children. For one, the right man didn't come along early enough in my life—though, I suppose, if I'd felt strongly enough about it, I might have had children even without the right man. But secondly, and most importantly, for a long time, I've felt that I've raised my children, and they are all grown now. Their names are Sharon, Dawn, and Herb Jr., and they are my two younger sisters and my only brother.

"My parents, being pastors and activists, were away from home most evenings, leaving many of the parental chores to me as the oldest child. That meant making sure everyone was home from school, that everyone did their homework, that dinner was on the table, that we all ate dinner together, that the kitchen was clean and chores were done, that everyone went to bed on time, solving fights along the way—and okay, participating in a few myself. And then there were Sharon's plays and dance shows, Dawn's track meets, and Dan's—what we called him before he got grown and decided he wanted to be Herb Jr.—biddy basketball and Little League games. My parents were rarely able to attend those things unless the events were held on weekends, so I went and watched and cheered. Every kid needs someone to watch them do stuff.

"When I went to college, it was my first time away from the younger ones, and I'd never felt such freedom in my life. I didn't know such a feeling of lightness existed—where you're only responsible for yourself, where your schedule is the only one to be considered, and where your own work wasn't an accoutrement to the main course of the kids' much more important priorities. What a novel idea and what a beautiful thing!

"So, once I was an adult, the appeal of child rearing had little luster. I felt like I'd done it all, except be pregnant. Now, my conscious mind knows that the role I played is far from all that parenting requires, but whatever more there is, I'll take a pass—the part I did was hard enough work. But that doesn't mean I stopped filling in, or being a third parent for my siblings. After all, there were college applications to help with, résumés to write, references to get, weddings to plan (and pay for), apartments to decorate.

"And then, joy of all joys, my sister Sharon had a son: my beautiful, smart, talented nephew Lorenzo. I could absolutely eat a pound of him, as my grandmother would say. I remember the day he was born—November 16, 1989," she says. "I was fortunate enough to be living in New York in his earliest years, so we spent countless hours together. His mother, my sister, traveled a lot as a singer post-divorce, and when she was away, Lorenzo stayed with me. And even when she was in town, she would bring Lorenzo to my apartment every Saturday morning and we'd spend the rest of the weekend together, just doing stuff. I reprised my role with Sharon, Dawn, and Dan, but it was way more fun this time. Today, he would tell you that I am his second mother. We have long conversations about everything and nothing. I am so proud of him. My biggest struggle is fighting against all societal elements to support him in being a real man who handles his responsibilities, pays his bills, and honors his family and his God. Some days it is easier than others."

Leah's brother and his wife have two sons: "Herb III (whom we call Daniel) and Myles. They are thirteen and ten years old. Daniel and Myles are so smart and funny. I could easily spend hours with them. I regret that I live so far away from them and miss out on their school stuff, unlike when Lorenzo was a kid and I went to absolutely everything. But I try to make it a point to have them spend their school breaks with me every year, just like Lorenzo did when he was a kid. They come to Washington and we do stuff. I have about a four-day limit before my patience runs out and they have to go." She adds, "I'm blessed now to have enough disposable income to be able to buy them stuff like the Wii, or to go and get them and bring them down for the White House Easter Egg Roll in the Obama days, or to buy Lorenzo a car or his first couple of business suits, or to help with school bills, or to set up college funds, or take them on trips."

There's a sign in Leah's kitchen that reads, "A Perfect Aunt Loves Them, Spoils Them, and Sends Them Home." She says, "That is totally me. As long as they are polite, well mannered, study hard, love God and their parents, and get good grades, I will move heaven and earth to get them anything they want, whether material or experiential. I am determined that they have the kind of experiences and exposures that enable them to move confidently in the world. So they can go to restaurants and know what fork to use, so they have passports and understand that not everyone in the world speaks English; so that they know what it feels like to sit in first class on an airplane, or to watch a basketball game from the stands *and* from a suite; so that they know how to eat Popeyes fried chicken in the backseat of a car *and* also order from a menu in a white tablecloth establishment—all so that they feel prepared to compete on as level a playing field as I can help provide.

"Every now and then, in rare moments of stillness and silence, I wonder if I made the right decision by choosing to be child-free. (I detest the term *childless*.) But then I remember the time I overheard a six-year-old Lorenzo tell someone that Auntie Leah was not allowed to have children, and when I asked him about it he said, 'Because, Auntie Leah, I'm all the children you need. And don't worry, I'll take care of you when you get old.'"

"I think the one thing we had in common," says Minyon, "was, with the exception of Yolanda, that a yearning for children was not our goal. It certainly was not mine. I can speak for myself pretty clearly on that point. Having no kids for me has been a choice and not an option. I didn't grow up with this burning desire to have kids. I have always thought being able to help provide and love my nieces and nephew was more than enough maternal instinct for me. It's been great to see them grow and mature into young adults."

Rather, as an aunt, Minyon found great joy in helping her brother and sister. She put one of her nieces through college. "She was the first one to go to college, and I wanted to help, because I wanted her to come out with an advantage of not being saddled in debt.

"She is smart as a whip. She's lovely, she's been married for years now and has her first child. My other niece is studying to be a nurse and traveling abroad. She was in the UK this winter learning about their health care systems. She is the compassionate one. My nephew is working for a prominent business leader. He is always mistaken for a basketball player, but he is maturing into a great businessman. They are all doing really well. My sister is a master's degree social worker. She works harder than any person I know in any profession. I mean she is just a hard worker—not just at her job, but with the church, with my family. She is the point person for the family problems and the family drama. She and her husband are both college graduates, had good government jobs, and retired early. My brother was the computer whiz—don't know where he got that gift from, but there wasn't a computer he couldn't fix. But even with degrees and great professional experiences, the thing I discovered was that those really hardworking people have to work twice as hard just to stay in the middle class. They made a comfortable living, but having a little bit of extra help didn't hurt. We don't reward the people that are doing the toughest jobs in this country, and so I was happy to be able to play the PANK role." It was the same for Donna. Being a part of a large family meant you had to take care of others, including her nieces and nephews—all seventeen of them. The oldest, Janika, was special. After Donna's mom, Jean, died, Donna took on the responsibility of motherhood by raising her niece.

• • •

In 2012, when Donna's father, Lionel, was dying, she looked to Tina and Leah for guidance. They taught her, both in word and by example, how to say good-bye. DC can be distracting. All of us can tell stories about being in rooms with presidents and power brokers, of all the holidays, weddings, christenings, and birthday parties missed. When Donna's father was sick and things took a turn for the worse, the Colored Girls urged her not to let the distraction of the work in DC make her miss the opportunity of traveling this last road with her father. Donna remembers, "Tina went home to see her mom until the end. And I did the same for my dad. I didn't know of the importance of having a good relationship with Lionel Brazile Sr. until I saw how Leah interacted with her dad, the Reverend Herbert Daughtry."

Leah has been praised for the subtle way she is able to be a presence of faith in the Democratic Party. She played, and continues to play, a similar role with us. An ordained minister, she is able to be both the keen political strategist and the hang-out-on-a-Saturday-night girlfriend the Colored Girls need. Her faith is on tap, available if you ask for it, but never something that she shoves down your throat. Donna says, "Leah is the holy Christian warrior woman. Her devotion to God, her love of family, her faithfulness keep us praying and praising God, an awesome God. Her friendship through fellowship has helped me love my own faith and get closer to thee. By the time my dad passed on, Leah had taught me not just in word but example how faith works in action, not just in prayer.

"Leah and I never could have been running buddies," Donna continues. "She's not a bar stooler, a profanity queen or Southern girl. She's remarkable in both character and wisdom. She's like a solid rock. So grounded that you can't see her blood veins. Thus, I never try to read her like I do my other friends. I let her thrive and then try to learn what she has said or the meaning behind it all."

Leah was on the phone with Donna as Mr. Brazile took his last breaths. "She was there with me as he was transitioning," Donna says. "Her words would be the last that he heard. Though we are Catholic and she is not, her prayers helped my family absorb the loss, and it strengthened us at a time we could have come unglued. Obama called my father a day before his death. My dad was still in a defiant mood. The president wanted to thank Lionel for his service. Before the president could finish, he chimed in: 'Mr. President, I'm so glad you killed that bitch. I would have killed him with my bare hands.'

"Soon after the president hung up, he called me back. 'Is everything okay?' I had to tell the president that my dad was referring to Osama bin Laden!"

After her father passed away, Donna turned to the Colored Girls even more profoundly. She had saved her biological family once, and before his death, her father had made her promise not to let their problems consume her. "Of my siblings, he said, 'I don't know how many more times you're going to bail them out. Let them fall, Donna. They've got to fall. You can't pick them all up. You've done enough.' My dad kept telling me that.

"He said, 'You've got to let go. You've got to start living your own life.'"

Donna says that living her own life took time. "It was hard, but I finally got the message. I bought a newly renovated house for me, and I've got a beautiful garden. And the garden is full of trees, shrubs, and flowers that I plant to honor my mother and my sister Sheila, who died a few months after my dad. Whenever a family member calls me back to duty, I plant flowers or trees. I got them out of New Orleans. I got them out of the flood and into warm clothes and decent houses. So now, every time they call with something, I say, 'You know, I'm planting some more trees.' I can tell you every part of this garden that [represents when] a family member called about some issue and I planted something rather than rush off to save them. I've got three varieties of different rosebushes. Then, back there, those are all my nieces and nephews. Every time they call up with something else, I plant more. And then when my older sister called with her blues, I got them plants; I planted tomatoes, I planted broccoli. My entire family is all throughout this yard."

All of us seemed to have absorbed the lesson August Wilson sought to teach when he wrote his play *Two Trains Running*. In the play, a character advises another: "You walking around here with a ten-gallon bucket. Somebody put a little cupful in and you get mad 'cause it's empty. You can't go through life carrying a ten-gallon bucket. Get you a little cup. That's all you need. Get you a little cup and somebody put a bit in and it's half-full."

For Donna, that little cup is her Friday nights. Sometimes she has dinner with the Colored Girls, but sometimes she has it alone. She says, "Friday night is my fish or shrimp or oyster night. Whatever is fresh and in season, I just go out. I find myself a place where there's good fish or oysters, and that's how I treat myself. I have to treat myself. I grew up with shrimp, crabs, oysters, and crawfish. I replenish my soul with good seafood. Good food and good company—that's a good life."

19

Homegoings

When Whitney Houston died unexpectedly in February 2012, we felt like we'd lost one of our own. We were all of an age such that we could have gone to school with her. Houston's music had been the soundtrack to our lives. The day of the funeral, Yolanda, in her role as the group's Martha Stewart, hosted a brunch at her home on Corcoran Street so that we could watch the proceedings together. Donna remembers that, on that day, none of the CGs wanted to be alone: "We wanted to be together, to laugh and cry. Unlike burying so many of our leaders, Whitney's death went to our own mortality and legacy."

The brunch was an unexpected gift. Getting together for a meal was always a herculean effort, with dozens of emails zipping back and forth about who would be in town and when. Leah says, "When the funeral date was announced, I originally figured that we would do our usual, and watch from our homes or hotel rooms and talk and text each other the whole way through. But when Yo offered to make brunch—well, who could turn that down?"

Yolanda remembers that "we all gathered in the kitchen, as usual, and watched the funeral on the small TV. We could have gone upstairs and watched on the big TV, but everyone loved that kitchen." Adjacent to the open-plan kitchen was a big leather sofa that everyone flocked to; there were bar stools at the counter.

Yolanda prepared a Southern-style feast: bacon, scrambled eggs, challah French toast, and fruit salad. The star of the table was her famous shrimp and grits. She remembers, "*That* was the day I found out Leah doesn't like grits, just the shrimp."

It was one of the rare occasions when we were all in town at the same time. "We drank champagne and had a wonderful meal," Yolanda says. "We talked about Whitney's journey and our own." Leah says of the Colored Girls, "We got there early enough to hear the commentators try to explain the rituals of black funerals to a television audience. Now, *that* was hilarious. Of course, there was the drama with Bobby Brown trying to be seated. The speakers were wonderful and gave us glimpses of a Whitney we didn't get to see."

When Donnie McClurkin sang "Stand," we stood and cheered. When CeCe Winans sang "Don't Cry for Me," the Colored Girls said they all "cried like babies." And, Yolanda notes, "we chuckled at the politicos who were jockeying to be seen."

Leah remembers being unexpectedly moved by Kevin Costner's story of Whitney's first big movie: "Costner was talking about how nervous she was during the filming of *The Bodyguard*. She wanted everything to be right, so she did her own makeup. But her regular makeup wasn't suited for studio lights, and it literally ran off of her face, to her great embarrassment. In my mind's eye, I could see her—her earnestness, her eagerness, *our* nervousness—as she stepped onto a new stage."

For Minyon, it was a vital, healing feeling to be with the Colored Girls on that day. "I grew up on Whitney's music," she says. "You immortalized these people in your mind, and they become family members. When they die so unexpectedly, you grieve, you cry, and you ask why. She seemed to be on such a great path at the time of her death. She was part of the iconic group of black women who taught us how to exhale."

Minyon was a longtime friend of gospel star BeBe Winans. Winans told a story at Whitney's funeral that spoke to Houston's heart and kindness. He recounted how he and his sister, CeCe, were about to embark upon their first major concert when they received a call from Whitney asking them to come over to her house. When they arrived, she took them to her closet, which BeBe said was as big as a church, and started showing them the outfits she had made for their tour. She had gotten the backup singers dresses, and had a suit made for BeBe and a dress for CeCe. Then she showed them her dress, because, she told them, she would be including herself as backup singer on their tour! Both BeBe and CeCe proceeded to tell her she couldn't come with them on their tour. It was the early nineties, and Whitney was at the height of her career. But Whitney wasn't having it. She told them that their friendship "wasn't a material relationship," that they were her brother and sister. She also told them, "Y'all are broke and I'm rich, so I *am* doing this." BeBe said that was the Whitney most people never got a chance to see.

Donna remembers that she brought her "old vinyl records" to Yolanda's house that day. "Whitney and some Michael Jackson, too. Whitney and Michael represented, in musical terms, what we had become in the political world: crossovers. Their music made me feel that the rainbow was alive and hope was still on the horizon."

Leah, the youngest Colored Girl, remembers, "Whitney came roaring onto the music scene in 1985, the year after I graduated from college. She was climbing the charts as an artist while I was coming of age as a full-grown woman, so it often felt like she had a song for every high and low of my life. Also, she'd cut her teeth singing in the church choir, so I felt a certain kinship. That voice—for me, you can tell a good singer by whether they can sing while accompanied by only a piano. No other instruments and no Auto-Tune. She was a wonder, and that voice was truly a gift from God."

It was precisely because Houston's struggles were so public that we knew that underneath the glitz and the glamour, when she sang songs like "I'm Every Woman," she meant it. Leah says, "When she got into trouble with drugs—I had friends and loved ones who were also struggling with addiction, so I recognized the 'look,' even though she was denying it. I hoped and prayed that she would conquer it, and I knew that, if she did, the Voice would be different, probably a lower register, and the world would have to adjust. There was a period when she seemed to be really, fully in recovery, and I was so happy and so hopeful. Then she died. It truly felt like the day the music died. I couldn't imagine anything more traumatizing."

At the end of the service, Leah remembers, "Ms. Cissy [Houston, Whitney's mother] was leading the recessional, and Whitney's voice came over the sound system, singing 'I Will Always Love You.' The kitchen got quiet, and we were all transfixed. The room was silent but for the sound of tears."

Two years later, in 2014, Minyon, Donna, and Leah made the drive from Washington, DC, to Winston-Salem, North Carolina, for Dr. Maya Angelou's funeral. Tina was already there, with President Clinton. Yolanda was with them, virtually and electronically, by text, email, and phone, and sometimes all three within minutes. Minyon says, "Funerals don't define our friendship, although we have, in recent years, found ourselves at the center of them—Ms. Coretta Scott King, Rosa Parks, Dr. Dorothy Height, Dr. Betty Shabazz, not to mention our own mothers and grandmothers, as well as Donna's father. And as we prepared to send yet another one of these women on their homegoing journey, the word that comes to mind is not *grief*, although that is surely present, but *courage*. These are the women who gave us the *courage* to live authentic lives through service and serving others. These women gave of themselves against amazing odds, and they met each day and each hurdle with a dignity, justice, and amazing grace that couldn't be questioned. It *disturbs* the soul to know that we don't have them anymore. As we drove from state to state to say good-bye to yet another of these titans, we were also reminded, as the words of Dr. Maya Angelou ricocheted across the country and around the world, how vital it is to write down what we know, because the truth is we lose a part of history every time one of these great women takes their last breath. I feel as though that would be a disservice to Dr. Angelou's memory and all that she taught us over the years, the greatest of which was her lesson on courage. As she would say, without courage, you can do *nothing* else."

It had been more than ten years since Dr. Betty Shabazz passed away, but for us, Maya Angelou's death evoked her memory as well. "I mean, we adored her," Minyon says of Shabazz. "I don't know why, but I miss her every day. It was something about her that was very innocent and sweet-like. I was much older when I got to know her, so I wasn't a kid, like growing up under Reverend Barrow, so I really felt like I had an adult friend in her. I don't know if it is because of the unexpected way she died, but I think I cried from the minute I stepped in that service until the minute I left. I cried the entire two and a half hours. I know I did."

These women were all different to us, and yet they are an important thread in our story. Minyon says, "These women, these legends, taught us that we were important, and that our service to our people and our country was not in vain. They were our connectors and protectors. You can't help but think about what is needed in this contemporary day to prepare our next generation."

During Dr. Angelou's service, Minyon says, "All I could think about was how grateful I am to have known her personally and have been the recipient of her teachings, her lectures, her love, kindness, and graciousness. It was a relationship for me that dates back several decades and that was developed through our family retreats, our conferences, our marches. There was never a time that a Dr. Angelou or a Dr. Shabazz didn't take any of my calls. Dr. Angelou in particular would always give of herself. You didn't need a title for any of these women to talk with you.

"Funerals aren't episodes for us," she adds, "although we have been at the center of them."

Just a few days after Dr. Angelou's funeral, we lost the great actress and activist Ruby Dee. Minyon wrote an email to the group that said with Dee's loss, "We can see, with clarity, that God is not whispering to us about the moment we are in. As the Scripture states, He is teaching us to number our days, that we may gain a heart of wisdom. These women held our hands. They lifted us up when we were low and they lifted us higher when we did as Zora Neale Hurston implored us to and jumped at the sun. During those years of quiet, when people felt that civil rights was a closed chapter in our nation's history books and these warrior women grew older, we invited them to lunch and made sure they knew how much we valued the roads they had paved. Now it is time for us to put them to rest."

It was within that context that we gathered for a Sunday supper, again at Donna Brazile's house, in 2014, shortly after the death of Maya Angelou. It was one of those rare occasions when we put down the mantle of purpose—"to whom much is given, much is required." There is a lightness to all of us being together that belies the constrictions of any numerical age. Donna was making gumbo in the kitchen, and Yolanda was dancing to Pharrell's "Happy." Minyon was giving the latest on what's going on, book, chapter, and verse; and Leah was cutting through the chitchat with her razor-sharp wisdom and wit. Tina Flournoy was there, too, her presence both beloved and appreciated. As Donna says, "We love to get down, but we need a Tina to keep raising the bar. Or, to put it more bluntly, Tina keeps our asses out of trouble."

Shonda Rhimes's *Scandal* was at the height of its popularity. It was a show we watched with interest, as we were all real-life fixers, Olivia Pope–like in our own realms. The actor Joe Morton, in his captivating turn as Papa Pope, doles out wisdom that rings true to how we had been raised: "You have to be twice as good as them to get half of what they have. . . . Get yourself some power." And always the threat that there was nothing worse than the wrath of your people, as Papa Pope reminds Olivia: "I am the hell and the high water."

While many black women share the experience of largely absentee fathers, it's notable that the Colored Girls do not. Each of us had strong and present fathers who helped build her confidence, shape her values, and guide her path. Rev. Herb Daughtry is beloved among the Colored Girls because, as we are fond of saying, "He's the last father we have left."

Leah speaks about the journey that led the Colored Girls from the voting booths of Louisiana and Alabama to conventions and the Capitol, all the way to the White House. She says the making of a Colored Girl begins with "the ethos of black people that black children learn from their parents from the beginning: 'You've got to be better. You've got to know more. You've got to study harder. You've got to be twice as good.' I think, in every instance, that's what you had: You know you've got to wake up earlier. You know you're going to have to work longer. You know you're going to bed later. You know that you have to know more than your white counterpart to be considered equal, even sometimes to be considered *almost* equal."

Leah saw the bar raised during the days of Jackson '84 and '88: "With Reverend Jackson, he couldn't just run for president talking about social justice. He had to master foreign policy, economic policy, and be able to get on a debate stage and talk about those intelligently. He had to." As for Ron Brown, if he had been white, there would have been no question about his being DNC chair, but "because he was black," Leah says, "he had to be able to navigate the big political discussions. Ron had to deal with the Hill and all of their insecurities, their craziness, and the leadership. I think that's the same thing with us. I don't know that we had anything more than anybody else, other than opportunity. The same rules apply. You better get up early. You better know the issue. You better read that brief and read it again, read it twice. You've got to know everybody's name, where they came from, where they're going. You have to, because you are black in America, competing in white spaces. The job requires you not to be prepared but overprepared."

Yolanda agrees: "I've grown a lot. I just think your confidence grows when you have successes. If you're never successful at anything, why would you have any confidence, and why would you think you can do anything? I think I had great confidence as a teenager. Then I went through a bad first marriage and lost it all. But I got it back because I had a solid foundation and lots of people who loved and believed in me."

"Then we happened to move in circles, in divine order, where an opportunity to play on the national stage was open to us," Leah says. "We took that same ethos that every black child in America has and walked through the door with that ethos. We always say you can't outwork us. One thing about it, you're not going to outwork a Colored Girl. What we don't know, we're going to make up for it in hard work. The Jackson campaign—we didn't know a thing about running a presidential campaign, but we knew how to work hard. Just being black in America means you have to be versatile, and you have to have a dexterity of language and a dexterity of movement, and be able to shift. Read the tea leaves of what's ahead, but also deal with what's in the cup right now. That's just how you are when you're black in America, because we deal with multiple cultures, and we are bi- and tri- and quadrilingual in this nation. I can speak black people. I can speak urban. I can speak old people. I can speak church people. I can speak white people. That's just how it is when you're black in America. By requirement, you develop this ability to navigate multiple worlds. That's what you saw with Ron, with Alexis: this ability to navigate these multiple worlds at the national level. For us— Minyon and me and the other girls—it was a matter of this was the door that was open to us. We took that skill and just walked through the door." Minyon adds: "We knew we had been given an enormous opportunity to not only make something of ourselves, but we also knew we were paving the way for other generations coming behind us. There was this unspoken assumption that these positions didn't just belong to us. Just like we had been nurtured and groomed by our leaders, we could do no less for other women and people of color. It was our duty."

The story of the Colored Girls could have been just individual episodes of *The HistoryMakers*, entries in the Who's Who of American politics. But the way we came together created something more powerful than our individual parts. We found in one another a lightness that counterbalanced the heft of the task before us. And in that lightness, we found a steadiness in a town known for double dealing, a "take off your shoes and stay a while" kind of friendship and joy.

On occasions like that gumbo supper at Donna's, if you'd visited with us, you'd have seen us not as power brokers or politicos, not as public servants or political hidden figures. You'd have seen us simply as girl-friends, standing in that rare magic-hour light, that time when being black and female meant every good thing that being a Colored Girl has ever meant or could ever mean. As Toni Morrison so eloquently writes at the apex of *Sula*, her masterful novel about women and friendship, "Girl, girl, girlgirlgirl . . . We was girls together."

20

Shoulders

One evening at Ruth's Chris Steak House in DC, we gathered for one of our catch-up dinners. We were gathered in the private room, better for privacy and uncensored conversations. It was 2015, and the nation was in the throes of celebrating the fiftieth anniversary of the Selma-to-Montgomery March. Donna had attended a small reception at Speaker John Boehner's office. The honored guest was Amelia Boynton Robinson, a voting rights activist who was called, by many, the matriarch of the voting rights movement. It was Robinson who convinced Dr. Martin Luther King Jr. to focus his efforts in Selma. During the first of three marches, each of them organized to gather crowds to walk the fifty-four miles between Selma and the capital, Montgomery, to register to vote, Robinson was gassed, beaten to the point of unconsciousness, and left for dead as she crossed the Edmund Pettus Bridge. The photograph of Robinson being cradled by a young man was shared around the world, a forever-enduring image of the day that would come to be known as Bloody Sunday.

Robinson survived the whips and billy clubs of the Alabama lawmakers. When President Lyndon B. Johnson signed the Voting Rights Act into law, Robinson was a guest of honor in the White House. Now she stood with Donna and other guests in Speaker Boehner's office. As Donna tells the story, Eric Holder, then attorney general, approached the 103-year-old Robinson and shook her hand, saying, "I'm so glad to meet you. We all stand on your shoulders"—to which the centenarian activist replied, with a slightly wicked smile, "Get off my shoulders! Get off and go do something." And we all burst out laughing! Donna says, "I loved it. It was so true." Minyon who was doubled over, saying, "Picture that. Get off my shoulders!" Leah chimes in, "Go get your own shoulders!" Minyon later noted, "Of all the people who fulfilled the mission of 'do something,' it would certainly be Eric Holder. Countless people stood on his shoulders throughout his tenure as U.S. attorney general. From our vantage point, he was one of the best U.S. attorney generals in modern history. He was also one of the most beloved cabinet members in the Obama administration."

It was a funny story in and of itself, but especially funny to us because, as black women who worked largely behind the scenes, we knew a thing or two about people standing on our shoulders. We're not matriarchs of the movement, not yet. On average, we're about the age Robinson was when she began to plan the march to Montgomery. But we identified with her because voting rights is a cause we never take for granted. Every election, each of us spends hours working the phones: How are they getting the word out about registering people to vote? Were people having problems at the polls? Were there carpools and ride services in rural areas? Were the polls open up late enough in urban areas? Did people know how early and how late the polls opened? And always, in every aspect of our work, we're looking to add women and people of color to the conversation, because, as Donna likes to say, "If you're not at the table, then you're on the menu."

We talked that night, at dinner, about Fannie Lou Hamer and how she had once said, "There is one thing you've got to learn about our movement. Three people are better than no people."

Minyon leaned across the table and nodded in agreement. "Hello, hello! You know, that's biblical: 'Where two or more are gathered together in my name, there am I in the midst of them.'"

There were four of us in the room that evening, and together we had moved mountains. We knew whose shoulders we stood upon: Rev. Willie Barrow, Fannie Lou Hamer, Coretta Scott King, Dr. Betty Shabazz, Shirley Chisholm, Dr. Dorothy Irene Height—the list was seemingly endless. But we were also crystal clear on one point: we had gotten up on our own two feet and done the work.

The planning for the 2016 Democratic National Convention started in 2014. Leah was named the CEO in April 2015, responsible for all aspects of the planning and execution of the party's quadrennial nominating convention. This was her second time in this role, and the first person in Democratic Party history to hold the position twice. Leah said at the time, "This cycle's campaign (Clinton versus Sanders) has uncanny similarities to the 2008 campaign (Clinton versus Obama) and is, interestingly and in many ways, a redux."

Leah notes now, "When I became the CEO, I had three candidates: Hillary Clinton, Bernie Sanders, and Martin O'Malley. It's really important, as the convention CEO, that you are evenhanded with everybody because you don't know who the nominee is going to be. I had the same situation in '08, when I had Obama and Clinton. You don't know." Two others had already dropped out: Lincoln Chafee of Rhode Island and James Webb of Virginia.

Everything about the convention has to be ready before the nominee is decided, and yet the plans have to be malleable enough to adapt. "You have to make a decision about a podium design before the first primary has occurred," Leah says. "You have to contract a producer for the convention before the first vote has been taken. You're making decisions about the shape and the construct and the foundational things of the convention when you don't even have a candidate yet."

Leah's role required her to be extremely neutral when the rest of us were already picking sides. She took regular meetings with O'Malley's team, with the Sanders people, and with the Clinton people to say,

"Here's where I'm at with the planning. Here's what I'm thinking about. Do you have suggestions? Do you have objections? What can I count on you to help with? Is this an area where you're interested?" She adds, "I had to do that all the way through till we had a nominee."

There was already dissension within the DNC ranks, and Leah did her best to navigate it. "There came a point, as we were getting into the platform process, that the Sanders people refused to talk to Debbie [Wasserman Schultz]," she remembers, referring to the then DNC chair. "Just out-and-out would not talk to her. They said she was unfair. So, they said, 'Leah, we will talk to you. We will not talk to that woman.'" It was a difficult spot to be in. I did and do consider Debbie a friend; she's one of the strongest women I know, and I believe, to this very day, that she did not get a fair shake during the 2016 cycle.

Because of Bernie Sanders's contentious relationship with the DNC, Leah became a key point person for his team, trying to understand their concerns, their issues, and their preferences, and sometimes having to engage in a bit of shuttle diplomacy between the two campaigns. "When we were naming the Platform Drafting Committee," Leah says, "I was the go-between as they each named their appointees, ensuring that each was comfortable with the other's picks, and navigating a solution when they weren't. People don't know that because it's not the sexy stuff and it's not what people focus on. It was that sort of balancing act I had to carry all the way through until we had a nominee."

Even the booking of hotel rooms became a point of contention. "Both candidates were preparing for the convention, and I had to figure out, so to speak, how to split the baby. So, I said the same thing to both camps: 'You get a hundred fifty rooms and you get a hundred fifty rooms. I'm holding on to an extra three hundred rooms. Whoever's the winner gets the additional three hundred.'"

Charlie Baker, whom Leah calls the "other white man in our lives" (after Terry McAuliffe and Howard Dean), was her main contact for the Clinton team. Minyon says of Baker, "Charlie has a heart of gold—he'll give you the shirt off his back. We became even closer when we worked for Hillary. He took a leave of absence from the firm to work full-time. Charlie is deceptively low-key. He likes to give everyone the benefit of the doubt, which is an admirable trait. But don't let the choirboy look fool you. He doesn't mind doing what it takes to reach his goals. Charlie, for me, has always been my foxhole buddy. He is definitely the person you want in a foxhole when things aren't going well."

Just as her father navigated the police brutality and civil rights campaigns of the late 1970s and the Reagan years by forming the Big Four, Leah did some navigating of her own by becoming a leader in the DNC. "I was trusted by all the camps," she says proudly. "I think that's the thread I get from my father. I can navigate through all of these players— which is not to say we were ever best of friends. But at least, when I called, they would take my call. I could call them and say, 'This is what we need.' We had a responsive, reciprocal relationship, which went through the convention."

Leah's role as the go-between became even more powerful in 2016, when the convention unfolded and Sanders wouldn't immediately concede. Instead, he insisted on a full roll-call vote. "Traditionally, you do a roll call, and then the nominee (who we all knew would be Clinton by that time) picks the state—usually it's their home state—that takes them over the top, and then the roll call stops," Leah explains. "That's what you normally do. Balloons come down, and everybody's cheering, and 'Yay, we have a nominee.' Sanders said no, 'I want *every* state to vote.' We had to engineer this whole thing to allow it to get all the way to Wyoming, to allow Wyoming to vote, which meant we had to do a calculation that would say, 'Okay, New York will pass, or Vermont will pass, or somebody's going to pass so that there's no winner.' It was just crazy. That's the sort of dynamic that we were dealing with."

"Hillary admired Leah's artfulness in terms of being able to work with all kinds of people," Minyon says. "But she also admired the fact that Leah knew how to put an infrastructure together. And in that infrastructure, she knew how to choose the right people and how to make sure that you had the right directors leading the departments. Leah has an unusual gift when it comes to leadership; because, first of all, she doesn't mind getting really, really talented people. It does not take any shine off of her. She doesn't mind giving people the shine. At the same time, she holds people accountable." Minyon notes that she and Leah had similar skills and have both run complex organizations with complicated infrastructures. "I think this is where Leah and I differ," she says. "I'll spend a lot of time managing egos and personalities. I don't mind listening to people's complaints, especially if people believe they haven't been heard. But in the end, work has to get done, and I am pretty matter-of-fact about that. Leah will only listen so much before she wants to get to the bottom line, which, frankly, works, too, when time isn't your friend and there are deadlines to be met."

Then, on the eve of the DNC Convention, Debbie Wasserman Schultz resigned, and Donna became the interim chair. "Under the DNC rules, Donna is automatically the chair," Leah points out. "There wasn't a conversation that went, 'Ooh, who should we get? Let's see. Here are twenty choices. Hmm, let's pick Donna.' No. The charter requires that the chair designate the next in line, if anything should happen to the chair. Donna was designated the next in line because that position that she held, vice chair for civic engagement and voter participation, is *always* the next in line. There's actually a document that the incoming DNC chair has to sign once they are elected. When Debbie became chair, she had to make that designation. And it was the same when Tom Perez became chair; two days later, he had to sign the papers that the vice chair, Louisiana state senator Karen Carter Peterson, who's the vice chair for civic engagement and voter participation, is next in line. When Debbie said, 'I'm going to step down,' Donna became next in line."

Despite the very real challenges coming into the 2016 convention, Leah remembers that "it was a very different experience for me personally than it was in 2008. I had a much stronger sense of my own power, my own personal power, and what I bring to the table, and my boundaries. In terms of staffing your team, I think it's something I learned in church. When you're in church and you are running an organization that is built on the contributions of volunteers, you learn how to treat people. When you are constantly aware that tomorrow this person could say, 'I'm not going to be here anymore, because I'm going to XYZ Baptist Church from now on,' or 'I joined the Cha Cha Church.' You learn to deal with relationships, and it's important how you treat people, besides all the biblical mandates. In the actual day-to-dayness of it, it's about how you treat people, and really treating people how you want to be treated."

Yolanda felt increased confidence as well. She says, "When Leah became CEO in 2008, I told her I wanted to do something. I have played many roles at conventions over the years, but I really wanted to support her. She said, 'I have the perfect job for you.'

"Speaker tracking and podium operations had traditionally been two separate roles. In fact, there was a whole fiefdom that had been created under years and years of white men running things. [Leah] said, 'We need to shake that up, and it's not rocket science; I have a memo.' And she was right: it was not rocket science. I combined the two roles and consolidated everything to fall under one umbrella. We got rid of what we didn't need, and I was able to recruit a slew of volunteers (including myself) to take over that operation. We brought in so many new people of color, who were either lobbyists or worked for members on the Hill, who would come to town for about ten days, pay their own expenses, for the most part, and they were all so grateful for that opportunity that never would have happened if the leadership hadn't changed. I've served in that capacity for the past three conventions, but I don't do it for free anymore." She adds, "In 2016, Leah was a different person. She was a real *boss*."

Once Donna became chair, she and Leah were "actually talking in person." Leah explains: "We were quiet on email because we were talking. At the convention hall, we could just walk over to each other and we'd talk forty-nine times during the day."

In October, then–FBI director James Comey decided to reopen the Bureau's case against Hillary Clinton, which stopped Clinton's momentum days before the election. The next few months proved to be hazardous for everyone involved. The hacking of the email accounts of the DNC, the Democratic Congressional Campaign Committee (DCCC), and John Podesta kept the noise between Clinton and Sanders supporters at a fever pitch as the Russians sought to discredit Hillary, destabilize the DNC, and help Donald Trump.

Even as a senior advisor to Hillary Clinton, Minyon depended on the training she'd received as a young organizer in Chicago. "Knocking on doors gives you a sense of where people are. I did a lot of door knockings for Hillary during the 2016 campaign, so it certainly hasn't gotten old. In North Carolina and South Carolina, it was me, Kiki Moore, Cheryl Mills, Ann Walker Marchant, Leah, Judy Bird, Marva Smalls, Ann Stock, Capricia Marshall—oh God, it was a ton of us door knocking. I think we did it just to figure out what people were thinking and how they would respond. We also wanted to see if people were energized. I did churches for her on Sundays, I did speaking engagements, I did it all. Partly because it's good when you're an organizer, your mind can't help but to go back to the ground. You really want to know what the pulse of the community is. The only way you do that is either you knock on doors or you speak at some of these community events."

Minyon explains that when you knock on doors, you're likely to get one of three responses: "You get the type of person that opens the door and they will say to you, 'I am already voting for her,' in this instance, or voting for him, 'but thank you very much for stopping by.' You get the second type of person, who's voting for your candidate but wants to tell you why they're voting for them, so you spend an enormous amount of time listening to them talk about the reasons why they're voting for their candidate and why they're not voting for the opposition. You have to have extreme patience. Then, of course, you inadvertently get the person that you know is not supporting you and they will not even open the door, and you know they're in the house. That's okay, 'cause you know what? We don't have to talk to all our friends. We try to talk to the people that are on the fence. Sometimes you can change their mind.

"I know we changed a lot of minds in Chicago working for Harold Washington, and we changed a lot of minds working for Hillary. We changed a lot of minds working for Reverend Jackson. Minds were certainly changed when President Obama ran his historic races. You've got to be willing to get on the ground. That's the thing. That's the danger in modern-day campaigns. Technology is such a heavy component of modern-day campaigns, it takes you away from interacting with people. I will assure you there is nothing like having a real strong field organization and having real skilled organizers on the ground that are going door-to-door and/or doing events in the community."

Minyon has been friends with the award-winning gospel singer BeBe Winans for years. "I love BeBe; he is like a brother to me. We both share a love for Nassau, Bahamas, where we often vacation over the Christmas holidays. In fact, that is where our friendship began to blossom decades ago. As the years progressed, BeBe has been there for me whenever I have needed a singer at an event, funeral, or simply needed a get-out-the-vote song for campaigns, which he did do for the election. He has no discretion on his kindness when it comes to his friends."

The Sunday before the election, Hillary Clinton was scheduled to speak at several churches in Philadelphia. "We were almost across the finish line," Minyon says. "I got this bright idea that she needed some stirring singing from BeBe to take her across the finish line. Mind you, this lightbulb went off that Saturday."

Minyon tracked BeBe down in Dallas. She says, "I told him I really needed him. Hillary needed him, although I don't know if Hillary knew just how much she needed him.

"The last couple of weeks had been tough. All I wanted was to hear BeBe singing 'Stand.' Without much coaxing, he agreed to take a very early flight out of Dallas. But he would have to leave, heading back to Dallas, for a Sunday evening event. He would be our surprise guest, in case something went wrong. Since this was [Hillary's] last weekend of campaigning, I thought, 'Let's go out on a high note. Let's give God the honor and glory.' We got BeBe from the airport and took him to a holding room. Senator Cory Booker was there. The congregation stood up with a Pentecostal welcome and applause. The senator gave a great 'sermon' before the sermon."

Cheryl Mills, Maggie Williams, and Maya Harris were all there. As Minyon puts it, "all of Hillary's girls were present."

The pastor took to the lectern and announced BeBe Winans. When he walked in, the church erupted into thunderous applause. Then he brought the house down when he began to sing "Stand."

When you've given your all and it seems like you can't make it through
Well you just stand. When there's nothing left to do,
You just stand. Watch the Lord see you through
Yes, after you've done all you can, you just stand.

While all eyes were on Winans, Minyon watched the candidate: "In Hillary's face, you could see a sense of peace as she rocked back and forth."

When the service concluded, Hillary greeted everyone in the holding room. But the show wasn't over. "Out of nowhere, Hillary and BeBe starting singing 'Amazing Grace.' We all just became mesmerized as we listened to them sing. She was glowing. There was a sense that she had done all that she could do. You couldn't help but believe God had this. Who knew that Sunday those two songs, 'Stand' and 'Amazing Grace,' would become a prophetic witness."

21

November 8, 2016

On Tuesday, November 8, 2016, Minyon was in the boiler room at Hillary's Manhattan office. She'd taken a partial leave from her job as a principal at the Dewey Square Group. She worked in DC one or two days a week, but she spent the rest of the time at campaign headquarters in Brooklyn. Joining her in the boiler room was a handful of colleagues, including Charlie Baker. She says, "It's so funny how Charlie ends up in our narrative all the time. Charlie was the guy we worked for on the Dukakis campaign when we did that sign 'We Are the Colored Girls, and We Shall Not Be Moved.' He was the one that was behind the scenes saying, 'Hey, listen, you guys stay where you want to stay. You come here to do this work. It's not about where you sit. He was our white boy advocate, and here he was again, still in the mix thirty years later."

Early that evening, no one in the boiler room mentioned conceding. Their focus was on what was unfolding in the states. They worked the phones, trying to get information from Democratic elected officials. Sometime during the evening, as results began to come in, President Clinton called. "Do we think this is going to close? Do we still have time to win this state?" Minyon explains that "the thing about President Clinton is that he *really* knows these states, so he was drilling us on areas. 'Have we gotten returns from this area? Have we gotten returns from that area?' He was just asking the strategic questions that you would ask in terms of where the votes were coming in from. Answering those questions gave him an indication as to whether or not we would be okay in a particular state. For example, he would ask, 'Have they come in from Broward County? Have they come in from Detroit? Have they come in from the suburbs of Detroit?' He looked at Michigan closely because, he knew how pivotal the state is in any election. He understood the demographics. Clinton had become adept at speaking to different audiences but delivering the same messages. His economic messages especially resonated with voters from all walks of life. That was particularly true in Michigan, where there was a large white working-class population and a large minority population. Clinton knew in order for Hillary to win the state, she would need both."

In those first few hours of election returns, Minyon did nothing but gather information. "We were checking in with our people who were out in the field," she explains. "Some of us have tentacles inside the campaign. Charlie, Michael, and I usually had operatives that were outside the campaigns, and they were elected officials and they were political people that weren't necessarily attached to Hillary's campaign, but they were running their own campaigns or connected to campaigns. So, we were checking in with them to see how things were going. Like in North Carolina, I met a group of activists and community leaders who were active in their state. So, we were checking in with folks that had their feet and ears on the ground. All day we were trying to figure that out. I called Congresswoman Gwen Moore from Wisconsin, and I kept saying, 'Gwen, what's going on?' and she said, 'Listen, we still have votes out in Dane County and the city of Milwaukee.'"

They worked the phones in Michigan, Pennsylvania, and states in between, but Minyon was starting to feel uneasy. "It doesn't feel right" was her gut instinct. "It's not closing right." She can't remember exactly when she and Charlie said, "Okay, we're in trouble." But even when they lost Florida, the mood in the boiler room was still "We keep going. We still have a path. We've just got to pull in Pennsylvania." As she remembers it, "We were still looking at Pennsylvania, Michigan, and Wisconsin. We were like 'It's not over till the fat lady sings.' Honestly, it was the wee hours of the night when they called Wisconsin and Pennsylvania. I don't know if they were deliberately holding, but the networks didn't call those states. They were like 'Oh, this is looking really close,' so they didn't call it."

Minyon stopped thinking "It's not closing right," and started thinking that there was a mystery to be solved. "This thing just feels undone," she told Charlie. "It feels undone." For over forty-five minutes, Charlie and Minyon spoke to President Clinton, trying to explain what they thought was going on. They didn't feel that they had accurate numbers in Wisconsin and Michigan and other states where the race was tight. Florida was in the balance, as it had been in 2000. Minyon grimaces: "We kept praying that we weren't going to have to deal with any hanging chads."

Several hours later, she got a call from the hotel saying Hillary was getting ready to concede. Two of her colleagues called from Hillary's hotel room and asked, "Minyon, can you get over here?" They believed that Minyon could convince Hillary to hold out a little longer. But Minyon said she couldn't. "By the time I get there," she reasoned, "no telling what else will be happening in these states." Minyon was resolute. "I just kept saying, 'Listen, it's too early, it's too early.'"

Then there was the matter of the thousands of supporters waiting at the Javits Center for what was supposed to be a victory party. Even months later, that visual is painful for Minyon. She says, "They put this plan in place to send John Podesta out there and to just shut it down.

Let the people go home, let us all take a breath, let's see if we can figure out what's going on." Right after John made his announcement, Minyon remembers that "I got a call from one of my colleagues at Peninsula that Clinton had conceded. It was numbing."

Yolanda began the evening at the Midtown apartment of a friend, Viacom executive Marva Smalls. "She's got a beautiful place on West Fifty-Seventh Street and invited people over for cocktails and hors d'oeuvres, and to watch the election returns early," Yolanda explains. "I got a hotel room right around the corner from where she lived."

Thirty people gathered in the apartment for what they thought was going to be a night of celebration. But as the results started to come in, another story was developing. "This can't be right. This can't be right," Yolanda remembers thinking. "It's the absentee ballots or something. Something's going to happen. This can't happen. It was traumatic."

Leah had gone over to the Javits Center earlier that day, since she had been tasked with hosting the hospitality suite, where close friends of the campaign would watch the returns. Everyone from the Mothers of the Movement to Governor Tom Vilsack to Vernon Jordan was there. The mood was jubilant and expectant as the crowd watched the returns come in. Leah greeted and hugged the guests, moving easily among them as they all waited.

As chair of the DNC, Donna spent her day in the boiler room, where Minyon and Charlie Baker had gathered, until she went over to the Javits Center. "My role was to monitor what was happening in the states and to field calls from the Voting Rights Institute," Donna explains. She began Election Day as she always does, calling into a slew of radio stations and urging people to get out and vote or simply stay in line until the polls closed. The call-in shows are valuable, Donna explains, because "when you're on the phone with people in various communities, they often tell you, 'Oh, there are problems. Our machines are not working.' Or someone showed up and they said they didn't have the right form of ID to vote."

Early that evening, Donna looked at the exit polls and felt that things still looked pretty good. Florida hadn't come in yet when she left the boiler room to make a round of media appearances. She told Minyon she would come back as soon as she finished. She remembers that she wrapped her last segment on TV at 10:49 and that she was "sitting there saying, 'Something is wrong.'"

She was looking at the numbers. In Detroit, President Obama got 591,000 votes in 2008, Hillary got 512,000. But there were more than 10,000 ballots cast provisionally. She says, "It felt too much like 2000. I tell people I feel like I'm the Ernie Banks of politics. I have great statistics but no championship."

By the time Donna returned to the boiler room, John Podesta had been dispatched to the Javits Center. Donna turned her attention to Flint, Michigan, and Philadelphia. "Donald Trump was clearly going to get to two hundred seventy that night if the results showed he had won those areas," Donna says, referring to the number of electoral votes Trump needed to win. "We didn't want to give up. And I don't think Hillary really wanted to give up, either."

Back at Javits, Leah's phone was going crazy. Texts coming in from the boiler room and from operatives across the country were contradicting the news reports. It was soon evident that the evening was not going well. "It was surreal. I had to keep my happy, optimistic face on because I couldn't and didn't want to alarm or upset our guests prematurely. But every time I looked at my phone, I was getting news that this thing was going south. I wanted to cry, but I had to keep smiling. I deserved an Academy Award that night."

Tina Flournoy, President Clinton's chief of staff, was at the St. Regis hotel with the Clintons. The night before, she'd been with the president for the fly-around. They arrived at 2 a.m. The team stayed in Westchester so they could vote the next day. She remembered that she had less than two hours of sleep. She got up, took a shower, changed, and the day began. Hillary and President Clinton voted, then went back home until that evening. Then the rest of the president's team dispersed for the rest of the day.

As fate would have it, Tina arrived at the St. Regis just as the Clintons were pulling in. She says, "You cannot imagine the level of security around her and Trump then. The street was blocked. There were tents around the entrance to the hotel, so you really couldn't see the entrance. I didn't pull up because my taxi couldn't get in there. But I got close enough to just get out and walk. And it was lucky: they were just pulling in, and I knew all the advance people, so I just rode up the elevator with them."

The Clintons had two whole floors of staff and working rooms at the hotel. The Clintons were all there, including Chelsea and her family. Members of the team were in and out of the suite all night long. Throughout the night, everyone was watching the returns, talking to people, moving around. It became clear, to the team, fairly quickly to us there, that there were problems.

Tina remembered, "All of us have lived through election nights. What you learn, particularly in one like this so tight and tense and fraught with emotion, what you know is that you'll hear and absorb a lot of different information and feel a lot of different emotions. All the balls are constantly in the air. Going into that night, we all thought she was going to win," Tina said. "So that night for me was just . . . you've got to take care of what's in front of you."

Tina was part of the conversation when Hillary's team decided they needed to send someone over to the Javits Center. She remembers they talked about who it should be once it was decided that Hillary wouldn't be going over.

That night, Minyon was scheduled to join the rest of the team at Hillary's hotel. She says that despite her close friendship with the campaign team and the candidate herself, once the boiler room was shut down, she didn't have the strength to swing by the hotel to make what would have been little more than an appearance. Instead, around 4 a.m., she asked one of the young advance team members who was at the hotel to go to the room they had reserved for her and retrieve her overnight bag. By this time, the Trump security team had the streets on lockdown, so the taxi driver pulled over and she met the staffer at the corner. The thought of seeing Hillary that night was more than she could bear. Minyon describes her ride across the bridge to Brooklyn as one of the saddest and longest rides imaginable. She drove up to her hotel. "My faithful little watering hole," she called it. She stopped at the front desk because she knew how much they were rooting for Hillary. All she could say was "I'm sorry." She went straight to her room. "I didn't want to see them, I didn't want to talk to anybody. I wanted to process it. At that point, I still didn't believe it was real because I still believed something went dreadfully wrong." Minyon answered dozens of texts and calls. Just a few short hours later, she would make her regular early a.m. "Super Six" call, with the five other members of Hillary's inner circle.

After the decision was made to send John Podesta to the Javits Center to shut things down, Tina sat with other senior-level staffers around a dining room table in a suite. As Hillary reported in her book *What Happened*,

"Someone sent out for whiskey. Someone else found ice cream, every flavor in the hotel kitchen." And after Hillary called Trump, Tina and other longtime members of Hillary's team, as well as Hillary, had ice cream.

At around 10:30, Yolanda and a handful of guests headed over to the Javits Center, where Leah was holding down the fort. When they arrived, they called Leah, and she sent someone to bring them up to the VIP suite. The first person Yolanda saw was Isiah Thomas, who was a friend. They hugged, and in his embrace, Yolanda started crying. She and Isiah exchanged what became a dialogue of disbelief: "This really can't happen. This really is not happening, is it?" Then Yolanda went off to find Leah.

Once she found her, the tears started again.

Leah nearly lost it when Yolanda showed up. They hugged each other, and the tears started flowing. But the embrace didn't last long—we knew people were watching us, and our breaking down would be a sure sign that it was over.

Yolanda called Minyon, who was in the boiler room. "What are we doing?" she asked her.

Minyon said, "John [Podesta] is coming over to make an announcement."

Leah whispered to Yolanda, grabbed her dad, Rev. Herbert Daughtry, who was watching the returns with her, and they eased out of the room and down to the bleachers to be with the crowd.

Yolanda, Leah, and Leah's dad all sat in the bleachers waiting. There were television broadcasts on the Jumbotron but no official announcement. Yolanda began texting Minyon: "Okay, is she coming over or what? What's going on? People are starting to leave."

While she was waiting, she looked up and saw that the ceiling was tented with two hundred pounds of confetti. The plan had been that when Hillary made her victory speech, she would symbolically shatter the glass ceiling. Looking up, as so many did, was a constant reminder of what lay in the balance.

When Minyon finally texted Yolanda back, it was to say, "Podesta's on his way over." Yolanda remembers thinking, "Okay, I'm out." In order to avoid the crowds, she, Leah, and Reverend Daughtry left the Javits Center before Podesta arrived. It was two o'clock in the morning.

Yolanda called her friend Marva and said, "I'm on my way back. I can't believe this is happening. I can't stop crying." Marva urged her to come over and not be alone. Yolanda sat with Marva pretty much all night, along with Marva's boyfriend, Walter. She finally fell asleep on Marva's couch. When she woke up, they watched the concession on television together.

Leah's dad dropped her off at the Hilton, where she was staying. Their car ride was conducted in silence. There was just nothing to say. Leah remembers, "As I got out of the car, my dad said, 'I love you, daughter, and it's going to be okay.' I hugged him, went into the hotel, and went right to bed. I was physically and emotionally exhausted."

Yolanda says, "I'll start out with saying I've never felt so helpless. I just didn't know what to do. I think most people didn't know what to do. When the shit happened with Gore, we fought it. But this one—I just couldn't believe she conceded so soon. It just threw everybody off. We all wanted to fight. Who knows what would have happened if we had done that? Maybe we really would have found out about Russia earlier. Maybe we could've had more impact on the Electoral College. I don't know. Who knows? But I'm a fighter, and I was just so heartbroken when she gave in so early."

"We finished the ice cream," Tina says. "I don't recall any . . . there weren't tears flowing. There weren't people going, 'How did this happen?' It was kind of like 'Wow. Here's where we are right now.'" Tina notes that in these kinds of situations, "Hillary is always the strongest person. She keeps it together."

Then Hillary stood up and said, "Well, I think I'm going to go to bed." It was late.

The staffers put stuff on the cart, pushed it out into the hall. There was no time, Tina says, to "cry about this, worry about this right now. Hillary's team had shit to do. What are we going to do tomorrow? Is she going to do a concession speech? If so, where? All that had to be decided that night, because her appearance was the next morning. And then we had to get the word out to all the staff and supporters and to the media. We did what I want to ascribe, not just to women or to black women. We did what people do in those moments: you do the work."

Tina may have been the only person in the room who had experienced that moment before. In 2000, she worked on Al Gore's campaign, as Joe Lieberman's traveling chief of staff. She was with Gore and Lieberman on Election Day and that night at the hotel. In the almost two decades since that election, many have forgotten that on that night, Gore was declared the winner. Tina and the team started making thank-you calls. Then the news came back that Florida was being taken out of the "win" column.

There was what seemed like an endless back-and-forth. Then Gore called Bush and conceded. Tina remembers that "we got ready to go to the outside event, where he was going to do his victory speech, and it's now going to be a concession. We get there, and it's at the war memorial [in Nashville]. We go into a room underground. And by that point, word had gotten to us that those Florida numbers may not be right." She shook her head, remembering thinking, "You cannot concede. You cannot concede. Once you concede, it's over."

Tina continued: "So, we're in this little room, and I'm in there as Lieberman's staffer, but I was a Gore person and that's how I got to be on Lieberman's plane, because the Gore people put me on his plane. And so, I was standing next to the VP when he called George Bush and said, 'I'm taking back my concession. We're not conceding.' And, to this day, I think, 'How is it that, I, a woman of color, was in the room during the two most pivotal election nights in modern times?'"

The "Super Six" on Minyon's morning-after-the-election call was comprised of senior advisor Minyon, campaign chairman John Podesta, campaign manager Robby Mook, campaign strategist Jake Sullivan, communications director Jennifer Palmieri, and campaign vice chair Huma Abedin. The focus of the call, she says, was "we had to figure out how to pivot her out of this, making sure that she got her speech together and that she had the opportunity to say what she wanted to say."

On the call, Minyon notes, everyone made an effort to be supportive of one another. "Obviously, it was a tough time for the campaign manager. So, nobody dared to utter would'ves, could'ves, should'ves. We were still trying to say what happened. I think this was probably the only campaign in American history that I will always go, 'Something happened.' Outside of Gore's campaign—where we know for sure. But in that situation, there was a logical path for them to follow. They did the Supreme Court thing, so that kind of gave the American people some closure. I don't think we have closure in this election, and I think that's what's so hard and so troubling."

After the Super Six call, Minyon called Leah, and the two women agreed to meet over at the New Yorker Hotel's Grand Ballroom, where Hillary was getting ready to give her speech. It was in the ballroom, with Leah by her side, that Minyon cried for the first time. "When I saw all those young people who had worked on the campaign, when I saw their faces, it just tore me apart," she explains. "Up until that point, I had held it together because I was really in my head saying, 'Somebody's going to figure out that something went wrong, and this is going to be all right.' I was thinking, 'Any day now, we're going to figure it out.'"

Facing the volunteers in the Grand Ballroom pulled the election into focus in an entirely different way for Minyon. She says, "When I saw the pain in those young people's faces, Lord have mercy." It's clear that the emotion comes rushing back at her because she is not visualizing a crowd, but rather, individual young women and men she mentored and became fond of. "That's when I realized, for the first time, this campaign was bigger than any one person," she says. "It was never really about Hillary. It was about all those faces that we never see, we never get to talk about. It was all those young people that don't have a champion in the White House. I thought, 'Oh my God, what will happen to them?'"

Minyon and Leah saw Hillary on the rope line, and she asked them to come backstage after her speech. There, she told them, "You guys are going to have to help me, because I'm not really sure what I'm going to do now." Minyon says, "It was very girlfriend-like. Everything about Hillary in that moment was very pure, and the word they wrongly used against her so often during the campaign—untruthful—came to mind. It was very real, very authentic, and very crushing."

On Election Night, Tina went to bed so late she nearly overslept. (She'd slept less than six hours in two days.) She walked into the Grand Ballroom at the New Yorker with John Podesta; they were practically holding hands. Sitting in the front row with John and the rest of the campaign leadership, she said, was "the hardest moment for me. If you see pictures of me at that point, I'm really holding back tears. Because I'm looking at her, amazingly, again holding it all together. My boss [President Clinton] was having a tough time. I think Tim Kaine was crying. That was a very hard moment. I always say this to Minyon and my boss—Hillary and I are actually a lot alike. I get her up and down. I get that the thing you must do is move on, continue to put one foot in front of the other. Focus on the work and not on what just happened. I can imagine that in the moment, she was thinking, 'I will do that when I'm alone and have time to do it, but right now I will not break down.' I would not have expected anything else of her."

Like Tina, Hillary had been close to her mother and inspired by the way her mother made a way out of no way. "Hillary talks so much about her mother," Tina says, with admiration. "Her mother had a tough life. And out of that life, she managed to be an unbelievably loving mother and grandmother. She did it by always moving forward and not—I use this word carefully—not wallowing. And she hammered into her daughter, 'Don't wallow.' Because that's the only way she was able to survive. It may be a generational difference. I think my mother was very much like that. You don't wallow, you just get it done."

Hillary Clinton is not a Colored Girl, but Minyon believes Clinton recognized in them a steeliness that is at the very core of her own personality. "We have this steeliness about us that causes us to have to keep marching on—and so does she," Minyon says.

"Obviously, there's no way in the world that we will ever know how painful this experience has been for Hillary. Partly because, in her mind, she doesn't have the luxury of just stopping advocating for the issues she believes will help children and families. She continues to believe there is so much at stake. She will press forward no matter how tough it has been on her personally, because in the end, that's what true public servants do."

Looking back on that evening, we all realized that the decision to concede came swiftly, and once the decision was made, there was little Minyon or any of her like-minded colleagues could do to convince their candidate otherwise. "Part of Hillary's character, which makes her so admired, is that she's a very focused and disciplined person," Minyon explains, ". . . especially when it comes to her beliefs about democracy and elections. She believes in a peaceful transfer of power. She also believes deeply that America must live up to its greatness for all its citizens, especially our most vulnerable. In many ways, this made her the perfect candidate and a great public servant. She will do everything that she can to make sure that the left-out, the locked-out, the least of those among us are included. With her, it wasn't a matter of her saying, 'No, I won't concede.' It was a matter of her saying, 'Our country is built on a peaceful transfer of power.' So, her instinct was 'I've got to make sure we don't send our country into chaos.'"

Minyon saw things very differently: "My instinct was 'Let's send this country into a tizzy until we can find out what's going on.'" She points to the fact that more than a year later, the issue of what exactly happened in the 2016 election, how much interference and from what quarters, remains unresolved. She speaks in plain language when she says, "All these months later, we're still saying to ourselves, 'What the freak happened in our country?' I'll admit that I wore them out about the Russians. And by 'them,' I mean the other Colored Girls. I kept saying, 'I'm telling y'all. Y'all better wake up.' I'm sure I sounded like some kind of crazy conspiracy theorist."

For Minyon, the scrutiny that would follow the campaign was dispiriting. Not because she couldn't bear the criticism, but rather, because there seemed to be so little focus on lessons learned. "There's a lot of debate about what the campaign could have done," she says. "Being a person who has worked in presidential elections for a long time, you always figure out things you could have done better. This is just an absolute fact. We didn't do this 100 percent right. But there were so many things that we did do right that this just felt so unsettling, especially in the places like Pennsylvania, Michigan, and Wisconsin and Florida."

That morning, after the concession speech, Yolanda walked back to her hotel from Marva's house. She remembers that she was "literally crying. Walking down the street crying. I remember feeling like I was in a dream or, really, a nightmare. I walked just two blocks, but the people I passed all looked like the walking dead." When she got to her hotel, she fumbled through her purse, looking for the key. Two doors down, a cleaning woman noticed how distressed she was and opened the door for her.

Yolanda says, "I just broke down and started crying, and she just hugged me. She grabbed me and she hugged me. I said, 'I'm sorry.' She said, 'No, we're all so upset. We don't know what we're going to do.' I left that lady a hundred dollars when I left. I just thought she was so kind. She was there when I needed somebody, and I appreciated her kindness."

After leaving the Javits Center, Leah remembers that she was in bed for three days. Her father called to check on her, and she explained that this was not what she thought she'd be doing. He said, "Well, okay. I'm praying for you."

Then he sent her a note. It read, "I know this is hard. Not what we expected. Undeserved. You being in bed is perfectly understandable. But if you want to get out of your funk, what you have to do is focus on somebody else and go help somebody else." So, Leah called some of the young people she'd mentored over the years, and invited them to dinner. "It was four hours with my 'kids,' as I call them. For many of them, it was their first loss. So, they didn't know what to do. And for all of them, like so much of the rest of the nation, they were confused, disappointed, and angry. By the end of the evening of talking, crying, and laughing, they all felt better. After that, I went home and I cried. I thought to myself, 'If I believe all the things that I preach, if I believe in the God that I serve, that I have given my life to, then I have to believe what the Scripture says: "All things work together for good for those who love the Lord." I have to believe that. I don't like it. This is not what I wanted to be doing. But if God is God, then I have to say, "Everything in divine order." There is something in this for me and I might not know what it is for five years, six years, seven years, ten years. But I have to believe that, or else the whole construct of my life falls apart.'"

In the months that followed, we would struggle with the Democratic leadership as it tried to rebuild itself in the era of Trump. Donna had to return to Washington, DC, and the DNC. The white working-class voter became the voter most likely to be courted, and women of color felt painfully sidelined. "Black women turned out for this election," Yolanda fumes.

"We turn out for every election. Men didn't turn out the way they're supposed to turn out, but the women did turn out. And white women did not. But we're always an afterthought. We're still an afterthought. We're sick of it. We're sick of it. . . . I think it's too very, very difficult to start a viable third party. It takes a lot of time. Although, you know, we should study Macron, in France, because he did that in a year. He took over."

In the months after the election, Donna found herself knee-deep in the transition work of closing out the campaign and readying the DNC for a new roster of leaders, raising money, downsizing the staff, and preparing for a new day. She was worried that people would forget that the DNC had been the victim of a crime. She leaned on Leah and her organizational skills to make it through. "I had to keep the party going, and I couldn't run nowhere. I had no time," she says. "Leah said, 'I want to help you clean up. I want to help you get it ready for the next officers.' And by January, Leah basically moved into the DNC to help me out for the last two months of my tenure. Yolanda and Leah became my transition advisors. I needed that. I needed to walk away knowing that I could hold my head up high."

Donna busied herself with offering her support where she could. She met with the Black Lives Matter millennials, with Bernie Sanders's delegates, and with candidates such as Stacey Abrams, an African American woman running for governor of Georgia. "When you're in the revolution, you don't get a break," she says wearily. "You don't get a time-out. But I had to learn how to grieve, because I was wounded."

Leah went from helping Donna at the DNC to cochairing the transition of the newly elected DNC chair, Tom Perez. "I wasn't expecting to have that opportunity, but it gave me a time-consuming focus as I learned about Tom and helped him design a DNC that would be reflective of his goals and objectives." Diving into such a massive project following the November 8 loss helped Leah reset: "I'd really had no idea what I would do next—I had been director of presidential personnel for the Clinton-Kaine Transition Committee, tasked with filling the thousands of jobs, including cabinet posts, that would be available in the new government. Everyone's assumption—including mine—was that I'd go into the Clinton-Kaine administration, at least for a short time. But now I was at a loss. The DNC transition work consumed my time in a good way. The DNC; my ongoing work in McDowell County, West Virginia; my church work; and a bunch of travel filled in every blank. By the end of 2017, I had traveled to twelve countries and thirty U.S. cities, working on projects, lecturing, preaching, and working with clients."

When the first one hundred days of Trump's administration offered shock after shock to the democracy, the Colored Girls were the activism equivalent of Donna's grandma Frances. That Louisiana Catholic woman prayed without ceasing. We organized without ceasing, offering our wisdom, insight, connections, and experience to individuals and organizations around the country.

Minyon explains it this way: "I have always thought that public service was something that you either inherently or instinctually want to do, because it's hard. Public service is not like this sexy thing. I'm unapologetic about my advocacy for black people, people of color, and women because I believe that we have been the backbone of this country. But the work that lies ahead of us is clear: what we must do is turn our pain into power.

"A lot of the young activists get recognized fairly quickly through media appearances. I believe there is value to that as well. Your issues get on the front burner quickly. And they should be applauded for using these mediums to raise tough issues without fear. It is also a sign of how things have changed. We were behind-the-scenes players. We started out supporting the principal until we emerged as the principals. I've never woken up thinking, 'Oh, I'm helping to shape American politics.' I would wake up saying, 'Hey, we've got to make sure that this work gets done right and make sure that our people are included.'"

22

The Colored Girls
Bringing U.S. Together

In 1996, Dorothy Height had an audacious idea. She would purchase a building on Pennsylvania Avenue, situated right between the Capitol and the White House, to be the national headquarters of the National Council of Negro Women. Dr. Height, at the time, was eighty-three years old and president emeritus of the organization she had led for almost forty years. She sat in her office at the NCNW, dressed in a purple dress, a purple coat, and a matching hat, and told a reporter from the *Washington Post* that the boldness of her enterprise was more urgently needed than ever before: "It is the times in which we live. Look at it: Affirmative action is threatened, the whole welfare reform, the whole shift back to states' rights—that is a terrific change. The conditions facing our people today are such that we need to develop national strategies to produce grass-roots results." Height aimed to raise thirty million dollars to secure the purchase of the building and to fund a nine-million-dollar endowment that would ensure decades of future programming.

The building, at 633 Pennsylvania Avenue, had once been the headquarters of Sears, Roebuck. In the 1800s, a photographer had a studio on the lobby level. Abraham Lincoln sat for a portrait in the lobby. The chair he sat in was still there. Before the Sears Building was built, the corner of Pennsylvania Avenue and Seventh Street Northwest was home to the Center Slave Market. In 1848, two teenage girls, Emily and Mary Edmonson, along with their four brothers and seventy other slaves, escaped from the Center Slave Market. With the aid of Paul Jennings, who was a former slave of President James Madison's, the two girls and their party devised a plan to board a nearby schooner called the *Pearl* and make their way north to the Underground Railroad. The Edmonson sisters and their group almost escaped. But the next day, when the slave owners discovered they were missing, they formed a posse of one hundred men to find what they called the property of "41 of the most prominent families in Washington and Georgetown . . . valued at $100,000." Motivated by the ransom money and what he called a grudge against "uppity coloreds," a freedman named Judson gave away the location of the *Pearl*. The slaves were all captured.

But the story was far from over. Paul Edmonson reached out to a reverend named Henry Ward Beecher and convinced him to rally his church to raise the funds to purchase the freedom of his daughters—which they did. It was her interaction with Emily and Mary Edmonson that inspired Henry's sister, Harriet, to write *Uncle Tom's Cabin*, the book that did more to expose the evils of slavery and sway the American consciousness toward ending it than almost any other. Emily and Mary attended Oberlin College, and Emily went on to become one of the founders of Miners Teachers College, in Washington, DC. For the next seventy years, nearly every African American who taught in the public schools of DC was trained at Miners, an exponential gift of education that touched hundreds of thousands of African American students and helped shape the citizens they would become.

All this is to say that when Dr. Height set out to purchase 633 Pennsylvania Avenue, she was not only planting the seeds for the sovereignty of future generations of black women who would heed the call to public service as the Colored Girls, but she was also feeling the weight and strength of history. The Edmonson sisters' planned escape from Central Slave Market, while not initially successful, would set the stage for a chain of events that would be the undoing of slavery. Two black teenage girls, held in bondage, had, upon the very site Height had her eyes on, accomplished that. What else could black women do, envision, imagine, and accomplish on that same hallowed ground? By her ninetieth birthday, Dr. Height had not only purchased the building, but also managed, with donations from those who loved and admired her, to pay off the mortgage. The National Council of Negro Women owned the building's historic tower outright, and it is still the only building on Pennsylvania Avenue owned by African Americans.

In the summer of 2017, more than two dozen powerful African American women gathered for a meeting convened by Rev. Leah Daughtry and Minyon Moore. The question on the table was what could and should black women do to leverage their political, economic, and social capital to move their communities and the nation forward, particularly in light of what was happening in the country post–November 2016.

It was part of what we called "the unplanned year." If Clinton had won, most of us would have taken on different roles in Washington. In light of that loss, though, after the grief and the shock had subsided, we decided to do what we did best: organize.

The women were all dressed as befitted a meeting at the NCNW, the house that Dr. Height built. Leah's hair was tinged blond, and she wore a purple dress (Dr. Height's favorite color) and beautiful floral-patterned sling-back heels. Minyon wore a stylish cobalt-blue suit, a silk blouse, and simple gold earrings. Many of the women in attendance or joining by conference call had penned an open letter to the new DNC chair, Tom Perez:

> *Dear Chairman Tom Perez:*
>
> *Black women have consistently shown up for Democrats as a loyal voting bloc, demonstrating time and again that we are crucial to the protection of progressive policies such as economic security, affordable healthcare and criminal justice reform.*
>
> *We have voted and organized our communities with little support or investment from the Democratic Party for voter mobilization efforts.*

We have shown how Black women lead, yet the Party's leadership from Washington to the state parties have few or no Black women in leadership. More and more, Black women are running for office and winning elections—with scant support from Democratic Party infrastructure.

Well, like civil rights activist Fannie Lou Hamer, who testified at the 1964 Democratic convention demanding Blacks have a seat and voice within the Party, we are "sick and tired of being sick and tired."

The Democratic Party has a real problem. The data reveals that Black women voters are the very foundation to a winning coalition, yet most Black voters feel like the Democrats take them for granted. The Party's foundation has a growing crack and if it is not addressed quickly, the Party will fall even further behind and ultimately fail in its quest to strengthen its political prospects.

Investing in Black women's political leadership is a solid return on investment, one that is rooted in facts and data. In recent years, Black women have proven to be the most active voting demographic in the nation. In 2008 and 2012, 70 percent of eligible Black women cast ballots, accounting for the highest voter turnout of any racial or gender group, proving that our voting power can and has determined elections. A closer look at the data shows that in 2012 Barack Obama won re-election by 4.9 million votes.

Black women cast a total of 11.4 million ballots, providing the margin he needed to win. This past November, even with a clear lack of voter mobilization investment and a decrease in overall Black voter turnout, 94 percent of Black women voted to keep this country moving forward by casting ballots for Hillary Clinton. In addition, on November 8th we saw important elected-office gains by Black women despite the otherwise dismal defeat of progressives during the general election.

The 115th Congress has 20 Black women—the largest number in history. The group includes Kamala Harris, who is the second Black woman to serve in the U.S. Senate, a body that has not had a Black woman's voice in 20 years. In addition, Lisa Blunt Rochester became the first woman and Black person to represent Delaware in the U.S. House of Representatives.

Black women also made important progressive wins in Minnesota, where Ilhan Omar became the first Somali-American Muslim elected to the state legislature; Kentucky, where Attica Scott became the first woman elected to the state legislature in 20 years; Cook County IL, where Kim Foxx was elected state's attorney; Orange County FL elected Aramis Ayala the first Black state's attorney in Florida's history; the state of Texas elected its first woman Sheriff, Zena Stephens; and Jefferson County, AL elected nine Black women to the judicial branch.

This February, in the DNC elections, we saw an increase in overall diversity within the officer ranks, but no increase in leadership representation of Black women. Since taking office, you have met with and listened to key constituencies. But you have yet to host a Black women leaders convening.

Organizing without the engagement of Black women will prove to be a losing strategy, and there is much too much at stake for the Democratic Party to ignore Black women. Following your recent announcement of your top staff hire, we are left with significant concerns about how the Party is developing its strategies and allocating its resources. In the absence of our inclusion in discussions about the Party's forward movement, we question whether the Party values our loyalty and takes our commitment seriously.

In this termed "movement building moment," how will you lead the Democrats forward? Will Black women be among those at the helm, helping to design the strategies, craft the message, mobilize troops, and lead the way—as policymakers, political strategists, activists, and elected officials?

We respectfully request that you convene a meeting with Black women leaders and activists where you can hear not only our concerns, but also our thoughts on how the DNC can invest in Black women's engagement and leadership moving forward from hiring of key staff and consultants to investment in training and leadership opportunities.

The time is now for progressive power brokers and the very Party that we have carried on our back to the voting booth, year in and year out, to make a sustained and substantial investment in our leadership and priorities.

We have demonstrated our commitment to the Party. It is time for the Party to demonstrate its commitment to us. We stand ready to join you, your team, and Party leadership on the front lines—but not as silent partners.

The letter was signed "In Service," and its authors included the Women's March cochair Tamika Mallory, as well as seven congresswomen: the Honorable Marcia Fudge (D-OH), the Honorable Joyce Beatty (D-OH), the Honorable Bonnie Watson Coleman (D-NJ), the Honorable Eddie Bernice Johnson (D-TX), the Honorable Barbara Lee (D-CA), the Honorable Stacey Plaskett (D-NY), and the Honorable Yvette Clarke (D-CA).

Leah began the meeting by saying, "If I could wave my magic wand, I'd have a gathering of black women. How do we collect ourselves and move collectively into the future?"

Minyon added, "You can't move the policy if you can't move the politics. Part of this is about engaging elected officials and electing officials who will carry our strategy forward."

Yet, Leah noted, part of the message was reminding people of the power and heft of black women and their vote. "You can't harness power you don't know you have."

Yolanda added, in frustration, "We did what we always do: show up and show out." She continued: "Black women continue to be a consistent voting bloc. White women are not. But we're always an afterthought. We're still an afterthought. We're sick of it. Leah knows what my goal is, and it might not be hers. But however this summit comes out, the way I feel right now, I would like to see everybody leave there and make a commitment to register as independent, and just support good people, regardless of the party."

In that moment, Minyon got uncharacteristically sharp: "I don't give a crap if we put another penny into this party. Our vote is our power. Congressman John Lewis tells us all the time that our most precious asset that we have is our vote."

The room was transformed, and the conversation continued in earnest: What do black women owe the Democratic Party? What does the party owe black women? All of it seemed to be particularly powerful because this group of black congresswomen, legislators, activists, organizers, faith leaders, and Colored Girls had chosen to gather at this historic spot: 633 Pennsylvania Avenue.

It was, it should be noticed, far outside the scope of any stereotypical depiction of the angry black woman. Later, the Colored Girls put it this way: "If you were to look at it as a discussion about the economy or capital events, it would be a businessman saying, 'I have most of the equity in this company, so I don't need you to ask me what else I am going to put into this. Instead, I need you to tell me what are you going to do to make sure that my equity is worth something?' It's the same conversation framed in a different way. And that's what we can't lose sight of." They noted, "If the same point were being made in a different context by white men, maybe even white women, it would be viewed differently. But it's the same point. It's a cost-benefit assessment, overlaid with a belief system."

A few months later, the women had organized a summit for 2018 called Power Rising. But within the party, tensions were mounting over the place and earned power of the Colored Girls and their circle of women of color. In October 2017, at the fall meeting of the Democratic National Committee in Las Vegas, rumors swelled that some of the Sanders loyalists were going to attempt to strip three of the Colored Girls, Minyon, Leah, and Donna, of their at-large membership in the party to make room for additional Sanders loyalists. For some unknown reason, Symone Sanders, an African American woman who served as national press secretary for the Bernie Sanders campaign, was also among those being targeted for removal.

Minyon said, "If they think targeting black women who have

committed themselves to this party as an avocation and not a vocation and have given more than they've gotten is a smart idea, then God bless them."

Symone Sanders told BuzzFeed News, "Perhaps if we stopped tying our politics to people and started to look at the issues, we could put the battles of the 2016 primary behind us. That's what I did and that's what I'll continue to do. But for the life of me I still can't figure out how black women continue to get the brunt end of the stick in this party. It's disgraceful."

In Las Vegas, Leah took to the dais to give a report on the now-concluded transition. After her report, she gave a rousing speech that seemed to settle the matter of black women's place, if not forever, then for the immediate future:

> Now, before I take my seat, Mr. Chairman, I'd like to exercise a moment of personal privilege. I have had the opportunity of working for the DNC since 1989, when chairman Ron Brown hired me. And for nearly thirty years, I was coffee maker, gopher, fax fixer, paper-jam clearer, phone-answerer, mail-opener. You name it—it was my job. I served as a staff assistant, a project manager, director of administration, chief of staff to two DNC chairs, and CEO of not one but two Democratic conventions.
>
> Four years ago, President Obama and chairwoman Debbie Wasserman Schultz acknowledged my contribution by appointing me as an at-large member of the DNC. I could not have been more surprised or more humbled by the honor I never imagined would come to me. And for thirty years of my formal work at the DNC, I have made opportunity and inclusion a hallmark . . . pushing and pulling the doors of our party open. Sometimes kicking them down to make room for Democrats from all walks of life to have a seat at the same table where someone made room for me.
>
> I have done the work. I have paid my dues. And I have earned

my seat at the table. And yet, over the course of this meeting, some unnamed, shadowy, increasingly noisy faction of our party has suggested that I and a few of my like-minded friends are the wrong kind of Democrats to hold membership of the DNC. That somehow, maybe because of my race, maybe because of my gender, maybe because of the brashness that comes from the combination of the two, maybe because I actually had history and institutional memory of our party, maybe because I chose to support the nominee of our party—I don't know what their reasons were. Maybe they didn't know that black women are the strongest, the loyalest, and the most consistent voting bloc of the Democratic Party. Maybe they forgot that we show up when nobody else shows up. Maybe they didn't know that black women control $1.3 trillion in the economy of the United States of America. . . .

Maybe they forgot. Maybe they didn't know. I don't know what their reasons were. I don't know their rationale. And they've receded to the shadows. So maybe we'll never know. But let me tell you what I do know. I know that though my name, and the names of Minyon Moore, Donna Brazile, Symone Sanders, and Jim Zogby were called this week, it's really not about us. We were just this week's targets. Tomorrow, or maybe even later today, or maybe even before this meeting is over, it will be about different names, different people, who don't meet some imaginary, ever-changing standard of what it means to be a Democrat. Maybe it will be because of the color of our skin. Maybe it will be because of our gender or our sexual orientation or gender identity, or choice of faith, or choice of employer. It doesn't matter this week's reason or excuse, because there are always forces that are looking to exclude people at a time when we need to be drawing the circle bigger. We have to be on guard against these negative, divisive forces. . . . We have to root them out, call them out, and expel them from our midst.

Let me tell you what I do know. I know that the Democratic

Party is the party of opportunity, fairness, and inclusion. I know that the Democratic Party is the party that fights for those who cannot fight for themselves—the least, the last, the lost, and the left behind. Those who have little. Those who have more. And those who have much. This is a big tent that welcomes all who are willing to fight for the principles we cherish. There are no litmus tests here. If there were, we'd be the Republicans.

We don't care if you're liberal-leaning or conservative-leaning. If you're left of center or right of center. We don't care where you worship or where you work or who you love. We don't care if we don't agree on every single line of every single issue. We just want to know will you work with us to feed the hungry? Will you help us to house the homeless? Will you help us to clothe the naked? Will you help us to lift the lost? Will you help us to protect the vulnerable? And if the answer is yes, then welcome to the Democratic Party. Welcome to the party that understands we don't have to agree on everything, just the main thing. Welcome to the party that understands you don't have to be just like me to be just like me. And let me tell you what I do know. I know that Donald John Trump is the president of the United States. Defeating him is where our attention belongs. He is destroying the very fiber of our country, and his every action is an affront to the values and principles of our party and our country. We don't have time or resources to waste time fighting with each other. Fighting with each other about who's the most progressive. Who's the most loyal. Who's on what committee. Who's got what position. Help me, Holy Ghost! We don't have time! . . . We are going to battle for the soul of our country, for the lives of our people. And we do not have a single person to waste. We need every man, every woman, every gender, every non-gender, every single person on the battlefield. . . . So come on, Democrats: We got work to do. Let's stop majoring in the minors and come together.

23

Alabama Godd*m

In 1964, Nina Simone sat down to write what she called her "first civil rights song," in response to the murder of Medgar Evers in Mississippi and to the 16th Street Baptist Church bombing that killed four little black girls on a Sunday morning in Birmingham, Alabama. Simone said she wrote "Mississippi Goddam" in less than an hour.

Simone, a preacher's kid, was born in Tryon, North Carolina. A musical prodigy, the sixth of eight children, she began playing the piano at age three. She was six years old when Billie Holiday recorded "Strange Fruit," a song she herself would one day cover. When Simone was seventeen, she spent the summer at New York's prestigious Juilliard School, preparing to audition for the finest classical music conservatory in the country, the Curtis Institute in Philadelphia. She was denied admission on the basis of race, a rejection from which she never recovered. Vladimir Sokoloff, a well-known and beloved professor at the Curtis Institute who had campaigned heavily on Simone's behalf, took her on as a private student instead. She began her career as a pop musician as a way to pay for her classical lessons.

As one of our great mentors, Cicely Tyson, has said, "Challenges make you discover things about yourself that you never really knew." If Simone had been accepted into the Curtis Institute, perhaps she might have become a well-regarded orchestra musician most Americans had never heard of. Instead, she took her classical training, her gospel upbringing, and the jazz and blues of her teenage years and added to that mix a fire unseen before in black female singer-songwriters. She was, quite simply, mad as hell. And because she was the one and only Nina Simone, she made music out of her fury.

She first performed "Mississippi Goddam" at the Village Gate in New York's Greenwich Village. But the recording that became a civil rights anthem was the live version of her March 1964 debut at Carnegie Hall. She begins the piece by lightly playing the piano in a playful swing that calls to mind the kind of Broadway ditties that the mostly white audience would have known well—a tune by Stephen Sondheim or Charles Strouse. Halfway through the song, she tells the audience that the song is a "show tune, but the show hasn't been written yet." Then she continues the song, which includes these lyrics:

> *Alabama's got me so upset.*
> *Tennessee's made me lose my rest.*
> *And everybody knows about Mississippi . . . goddam.*

The song was an immediate hit among white and black listeners alike. It was banned in the South, where radio stations broke the album in half before mailing it back to the label. In 1965, Simone performed the song at the Selma-to-Montgomery March as part of an all-star lineup that included Sammy Davis Jr., James Baldwin, and Harry Belafonte. (The success of "Mississippi Goddam" puts an interesting spin on the old joke "How do you get to Carnegie Hall?" with the response "Protest, protest, protest.")

Cut to 2017. The facts were simple and clear. Fifty-three percent of white women voted for Trump in the 2016 presidential election. Ninety-four percent of black women voted for Hillary Clinton. The aftermath of the election, in which Clinton won the popular vote but lost the Electoral College, brought a season of confusion and hopelessness to a nation that hadn't thought a Trump presidency possible. As Simone sang in her prophetic song:

> *Lord have mercy on this land of mine.*
> *We all gonna get it in due time.*
> *I don't belong here.*
> *I don't belong there.*
> *I've even stopped believing in prayer.*

Weeks later, when a disparate group of women began to organize across social media platforms such as Facebook for a protest march to take place on January 21, 2017, the day after Trump's inauguration, race—and racism—quickly came to the fore. Teresa Shook, a grandmother from Hawaii, and Bob Bland, a fashion designer from New York, originally called their march "the Million Woman March." Black women who remembered well the march of the same name that had taken place a decade before immediately called the organizers out. As one critic wrote on Facebook:

> Someone sent me an invite to this. The Million Woman March first occurred in 1997 by and for Black women, following the Million Man March in 1995 for Black men. I have already expressed in the group that I take issue with white feminists taking the name of something that Black people started to address our struggles. That's appropriation. My understanding is that others have voiced this concern, but it has yet to be addressed. I will not even consider supporting this until the organizers are intersectional, original and come up with a different name.

The name was changed to the "Women's March on Washington." Jia Tolentino, writing in *The New Yorker*, noted that the very name "still evokes black activism, but deliberately this time." It was a moment and a reference that would be lost on many who attended the march—that the United States of America is a country rooted in the work, vision, and culture of African Americans. That the name "Women's March on Washington" builds on the historic civil rights March on Washington only highlights the fact that the struggle for equality in this country, from the abolitionist movement to the modern civil rights movement, has been the blueprint for civil disobedience and nonviolent change not only for every disenfranchised group in America, but also for those who seek liberation and equality around the world.

Three nonwhite activists, Linda Sarsour, Tamika Mallory, and Carmen Perez, were invited to join the leadership of the march. Bland released a statement that underscored that "these women are not tokens; they are dynamic and powerful leaders who have been organizing intersectional mobilizations for their entire careers." She then urged white women planning to march "to understand their privilege and acknowledge the struggle that women of color face."

The response, as Tolentino reported in *The New Yorker*, was a firestorm. White women wrote Bland to say, "Every woman in our culture is a 2nd-class citizen. Period"; "Whatever your race, you're no better than trump voters with that statement"; and "Fuck You is my immediate reaction."

Despite the inevitable conflicts and differences, the march was a resounding success. More than five million protestors in more than five hundred cities and towns around the world marched in protest of Donald Trump's ascendancy to the presidency. It was the largest organized march in U.S. history—a powerful reminder that the right to march is one of the most influential tools of our democracy and, as has often been quoted, the power of the people is always greater than the people in power.

In Atlanta, Congressman John Lewis addressed the crowd at the women's march in his home state. The legendary civil rights leader told the thousands assembled, "I know something about marching. When I was much younger, had all of my hair and a few pounds lighter, I marched in Nashville. I marched in Washington. I marched from Selma to Montgomery. I'm ready to march again!"

The euphoria among the marchers swept the nation that day, and the Colored Girls were ready to take that energy and channel it into the work of creating lasting change. We knew that in order for the moment to become a movement, the participants needed to be willing to make their protests, their struggle for change, "not an event, but a lifestyle," as Minyon so powerfully puts it. They all remembered the words of Coretta Scott King, who said, "You do not finally win a state of freedom that is protected forever. It doesn't work that way. Freedom is never really won. You earn it and win it in every generation."

Then came the photo that seemed to capture it all: the euphoria, the schisms, the mistrust, and the work that still needed to be done. In front of the Capitol, three white women in bright pink pussycat hats stood smiling, taking selfies, and looking down at their phones. In front of them, a black woman stood alone holding a handmade sign that read: "Don't Forget: White Women Voted for Trump." She wore a hat, too. Hers read "Stop Killing Black People." And then, as if to say, "I see your six hours of marching and I raise you six generations of black female activism," she was sucking on a lollipop, unamused, unimpressed, but ready for the fight ahead.

The woman was Angela Peoples, then the director of GETEQUAL, an LGBTQ rights organization. The photo was taken by her boyfriend, Kevin Banatte. In the aftermath of the march, Peoples told a reporter, "There have been a lot of white liberals who want to bring white women and black women to the table to talk, but we can't have that conversation until you acknowledge the power and the privilege you're bringing to the table, until white women do some work for themselves and by themselves. . . . It's less about showing up and standing in solidarity with folks of color and immigrants, and more about actually doing the work in your communities to change some hearts and minds."

The idea of bringing black and white women together is an extension of the "Wednesdays in Mississippi" Dr. Height held during the 1950s, when frank, uncensored conversations between black women and white women were a rare and necessary step forward. Though the mission of equality remained the same, now organizers such as Peoples were calling for a change in strategy. It was the same sentiment Leah expressed when, on a bright Saturday morning in August 2017, white supremacists descended upon the college town of Charlottesville, Virginia, and engaged in a deadly, violent clash with protestors. The next morning, Leah took to social media and said, "Dear White Politicians, please do not go to black churches today and tell us how much you hate racism. Go to white churches and tell them."

We often say that "history is unbroken continuity." From Harriet Tubman and Sojourner Truth to Shirley Chisholm and Cardiss Collins in Congress; from Mary McLeod Bethune and Ida B. Wells to Dr. Dorothy Height and Drs. Betty Shabazz and Maya Angelou; to the Colored Girls and their circle, including Yolanda Caraway, Leah Daughtry, Donna Brazile, Minyon Moore, and their longtime friend and soul sister Tina Flournoy; to women like Angela Peoples and Women's March organizers Tamika Mallory, Linda Sarsour, and Carmen Perez—you don't need an Ancestry.com DNA kit to trace the bloodline of the Colored Girls. It is evident wherever women are working to hurry history along. As Dorothy Height liked to say, "If the times aren't ripe, you have to ripen the times."

On December 12, 2017, Doug Jones won the Alabama Senate seat vacated by Jeff Sessions when Sessions was named attorney general. It was the first major election of the #MeToo era, that fall of 2017 when a series of well-researched exposés by journalists took down a string of powerful white men who had been accused of sexual assault and sexual harassment that had gone unchecked for decades.

Jones's opponent in the Alabama race was Roy S. Moore, a conservative Republican judge accused of a long history of molesting teenage girls. The *New York Times* called the election "a referendum on decency." The voter breakdown was significant: 57 percent of women who voted cast their ballot for Doug Jones, along with 42 percent of men. But it was the breakdown along racial lines that made headlines: 98 percent of black women voted for Doug Jones, delivering him the victory. Jones became the first Democratic senator to win office in Alabama in twenty-five years. Thirty-four percent of the white women voted for Moore *despite the charges of sexual abuse and molestation.* Cue Angela Peoples, her sign, her hat, her lollipop. One retired white woman voter in Alabama told the *New York Times*, "I voted for Moore. . . . I just want us to get back to life the way it used to be." As the Twitterverse is fond of saying, "White privilege is a helluva drug." Yet there were signs of change in Alabama, too. Madeleine Bell-Colpack, age nineteen, told the *Times* that she voted for Jones because "I'm from Alabama. The culture [of sexual abuse] is rampant. That's why this election is so important to me—we have to get away from that."

What made Alabama different in 2017 was that black women weren't taken for granted as loyal Democrats—the media, the DNC, and a generation of "woke" young people took the black women's turnout in that state as a lesson in leadership. "Thank black women" became the rallying cry on social media, and it was pure Colored Girls 101 in how Americans of every color urged the Democratic Party to study black women's strategy and fortitude in their activism, but also to invest in black women candidates such as Tishaura Jones in Missouri and Stacey Abrams in Georgia. Senator Kamala Harris, the only black woman in the Senate, took to Twitter and urged Americans not to just tweet their thanks to black women: "Let's address issues that disproportionately affect Black women—like pay disparity, housing & under-representation in elected office," she wrote.

In an op-ed piece in the *New York Times*, "Don't Just Thank Black Women. Follow Us," Angela Peoples applauded the fact that black women were finally being recognized, not just for voting but also for the grassroots work of mobilizing their entire communities to vote. Peoples lauded organizations such as In Charge: Black Women Taking Action, in Virginia, which had engaged more than three hundred black female volunteers and contacted nearly five thousand voters and gotten them to the polls on Election Day.

Many would remember 2017 as a harrowing year in American politics, when the very fabric of the democracy was systematically ripped at the seams by the president and his administration. But black women did what they had always done: they showed up and showed out. In Virginia, black women delivered 91 percent of their votes for Democratic governor Ralph Northam. In New Jersey, Phil Murphy seized the governorship with 94 percent of the black women's vote. DNC chair Tom Perez took to Twitter: "Let me be clear: We won in Alabama and Virginia because #BlackWomen led us to victory. Black women are the backbone of the Democratic Party, and we can't take that for granted. Period."

Leah was heartened by the power of Colored Girls at the voting booth. It reminded her of her days in Brooklyn, in the movement, when people didn't have devices so they were forced to interact. "Social media space allows you this illusion of relationships and this illusion of closeness. In some cases, social media raises awareness of critical issues, as in the case of Black Lives Matter, and that's great. But in other cases, social media is a detriment. It's not really the same as a real conversation with people. It's easy to post something. We've created this society now where you never have to leave your house. You can have everything delivered. You don't have to have any human interaction whatsoever. You don't have to see another person except the deliveryman. There are a lot of folks who 'like' people's stuff. You don't have to do anything. I don't have to go to the rally, I 'liked' it. I shared it with my network, so what else did you want me to do? Actually show up? OMG."

She says, "I think there is something in the way black women communicate with each other. Some of it is social media and all that. I think we get it. Once we understand an issue and sign on to an issue, we are not shy about talking to other sisters about the issue. Whether it's our salons—you know there's a whole salon culture—or our church, or our sorority, or whatever organization we're in, if we're not in an organization

[then] the people on our block, our neighbors down the hall, or whatever. We don't have a communication problem because we're verbal people. Black women, we're verbal. We're going to find somebody: 'Girl, did you hear about such and such? Did you vote?' Then we take everybody with us because we're going to tell the whole household, the neighborhood, the whole whoever. 'Did you vote? God help the children in the house because you're going to vote and you're going to vote for a Doug Jones or Hillary Clinton, that's what you're going to do.'"

Kimberlé Crenshaw, an acclaimed critical race theory scholar and professor of law at the UCLA School of Law and Columbia Law School, told reporters of the Alabama Senate race, "In any other context, people who get it 98 percent right, they'd be at the head of the class. It's time for black women to be at the head of the political class."

When Maya Angelou was helping Dorothy Height raise funds to purchase the National Council of Negro Women headquarters at 633 Pennsylvania Avenue, she told the *Washington Post*, "The spirit in the African American woman has always been lively, vital and that spirit has kept us [as a people] alive."

In New York, where she still works for President Clinton, Tina Flournoy seconds Maya Angelou's emotion. She is unwavering in her belief in what black women and black people have to offer this country. Like the rest of the Colored Girls, she wants to make sure that we are not only looking ahead but also looking back. Colored Girls, official and unofficial, their parents, their teachers, their mentors, their grandparents, have given so much to this country already: holding on to the hope of democracy when the democracy did not recognize either their humanity or their human rights. As we look ahead to the elections in 2018 and 2020, we are gathering a tidal wave of strength by remembering from whom and where we came. "Remember, we as a people in this country have had to find our power in different ways," Tina says. "Our power has been our faith. Our power has been our love. Our power has been the fact that we wake up every day and say, 'I'm going to keep going.' It's amazing. It's amazing that we keep doing it. But that hope and steadfastness is an intangible power that people can't take away from you unless you give it away. We are a hopeful people. We are a forgiving people. As my boss often says, 'We are a people who believe in a second-chance God.' And we are. So, we are constantly moving forward in faith."

Donna, who campaigned for candidates in states throughout 2017, including Alabama, says, "I think this is an awakening. We're at a period now where women are no longer going to be defined by their gender, or restricted by society's norms." She continues: "The tradition used to be that if a man said, 'Stand up,' you stood up. If a man said, 'Go,' you went. But now these women are saying, 'No, me too. I am not going to allow you to disrespect me and to harm me.' So, this is a moment. It's an awakening, and I think similar to the civil rights awakening. We're going to see an awakening with women in American politics. Perhaps, if you look at it in reverse, some people say, 'Well, Hillary should have come before Obama.' Well, maybe it took an Obama and a Hillary for us to now have a new politics in this country. And ultimately, the shit that we're seeing from Donald Trump will dissipate, and we're going to see this new moment once again, within the next two to five years."

The Colored Girls ended 2016 in a moment of unexpected, almost crippling defeat. By the end of 2017, we were ready and rearing to go again. As Donna says, "We have not left the battlefield. That's what you saw when you heard Leah speak up a couple of weeks ago when they wanted to rip us off the DNC roster. We have not stepped off of the battlefield. And in many ways our journey started early in our lives and our careers. But we have yet to put our marching boots in the closet or hang them up on the wall. Or hang our gloves on the wall, because we still see injustice and we want to fight it. And we still believe that the table should be set with everyone with a seat."

In some ways, the way we move forward—constantly, propelled with energy and purpose and a great deal of laughter—it can be hard to remember how exhausting it has been to build the kind of careers in public service that we have. Over nearly five years of interviews, not a single

one of us has ever said, "I'm tired." Or "I'm exhausted." Just the ability
to talk about being tired seemed like a luxury we didn't have when there
was so much work to be done. Minyon says, "I think the hardest part
about how to figure out how to carry out legacies like Reverend Barrow's,
Ms. Coretta's, Dr. Betty's, and Dr. Maya's is people don't understand
that these women were heroes, but day in and day out, they were mostly
unsung heroes. Every day of their lives they fought on a different front.
Whether it was for women's rights or civil rights, they never gave up. But
people don't see the toll it takes on you and what it takes out of you. I
hope we can continue to honor them and their work. I hope we remain
a constant reminder that the work they did allowed us to sit at the table
and enjoy freedoms that they fought for us to get."

When people ask Donna for advice, she tells them, "To never grow
weary, to stay focused, and to bring others along the way. To ask for help
and never take no for an answer. We are indeed captains of our own
careers. Take charge. When it comes to career advice, I always say, 'Do
you want the long version or the short version?' The short version is 'Apply.' You want to go on TV, just apply. The long version is go out and do
something. Go out and do something so that people know that you are
a person who can be called upon to take action. And get results."

With her characteristic frankness, she adds, "I keep thinking to myself, 'When in the hell am I going to just rest? What cycle am I going to
take a break? What cycle will Leah take a break or Minyon take a
break? When are we going to actually sit back and say, "Wow, we can
rest now because our work is done."' You know, like old warriors of the
past, like John Lewis . . . our work is never done. And that's what it
means. I was reading what the pope said today in his encyclical. And
what he said about politics is about service, it's about the common
good. . . . He also used the word *respect*. But I also said that he could use
the word *love*. Our service is about love. It's about love of our country.
Love of our communities which raised us and nurtured us. And love for
the future generations who will have these remarkable opportunities to

govern, opportunities that were once denied to us simply because of the way we look. That's the story."

Scholar and Black Liberation activist Anna Julia Cooper once said, "When and where I enter, in the quiet, undisputed dignity of my womanhood, without violence and without suing or special patronage, then and there the whole Negro race enters with me." It is a lesson the Colored Girls have carried with us from Leah's days as a teenager observing her father, the Big Four, and the Black United Front; to Minyon, Yolanda, and Donna's early days in Jackson '84 and '88. Ron Brown understood the power of black women when he appointed powerhouses such as Alexis Herman and Tina Flournoy to positions at the DNC and the Department of Commerce. Angela Davis once said, "Black women have had to develop a larger vision of our society than perhaps any other group. They have had to understand white men, white women, and black men. And they have had to understand themselves. When black women win victories, it is a boost for virtually every segment of society." It was that boost that swept the nation after Doug Jones's victory in Alabama. Black women brought to the polls and to their mobilization efforts the selflessness taught by Rev. Herb Daughtry and Reverend Jackson and the "come as you are" generosity of the Skinner family retreats. The tide started to shift in American politics in December 2017, quietly and powerfully, because of the elegance of a Dorothy Height and the relentless imagination and creative grace of a Maya Angelou. It had all come down to that moment when black women did more than vote; they showed this country who they were at the core. And many understood that something inside black women, that they had nurtured, protected, and kept alive even in the darkest of days, could change a state, a nation, and maybe the world.

Minyon looks back on the journey of the Colored Girls, on what happened in Alabama and all that lay ahead, and says, "It really doesn't require a lot. Public service in its truest form requires a little bit of selflessness, and a lot of courage. More often than not, you are not going with the popular sentiment. In fact, you are going against what is popular and what is politically expedient. You are creating new and different attitudes. You are creating new and different ways for people to see you and understand you. Your very presence in a room sometimes makes people think differently, and so I think, in many ways, yes, we have created a lot of history. We have built on history, and there is still more history to come if people are willing to take up the baton."

She continues: "My mind stays in the framework of Harriet Tubman all the time. She has this quote that says, 'When you hear the dogs barking, keep going.' That's a favorite quote of Hillary's as well. We say it to each other all the time. That's the story of Harriet Tubman, and it's what we do today. If you hear the dogs, keep going. If you see the torches in the woods, keep going. If they're shouting after you, keep going. Don't ever stop. Keep going. If you want a taste of freedom, keep going."

24

Broken Friendships and Healing Spaces

During our Power Rising 2018 summit, a ten-year-old girl named Allana asked our mentor and friend Cicely Tyson a most important and thought-provoking question: "How many true friends do you have?" Some will tell you that if you are fortunate enough to have one true friend in a lifetime, you are blessed.

Because this book is as much about true friendship as it is about our careers, we felt it would be important to share with Allana and our readers the journey of true friends and what it means when you hit a rough patch in the road. And while we recognize that rough patches take different forms and shapes when you are dealing with lifelong friends, the real question is: How do you deal with it when you are going through the storm?

Over the years, we have had our disagreements and our breaks. Looking back, we see that the most significant seem to be connected in some way to a presidential cycle. The 2008 election was bruising for so many reasons. It was a historic election season, featuring a newcomer whom we'd all met and gotten to know and a veteran fighter who had opened doors for so many. Despite the bumps, the commentary, and the back-and-forth, we got through it.

Election 2016 was a sucker punch, challenging everything we believed about the potential and the promise of our democracy. But what came later was much harder. We've dedicated our lives to public service, and we are skilled navigators in the world of politics. None of us will shy away from the political equivalent of a street fight in the name of justice. But it is another thing entirely, to use the words of the poet Sonia Sanchez, when you find yourself wounded in the house of a friend.

We often think about what people most admire about the Colored Girls. And for us, it boils down to one word: *friendship*. That is what we are known for and why so many young people, especially young women, look up to us. They see us as a group of black women who support one another. We lift one another up, and we are there for one another during the good, the bad, and the ugly. We have become these mythical figures that young women are aspiring to be. While they rarely get the chance to see our differences play out in public, it is important for them to know that we do differ. We aren't a monolithic voice. In fact, the four of us couldn't be more different. But in spite of our differences, the glue that binds us is the belief that we are all aspiring to make a difference.

Spoken and unspoken, we share a trust that has sustained us through some difficult times. But as with anything in life, even the best friendships will be tested. Sometimes the trust is broken. And when you reach that crossroad, you are forced to deal with some painful truths and ask some tough questions.

The aftermath of the November 2016 election brought us to one of those crossroads, no doubt the most difficult we'd encountered. The campaign itself was probably the toughest we'd ever worked on, and the loss to Donald Trump was extremely debilitating. His Electoral College victory was truly devastating. We each navigated the aftermath in our own way, from disbelief to depression, from anxiety to angst to anger, from prayers to tears. We ate too much, drank too much, slept too much, worked too much—or ate not at all, slept not at all, worked not at all. In the midst of navigating all the debris from all that came at us during the attack on our country, our nominee, and the party we'd all invested in, we also had to deal with our own turmoil.

Yolanda was trying hard to get focused on her day-to-day work, but admittedly, she recalls having a very difficult time getting over this particular election. "Every morning, when I woke up and turned on the television, I was suddenly jolted into reality. It became like *Groundhog Day*. I got to the point where I couldn't watch or read the news at all. I couldn't believe (and still can't) that this happened to our country."

Minyon returned to her work at the Dewey Square Group while continuing to work on the closeout of the campaign. She says that being back at work full-time was "a welcome relief, but it was also a reminder that we still have yet to 'break the highest and hardest glass ceiling.'"

Leah found herself back at the DNC for yet another sojourn. "I walked in the door for one reason, to finish the closeout of the convention, and ended up staying to assist by producing the Future Forums, four regional town hall meetings to help the DNC connect with local Democrats and to give platforms to the candidates seeking to become officers of the DNC. It was the same model that Terry McAuliffe had used in 2006, ultimately leading to the election of Howard Dean as chair of the DNC."

As Donna has stated, "So much was coming at me; I was juggling so many issues after the loss of this election, and Leah appeared one day from out of nowhere. I saw it as a sign that God had truly not abandoned me in this, the worst political storm of my life." Donna welcomed Leah's help. "She became a godsend when she stepped in to help with those forums and the officer elections." Donna felt as though the Colored Girls were coming to help her close down a miserable and painful chapter in her career.

As time passed, Yolanda, Minyon, and Leah got word that Donna had begun to talk with her former publisher because she had become disillusioned and worried that no one would remember that the DNC had been under attack from a hostile foreign government and adversary. She eventually decided to add her story to the volumes of those who were also writing about the 2016 cycle. Though Yolanda, Leah, and Minyon were concerned that the content might conflict with this book, at the time, Donna reassured us that her book would be focused primarily on Russian involvement in the election and the related information that she'd learned during her tenure as chair of the DNC.

The truth was that Donna's stint as chair was bruising and deeply painful, with constant harassment and attacks coming from every side. We all felt that she had been unfairly targeted and criticized during the election, and we wanted to help her rebuild the party and get her back to the political strategy work she does so well. If her book would help accomplish this objective, we were all for it.

When Donna's book was finally released, we found that it was about more than the cyberattacks. She had decided to forgo the original narrative and relive the entire campaign as an eyewitness to history. When the excerpts hit the newsstands, Yolanda, Leah, and Minyon were all in shock. It was not the book they were expecting; they felt blindsided, as if the personal trust between them had been broken.

Donna explains, "When I began my writing and research in earnest, my thoughts around the book evolved." In hindsight, she says, "I should have let them know that I was going in a different direction, because so much of their lives had been invested in the 2016 election as well."

Now, there was no big blowup, no table-turning dinners, no thrown wine bottles. Instead, all but the most cursory communication stopped. We were, at turns, angry, sad, confused, and disappointed. We were thirty-year friends unsure of how to deal with one another. And after fighting so many battles together, it felt odd not to be standing side by side through the outrageous daily assaults being made by the Trump administration on public policy we had all fought for. But the pain was real, and the hurt was lasting for all of us.

For Yolanda, Leah, and Minyon, it was a matter of feeling misled and hurt. As for Donna, the strain of dealing with the ongoing turmoil inside the party and the investigation into the hacking led her to become more and more reclusive, and she pushed us away. Donna admits that she was more alienated than she let on, adding, "They should have known

I was in extreme distress, naked pain, crying inside as I was trying to keep it all together. They didn't see it."

The irony is that we were all in distress and in pain. We were all trying to keep it together for ourselves, for one another, and for those who were looking to us for guidance, support, and nurturing. Though we checked in and on one another frequently, more pointed emotional support was offered in response to distress. If you said you were okay, we believed you. If you said you weren't okay, we believed that, too—and a visit, a prayer, a long, long talk would be in the offing. We'd always been "say what you need to say" friends, and if ever there was a time when emotional honesty was easy to express, this was it.

That said, maybe we missed one another's signals, and maybe we didn't tell one another the whole rotgut truth about how we were feeling post–Election Day. We tell this story not to air our dirty laundry, but because we hope, more than anything, that this book will be instructive to the young women and men who are emerging as future leaders and friends. We have tried to lead our lives, in public and in private, guided by the highest ideals of integrity, character, trust, and honesty. But Lord knows, we have stumbled. And when we have, it has always been another Colored Girl who has helped us stand back up.

As we take steps to heal our friendship, we acknowledge that our circle is frayed. The outlines are still there, but the edges are faint. We build families wherever we go, and it hurts to have our little family in turmoil. We never have imagined an *us* without *all of us* in it. Of course, we're moving forward and getting our stuff done, but it's in spite of, not because of. Yolanda, Leah, and Minyon were happy that Donna attended the inaugural Power Rising 2018 summit. The moments we were there, all together in one room, felt good, not great—we all knew we had healing work to do with one another—but good enough to push us toward those hard conversations.

Now, we would not be us if we couldn't find a reason to crack a smile through the tears. We all had to laugh when Leah said that we had to fix this, fix *us*, sooner rather than later because "dammit, it's wreaked havoc with my email life. Can't use the shorthand group 'Colored Girls,' so I have to type out each individual address."

The renowned Buddhist monk Thich Nhat Hanh said, "Forgiveness is giving up all hope of a better past." Oprah expounded on this in one of her Super Soul Sunday tweets: "You think forgiving means accepting what has happened to you. It is accepting that it has happened to you. Not accepting that it was ok for it to happen. It is accepting that it has happened and now . . . 'What do I do about it?' . . . Forgiving is giving up the hope—not holding on, hoping, wishing that it could have been any other way than it actually was. . . . It's letting go so that the past does not hold you prisoner and does not hold you hostage."

In the end, we are a faithful people. Our faith compels us to forgive, and the hope that springs from our faith makes us know that there is a path forward for us and we are willing to walk it. That, for us, is the essence of true friendship! It might be slow going as trust is rebuilt. Baby steps. Baby steps.

Dinner is Tuesday. The place where friendships are made, broken, and healed. Yo and Donna are cooking. See you there.

25

Dear Sister Candidate

We are women of color in America, which means our lives, our very existence in this country are political. It is political because of the decisions that have been made for us and our community, decisions that influence and impact our lives and the options available to us. We have not had the pleasure of living our lives distinctly separate from the political decisions that were made before we were born, decisions that determined where our ancestors (including those who were enslaved), grandparents, parents, and we and our siblings would live, the opportunities that would be afforded to us, the schools that would be available to us, and the career choices that would present themselves.

We remember, as little girls, watching Barbara Jordan during the Watergate hearings—a strong, intelligent, persistent, powerful woman using big words and asking important questions. We asked our parents, "Who is that lady?" And they explained who she was and what she was doing and why she was doing it. We knew that we wanted to be smart like her, and strong like her, and persistent like her.

Over the years, we've thought about Shirley Chisholm, Barbara Jordan, and Ida B. Wells; about Fannie Lou Hamer and Wilma Mankiller and Patsy Mink; about Elizabeth Cady Stanton and Dolores Huerta and countless, *countless* others, and marveled at their tenacity and their fear-lessness. We might have once thought they could not possibly have imagined this time and this day, with women at the helm of business and industry, as governors and mayors, as teachers and police officers, as the nominee for president of the United States.

But that is simply not true. We have come to believe, with a deep head knowledge and heart knowledge, that the reason they fought so hard, that they made so many sacrifices, was precisely because they *could* imag-ine us, because they believed that one day we—activists, operatives, and organizers; elected officials and executives; married and unmarried—would be possible.

Because they believed that one day we—strong, accomplished, powerful—could and would *be*. They held a vision that, one day, a black girl from Brooklyn, like Leah, could and would be CEO of the Demo-cratic National Convention not once, but twice, the same convention that once refused to seat Fannie Lou Hamer. That a girl from the South Side of Chicago, like Minyon, would not only rise in the ranks of Jesse Jackson's Rainbow Coalition and become CEO of a major political party but also hold two major positions at the White House—assistant to the president and director of the Office of Public Liaison—and then go on to become the first African American assistant to the president and director of political affairs at the White House.

That a girl like Yolanda, from Rochester, New York, would go on to hold key leadership positions in every major presidential campaign, to advise and counsel such organizations as the Congressional Black Cau-cus, the Congressional Hispanic Caucus, the U.S. Department of Com-merce, and NATO's fiftieth-anniversary summit. That little Donna Lease Brazile, from Kenner, Louisiana, would become not only the first black woman to run a major presidential campaign, but also, not once but twice, serve as interim chair of the party that Bull Connor and George Wallace once called home.

Our foremothers *knew* that we could be union presidents and college presidents. That we could be members of Congress, and governors. That we could be on the presidential ticket. Hell, that we could *lead* the presidential ticket. They believed in this country and they believed in us and what we could and would become. That one day we would stand together, in one voice, fighting for the soul of our country. And make no mistake, we are fighting for the soul of our country. We have only to recall the events of Charlottesville, the ongoing travesty of Flint, the attempts to end DACA, to know that the soul of our country is at stake.

In the most recent elections, from New Orleans to Minneapolis to Charlotte to Framingham to San Francisco, black women had impressive wins in city council, mayoral, and state legislative races—and again, black women voters turned out in record numbers, helping ensure decisive victories in New Jersey and Virginia. But for far too long, the generational concerns of black women and girls continue to be underprioritized and ignored—often lumped into broader conversations without the necessary focus from decision makers. We have been campaign leaders in every major election since Jackson '84, supporting candidates who shared neither our race nor our gender; rarely seeing candidates in our own image. But the time has come to bring to the front of the pulpit all the wisdom, compassion, and leadership that comes from our unique intersectionality. As Professor Brittney Cooper writes in her book *Eloquent Rage*, "America needs a homegirl intervention in the worst way."

In 1977, the visionary black feminist Combahee River Collective wrote, "If Black women were free, it would mean that everyone else would have to be free since our freedom would necessitate the destruction of all the systems of oppression." Forty-plus years later, women candidates are stepping up to call out the powers that (for the time being) be on the destructive effects of their racism, sexism, classism, homophobia, willful environmental myopia, and polarizing ignorance.

Omeria Scott, a twenty-five-year veteran of the Mississippi state legislature who represents District 80, told a reporter that "In Mississippi, there is no color when it comes to being 50th in health care. There is no color when we're 46th in education, when we're 48th in the economy, when we're 49 among 50 states for opportunity. That's why we need to do something different."

We have elected an African American president, and yes, we have put a woman at the head of the ticket. But if communities of color were elected commensurate with their numbers, there would be 12 African American elected senators instead of just three: Senators Kamala Harris, Cory Booker, and Tim Scott. There would be 89 Latinos serving in the House of Representatives instead of only 30. There would be 31 Asian Americans in Congress, not 15.

And what about the women? If women were elected commensurate with *their* numbers, there would be 51 women senators instead of just 25. And there would be 275 women seated in the House and Senate instead of just 127. This is important because we claim to have a system of representative government. But you can't have representative government if the people aren't represented in government. You can't represent the people if the people aren't represented.

We must dare to enter the halls of power. We must match our rage, eloquently, with hands-on, practical activity. As Leah often tells her congregation, "Sitting in church all day won't make you a Christian any more than sitting in a garage will make you a car."

No one wants a heart surgeon who's never seen a heart. You cannot call yourself a musician if you've never held an instrument or sung a melody. Real athletes don't watch the game; they play the game. More and more of us must consider careers in politics: sign up, join up, get in the game. Practical, hands-on experience makes a difference and separates you from the pack.

At its "Run to Win" training sessions, focused on helping pro-choice Democratic women around the country run for office, and win, the PAC Emily's List has reported that black women are outnumbering other participants by huge percentages. Spokeswoman Vanessa Cardenas told reporters, "We know that black women are really driving the support when it comes to Democrats. It's very evident that they're supporting progressive policies, and they're the backbone of the Democratic Party when it comes to voting and participation. It is very real."

Women are making greater strides than ever. We are in the Congress, the C-suite, and the classroom. We are in the pulpit and the pressroom. We are everywhere, on every level. But as we climb the ladder and get our long-overdue seats at the table, we can never forget the sacrifices that were made for us to get there. The women who went before us, who cracked the glass ceiling so that we could shatter it. They did the hard work, and we owe it to them to continue the tradition.

First, Let's Remember Our History

When Donna was starting out as a young grassroots field organizer back in the early 1970s, it was difficult to imagine there was ever a time when women did not have the right to vote. It was even harder to visualize women not having a seat at the political table where key campaign decisions are conceptualized and implemented. Today, as women celebrate nearly a century in the political arena, we must remember that the road to empowerment was paved by activists willing to take on the old-boy network.

Back in Kenner, Louisiana, Rosemary Minor, a local civil rights pioneer, became an early mentor for Donna's generation of grassroots organizers. Raised in Jim Crow's segregated South, Minor taught the kids in her neighborhood to take their right to vote very seriously, to stand up for our communities, and to take on the responsibility of helping others. To many working-class families of that period, politics had little meaning, but with the encouragement of women such as Ms. Minor, people like us began to take pride in civic engagement.

By the time Donna turned nine years old, she was actively involved in her first political campaign. Minor assigned her to go door-to-door to remind their neighbors to register to vote, and to vote. Donna relished her responsibility to talk up the right to vote. As she rode her bicycle, she met many new people, and a year later, she received her first patronage job in politics: coaching a girls' softball league in her hometown. What a fabulous reward for political activism.

"Voting," Minor would instruct the parents, "would help to improve our daily lives and to empower our neighborhood." She was right. Rosemary Minor was not alone in her struggle to educate, register, and motivate citizens to get active and vote. Throughout our early career in politics, women played key roles in the electoral process—from volunteering for campaigns to fund-raising, to doing community outreach, to serving as poll workers on Election Day. Most of these women worked without the benefit of a campaign title or the formal recognition of their success, but their contributions often made the difference. Today, women campaign professionals have made great progress, yet some serious obstacles must be removed in order for us to be recognized as significant political players. These obstacles are not enormous, just burdensome—especially in the middle of a presidential campaign season.

For starters, most men in senior-level campaign positions refuse to allow women to develop winning campaign strategies. Often, men seek the advice of other men in developing campaign position papers or in writing scripts for paid advertisements. Women are often out of the loop when polling data are shared or meetings are held to discuss recent findings from focus groups. While women have made great strides in areas such as finance, communication, advance, and scheduling, the majority of nationally and statewide-recognized pollsters and media consultants are men.

In order for women to take their permanent seats, and not just the folding chairs at the edge of the room, it's time for women to be recognized for their talent and wisdom. We praise the work of veteran pollsters such as the late Linda Faye Williams, who worked at the Joint Center for Political and Economic Studies and taught political science at the University of Maryland. Dee Brown is a pollster and data analyst who works at Brilliant Corners with Cornell Belcher. She's the only African American woman we know of currently in that field. Thus, for women campaign professionals, the artificial barriers of exclusion must be torn down and removed. The best way to achieve this goal is for women to form the equivalent of the old-boy network and to create a new circle of empowerment.

The old-boy network has allowed men to assume critical leadership posts in government and in the private sector. Our advice is not to destroy their network, but to create a new national network to help advance women's careers in politics. From our perspective, the old network enabled men to move easily from campaign to campaign until they reached the top. Men also continue to push and support one another—and provide their male associates with business opportunities and contacts outside the campaign. Once the girls' network is established, we can use our growing power and influence to promote one another and to hire other women, especially young women. This network could be very useful in other strategic ways to advance women in American politics. The girls' network could easily help expand the number of women in the pipeline to run for public office. In addition, women campaign managers and other senior-level campaign professionals would be able to attract public attention and could help secure funding for female candidates. The network could train young women and help them secure jobs in campaigns or nonprofit organizations. As role models for young women, we could encourage a new generation to choose careers in public service. Women's organizations—such as Higher Heights, the Black Women's Roundtable, Emily's List, the Women's Campaign Fund, Emerge America, the National Council of Negro Women, the National Organization for Women, and Planned Parenthood Action Fund—could lend their expertise to help expand the network into a powerful political entity. This new network could help broaden the support for issues important to women and working families.

Minyon notes: "We have to re-excite the power of voting. When President Obama was running, there was sheer excitement. There is a theory that people will elect people that look like them, talk like them, or at minimum, speak to the issues they care about. For President Obama, I fundamentally believe that not only did they engage young people, young people saw someone that looked like them. Someone that spoke directly to their aspirations. People of color saw him. He embodied the power that we know we have when we vote. We have to start looking at how we elect people that reflect the population in which they serve. There's no reason why we should not have a woman as president, if for no other reason than our voting strength."

Finally, women campaign professionals need a network of our own to console, nurture, and inspire one another to keep going. Throughout our tenure in politics, we have leaned on our older sisters for advice and guidance. They have enabled us to grow, and to learn from our mistakes. Without the help of Rev. Willie Barrow, Coretta Scott King, Dr. Dorothy Height, Dr. Betty Shabazz, Dr. Maya Angelou, Myrlie Evers, Alexis Herman, C. Delores Tucker, Addie Wyatt, Lottie Shackelford, Lois DeBerry, Mary Frances Berry, Eleanor H. Norton, Alice Huffman, and Auntie Maxine, who often shared our pain and guided us with strength, wisdom, and imagination, it would have been tough for us to hang in there.

As the old slogan goes, we've come a long way, baby—from early women's rights advocates in the nineteenth century to second-wave feminists in the twentieth. And this new century will produce another set of remarkable women leaders, leaders who will usher in a new era of American politics. In each era, women have faced an uphill battle in challenging the status quo. It has never been an easy process, but the benefits to the succeeding generations are great. We owe it to those who have gone before us to continue the struggle. Ultimately, women campaign professionals will succeed not only in bringing more women into the electoral process, but also in helping to break the glass ceiling for women to achieve new heights at every level of public service, including as the first female president of the United States. Rosemary Minor would be proud to know we are still excited about spreading the good news about the right to vote and the need to bring other women into the room to take their seats at the table.

Power Rising

At critical moments in history, black women have always found a way to come together, define a new path forward, and make an impact in ways that change the world. However, not since the Combahee River Collective statement, written forty years ago, have we assembled with the purpose of crafting an agenda explicitly for black women, one that recognizes our unique needs. And yet, there is so much more to do to ensure equity, opportunity, and representation for ourselves and our communities.

It was in the tradition of the women who had gone before us (our grandmothers, mothers, sisters, and aunties) and in the interest of those who will follow our path (our daughters, our sisters, and our nieces) that we came together again, for the Power Rising summit, held in February 2018. Young mothers brought their newborns; at one point, the youngest in the room was four months old, the eldest ninety-eight. Congresswomen turned out: Representatives Yvette Clarke from New York, Marcia Fudge and Joyce Beatty from Ohio, Robin Kelly from Illinois, Brenda Lawrence from Michigan, Stacey Plaskett from the U.S. Virgin Islands, and Bonnie Watson Coleman from New Jersey.

We gathered there in Atlanta to create an actionable agenda to be implemented in our communities and nationally that leveraged our social, political, professional, cultural, and economic power and influence for the betterment of ourselves, our communities, and our country. We'd called our gathering of over a thousand women Power Rising, but as our friend and mentor Cicely Tyson reminded us, we've always had the power; the question was what were we going to do with it?

What Are You Going to Do with All This Power?

These women who've climbed to new heights, these women who are through the door and at the table, we want to say to them: Congratulations, you've made it! So what are you going to do with all this power, all this entrée, all this access? What are you doing to open the door wider for the women who will come after you? What are you doing to make more room at the table? How have you made the path easier for another sister? Whom have you helped? If you can't answer the question, then you're not in the business of public service, you're in the business of self-service. If you can't answer the question, then what's your point?

Yolanda says, "I can't remember the first time I met Kamala Harris, but I do remember she was still a student at Howard University. It was probably between 1984 and 1986. She was a part of Licia Green's crew—Licia who was the Ethel to my Lucy during the Mondale general election campaign. They were a decade behind me, but Licia adopted me as big sister, so I was pretty cool with her friends. I interacted with Kamala, through Licia, over the years, and we found ourselves together in Houston at Licia's fortieth-birthday party. It was a 'girls' evening' at Licia's house, and Kamala announced that she was thinking about running for San Francisco district attorney. My reaction was 'I'll come and run your campaign.' Fortunately, she had better sense and chose a person who knew the district and could hit the ground running. She won that campaign, and she's been winning every one since then. Minyon and I organized the first DC fund-raiser for her when she first ran for attorney general of California. (I did it at my home on Corcoran Street.) I continue to take pride in watching her become the leader she is meant to be."

Leah first met Stacey Abrams about five years ago, when Abrams was minority leader of the Georgia House of Representatives. She was visiting DC and wanted to have dinner with the Colored Girls, but Leah was the only one in town. The two had a long, leisurely dinner at Corduroy—excellent food, great service, and a quiet atmosphere; perfect for good conversation. Stacey and Leah soon realized they had a lot in common, including being preachers' kids. Stacey's also fairly no-nonsense, and really, really smart. They talked a lot about politics—national and Georgian, friends in common, future plans, among other things.

They kept in touch over the years, and when Stacey announced for governor, Leah wasn't surprised. Abrams is immensely talented, and the

Colored Girls knew immediately that we would support her. We gave money, offered advice, attended events, and talked about her candidacy whenever we got the chance. Of course, we were disappointed when she didn't win, but we were thrilled to see her take her place on the national stage.

Minyon met Aja Brown shortly after Brown was elected to mayor of Compton, California, in 2013. "Alix Dejean, on my staff, brought it to my attention," Minyon says. "Of course! I wanted to meet *her* as well. She had just pulled off an impressive victory by defeating Eric J. Perrodin, the incumbent mayor, and Omar Bradley, a former mayor.

"The day we were scheduled to meet," Minyon says, "I was immediately struck by how young she was. . . . She was just thirty, but appeared even younger. Yet she was very poised and self-confident—not in an arrogant way, but in a way that projected she would make a good leader.

"As she began to speak, I remember how clear she was about her vision for the city of Compton. During our conversation, I found her ideas to be fresh and forward-looking. She had a great understanding of the city and what was needed to get the unemployment down, to raise the hope of the young people in the city, and to make sure health care services were available to all. There was no doubt in my mind that she was ready to take on the tough issues of governing a city that, more often than not, had been forgotten."

In 2014, Aja Brown took the brave step of beginning peace negotiations with the Compton Bloods and Crips. Due to those regular meetings, violent crime in Compton has decreased an incredible 65 percent. That's the lowest it's been in twenty-five years, nearly Brown's entire lifetime. Her fans include Serena Williams, who grew up in Compton. "She just seemed to be a little bit different, her being a woman and her wanting to stand up and lead," Williams told *Elle* magazine. "She's talking about these big changes, and she's this young, driven individual in a way that's so inspiring for me, because I look at her and I think, What have *I* done? She's not doing a little bit. She's going all the way."

Minyon is also a fan of Ayanna Pressley, the first woman of color to win a seat on the Boston City Council. In 2018, she ran for Congress and won. Minyon says, "I met Ayanna Pressley when she was serving as the political director for then-Senator John Kerry. She soon became one of my mentees. She was very impressive right off the bat, and it certainly didn't hurt that she was a native Chicagoan. Ayanna has always had something in her spirit that has caused her to never rest on her laurels. When she sets her sights on something, she goes for it. When she decided to run for city council in a crowded field of fifteen candidates, she was the only woman and the only person of color. She won that race and became the first woman of color to serve on the Boston City Council. I know it shocked some of the establishment, but she didn't let the naysayers deter her. Her background, her upbringing have given her a steadfastness that makes her unflappable in all circumstances. I am so proud to see that she decided to seek higher office. She is everything we want on a national level. I expect to see her soar."

Lucia McBath lost her son, Jordan Davis, to gun violence in Florida. He was shot and killed at a gas station by an assailant who complained that Jordan was "playing his music too loud." Jordan was only seventeen years old. Lucia has done incredible work in the public sector, turning her pain into power.

She is now running for Congress in the Sixth District in Atlanta. The Colored Girls held a fund-raiser for her. We believe that the Parkland school shootings, along with the activism McBath is witnessing with students and moms, convinced her that she needs to be a part of helping to shape federal laws when it comes to the health and safety of families and children. She is also one of the "mothers of the movement," and campaigned vigorously for Hillary Clinton.

Yolanda feels a particular kinship with McBath: "She struck me so because we are both members of that dreaded club, parents who have lost a child. I know the kind of pain she's in, but she keeps it moving to honor her son. It's an amazing sight, to see someone go through the worst of tragedies and not fall into a sunken place. I've been there. I know how hard it is."

If You're Ready to Take Your Seat at the Table

For those of you who choose not to serve in elective office or even get involved in party politics, don't let that become a deterrent to becoming actively involved in public service or activism. Minyon notes, "I am reminded of my own sister, who has spent her entire career as an administrator and social worker. She is a daily advocate, working on behalf of our nation's vulnerable children and families. Saving children, searching for the right environment and homes for them to live a productive and healthy life—hers is a profession so noble and honorable."

We hold up and celebrate the women who are now serving in the military, on the police force, and as first responders and teachers. Every day, they sacrifice their lives so that ours can be better—public service at its finest. They remind us to heed the words of Maya Angelou, who said, "I've learned that you shouldn't go through life with a catcher's mitt on both hands; you need to be able to throw something back."

We also watch with great enthusiasm and joy the young women of color taking up the sword—their pens. They are writing our history and studying our history. They are becoming the new Toni Morrisons, Zora Neale Hurstons, and Dr. Maya Angelous. We are thrilled by the rise of so many black women filmmakers, too: Gina Prince-Bythewood, Felicia Henderson, Mara Brock Akil, Dee Rees, Lena Waithe, and Ava DuVernay, to name just a few. They stand on the shoulders of such pioneers as Oscar Micheaux and our very own Julie Dash. These newcomers are looking at the images and words of black women in particular, and women in general, in a way that we have longed and hoped for. They are using their power to write and tell authentically beautiful stories about who we are.

We also watch with joy the new young political TV commentators. We look at them and say, "We are in good hands. This next generation is conscious and fearless." They are ready to take on tough issues and policies that will impact generations of children not yet born. They are setting the record straight and using their voices to help amplify our truths.

And we are thrilled to see that people are thinking about not one black woman for president, but *several*. Isn't it a glorious day when you aren't discussing "the only one"? Whether these potential candidates share our dreams and hopes is left to be seen, but it is encouraging and noteworthy to know that this, too, is a first in history—to have not one, not two, but *several* black women held in this high regard. Senator Kamala Harris, a brilliant lawyer and advocate for human rights, was touted as a presidential candidate from the moment she set foot on the national scene. As a senator, she continues to be an outspoken advocate for equal rights and equal protection under the law.

Oprah Winfrey has spent most of her years as a business leader, TV talk show host, and philanthropist. Although she is currently saying she won't run, she is one of the most recognizable women in the world. She has emerged as a voice of reason at a time when the country seems to be looking as much for moral leadership as for political leadership.

While our former First Lady Michelle Obama has expressed no interest in the job, it is still significant that young women know that not only did she serve our country with distinction as First Lady, but also the credentials she earned before becoming First Lady more than qualify her to be considered a presidential candidate. Whether one of us becomes a First Lady of the United States or the first black female president, it is a life to be emulated.

As Dr. King reminds us, "Everybody can be great . . . because anybody can serve. You don't need a college degree to serve. You don't have to make your subject and verb agree to serve. You only need a heart full of grace and a soul generated by love." We have hope that tomorrow will be better than today because we can *all* serve.

We hope that at least some of you who read this book will decide to run for office. That's a good thing. Overdue, we say. But first, a question: We know you're ready to lead. But are you ready to serve? Do you really want a life of public service? Of putting the people's interests before your personal interests?

This idea of service goes far beyond elected office. Wherever you are, in whatever industry or sector, you must ask yourself: What am I doing to make the world better, to make life better for the people in my community?

Service is inherently about other people. Service centers on those who are being served, not those who are serving. It requires selflessness and a heart for giving. It is this that undergirds the idea of servant leadership, an old concept in the Christian church now made new: servants who lead, leaders who serve. The notion of servant leadership assumes that no matter where we find ourselves on the spectrum, leadership must be seen, in word and deed, as a form of service, and our service, likewise, as a form of leadership.

You need to know that sexism, like its related cousin racism, is part of the DNA of this country. The Europeans who made the trek to the Americas did so in large part to have freedom to practice their religion as they saw fit. Unfortunately, much of their practice centered on an embrace of patriarchal tenets, including the domination and submission of women and the view of women as not equal to men. These ideas bled into the fabric of the new United States, with the founding fathers creating a constitution that did not contemplate citizenship for non-whites, or the right to vote for women. It took nearly 150 years for women—well, in practice, those women *allowed* to register and vote; so, white women—to win the franchise.

In Europe, on the other hand, while neither the Protestant nor Catholic religious traditions included women in leadership, women were, in fact, part of the governmental processes. Britain's Queen Victoria and Queen Elizabeth I, Spain's Queen Isabella, Mary Queen of Scots—all led not only governments but also armies in their quest to defend their borders and expand their "queendoms."

And in Liberia, a somewhat conservative nation, President Ellen Johnson Sirleaf managed a country that had come out of political strife, navigated the Ebola epidemic and an international health care crisis, and set the country on a path to rebuilding. What can we, as women, learn from her story?

Whole nations, then, are accustomed to the leadership and authority of women. It has never been so in the United States, and until we deal forthrightly with the issue of sexism, it can never be. It is nearly exactly the same with racism—until the nation deals with the original sin of racism and faces the reality of racism's DNA in our nation's founding, we cannot overcome it. As inspirational speaker Iyanla Vanzant says, "You cannot heal what you won't acknowledge."

You must know your own worth, because there are days when you're the only one who will trumpet your own horn. That is why you see black women today avidly voicing their opinions in the public square, because we know that we are the most consistent voting bloc in the country, surpassing even white men.

Understand that you shouldn't and you need not participate in your own degradation or diminishment, or the degradation or diminishment of another, in order to succeed. You wouldn't know this from watching the nightly news or the latest lineup of reality television shows. But we will tout the high road with our last breath.

Before you dive into the big campaign (or the big job, the great opportunity, the exciting project), before you step in to lead, particularly in the public arena, it is imperative that you know, absolutely *know*, who you are in your core. Who are you without the lights, the camera, the podium, the Instagram feed, the audience? What do you believe? What are your values? What are your guideposts? If you can't define your center and your values, you shouldn't be pursuing leadership. One thing we Colored Girls know is that the glare of the lights can be both intoxicating and blinding—either way, it can confuse, mislead, and distract you from your real purpose, especially if you are not clear about your center, your values, and your purpose before you stand on the stage, under the lights, before the crowds.

And in this age of social media, where we post all the details of our lives, let us remind you that some of the biggest acts of service are done in the background, in the shadows. The great social movements of the ages were made possible by the big out-front voices, yes, but more important by those in the trenches, who did the work that made the big voices possible. Not everything needs to be in your Instagram feed! And if you think it does, we invite you to reexamine your motives.

We want you to know how proud we are of you for taking this major step. Deciding to run for public office is daunting on a good day, but in these times, it's downright scary. But we so need great advocates, like you, to take up the mantle for our children, for the environment, and for people who can't stand up for themselves. We look forward to supporting you any way we can.

More advice: watch who's around you—as in who's in your squad. You need a cheerleader, a coach, a compass, and a confidante.

The cheerleader will keep your spirits high and keep you encouraged when your self-doubt rears its ugly head. Cheerleaders always speak in exclamation points and think you're the best thing God ever made.

The coach will push you—and sometimes pull you—when you get stuck; will help you map a plan and stick to it. A coach surveys the landscape, helps you see the big picture and how you fit in it, and then helps you craft a strategy that helps you win.

Your compass is your truth teller. A compass helps you keep it real . . . not in a denigrating, demoralizing way, but in a keep-you-connected-to-your-center kind of way. Your compass will remind you why you wanted the job and what you wanted to accomplish. Compasses are unaffected by the glam, the interviews, the stage. They see you, know your heart, and help you keep the main thing the main thing.

Lastly, your confidante is your keeper of secrets. This is the person to whom you tell the whole truth. With your confidante, you can be bare and raw and entirely yourself. This is where you unburden your fears, voice your dreams, and check your ego.

If you're aiming to accomplish anything big in this life, you need that core team: cheerleader, coach, compass, and confidante. But first and foremost, especially if you are considering public office, you must do a background check on yourself before you even *think* about announcing anything. After a certain age, we all have baggage, but if you want to be a public person, you need to know what that baggage is and be prepared to defend it. You don't want to be sidelined down the road with something you could have explained up front.

If you're setting up a campaign, there are a few key positions you'll want to fill early on. Get yourself a good, seasoned campaign manager who understands your goals, and, most important, *you*. You will be attached at the hip to this person for the duration of your campaign, so it needs to be someone you feel *that* comfortable with.

Get yourself a good lawyer, one who understands federal, or your state's, regulations around campaign fund-raising, filing reports—someone whom you really trust, who will handle your business and always keep you informed. And you'll need a CFO, someone who will pay the bills, sign the checks. Again, someone you really trust. Your CFO will handle the money and work with the treasurer.

You need a communications director who can also serve as press secretary. You want someone who is media savvy and who can handle stressful situations. (Think Olivia Pope.) And a treasurer who is honest, can handle money, and whom you'd trust with your life.

That's your core team. Put them in place, and they'll take it from there. By the way, don't make diversity and inclusion an afterthought. Having your team look like America should be a priority, not a slogan. It will provide you with richness and diversity of opinion, policy, and thought.

This is just the beginning of the conversations we want to have with you, our dear Sister Candidates. And we mean all of you sisters, not just those of you running for office. We want to encourage and support all the many millions of women working in ways big and small for a better future for themselves, for their families, for their communities, and for their country. We are committed to your victory. We are committed to victory for all of us.

Index

For
Colored Girls
Who Have
Considered
Politics

Discussion Questions

1. What are the qualities of a good elected official?

2. In the book, the authors talk about the "Bank of Justice." What is the Bank of Justice and how can you make a similar idea work in and for your community?

3. What did you learn from the dinners the authors had with various famous individuals seeking office? How can you replicate something like this in your community to help people get to know those who represent them and those who want to represent them?

4. Thinking again about the dinners the authors had, the rules of engagement for the salon dinners were:
   - The candidate pays for dinner
   - The candidate comes alone
   - The dinner is off the record—no talking to the press

   Which candidate running in the 2008 Democratic primary do you think broke two of the rules? How would you feel about a person running for office who broke rules you had set down? How do you think this person will govern based on that rule-breaking?

5. In the book, the authors talk about the concepts of "winner take all" and "proportional representation" in relationship to the Democratic Party's rules for the presidential primary. What do those terms mean? If you were a candidate, which would you favor and why?

6. What did you learn about politics by reading this book that you didn't know before?

7. How can you do "good" and do "well"?

8. If you are a woman reading this book, what unique challenges have you faced in your career?

9. What did you learn about the challenges facing people of color involved in today's political arena?

10. Why is it so important to "know your history"? The year 2019 is regarded by many in the African American community as a landmark because it's the four hundredth anniversary of the year in which approximately twenty African people were brought to North America against their will. In 2020, we'll mark the one hundredth anniversary of the signing of the Nineteenth Amendment, which gave women the right to vote. What historical event is personally important to you and how would you honor that event in your life and in your work?

11. If you decide to run for office, who are the four people most important to have around you and why?

12. What would help you become a more effective advocate for your community and the needs of others? What advice would you give others who aren't sure how to be an advocate?

13. What did you learn about "friendship" from this book?

14. For both men and women starting out, there is a big focus on the importance of sponsors and mentors in your career journey. How do you define the two, and what roles have they played in your own journey?

15. Who is the one person that all four CGs worked for, and how did he impact their lives/careers?

16. What is the most inspiring or helpful advice that you have ever received?